OUTSIDE THE LANES

OUTSIDE
THE
LANES

Blue Star Press.

Design by Brielle Stein

Swimmer silhouette illustration © Flatman Vector 24 / Shutterstock. All other illustrations by Brielle Stein.

This book was typeset in Degheest by Ange Degheest, Camille Depalle, Eugénie Bidaut, Luna Delabre, Mandy Elbé, May Jolivet, Oriane Charvieux, Benjamin Gomez, Justine Herbel. Distributed by velvetyne.fr.

The authorized representative in the EU for product safety and compliance is Authorised Rep Compliance Ltd., Ground Floor, 71 Lower Baggot Street, Dublin D02 P593, Ireland. www.arccompliance.com

ISBN: 9781963183115

Printed in Colombia

10 9 8 7 6 5 4 3 2 1

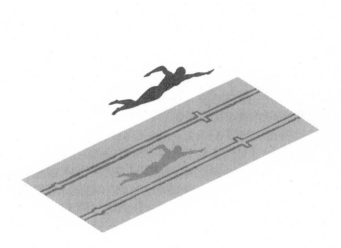

DEDICATION

To my mom, for making everything fun, even when you're throwing up for twenty-one hours.

And to everyone who struggles with OCD. They're just thoughts, no matter what your brain says to convince you otherwise.

CONTENTS

PROLOGUE

I hold a world record as the only person to swim the Maui Nui Triple Channel Crossing.

I was ranked eighth, sixth, and eleventh in the world in the 800 long course meters freestyle over three consecutive years. I placed in the Top 10 four times at World Championships.

I was on the USA Swimming National Team for eight years.

I was the youngest person to ever place in the Top 10 in four events at a single Olympic Trials.

Swimming brought me so much joy and so much pain.

It was invigorating. Empowering. All-consuming. It made me feel alive. It made me feel dead. It was—and still is—my favorite thing to do.

I gave everything to swimming. My body, my mind, my childhood, my soul. I poured every ounce of myself into it.

Did I get anything back in return? Yes. Absolutely.

Did I get everything I deserved? Depends on who you ask. The biased part of my brain would say no. But the rational part of me knows that I got more than I ever could have asked for.

I spent countless sleepless nights reconciling that my childhood dreams hadn't been—and would never be—fulfilled.

I transferred the skills I learned on my journey to failure into everything I do. Because is it really failure if I chased a fulfilling life along the way? Or if I became a better person?

If I had peaked at the right time—if the Olympics had been held in 2013, 2014, or 2015—I would have been labeled one of the best swimmers in the world.

But "ifs" are irrelevant.

1

THE AU'AU

I couldn't figure out what had possessed me to swim across the ocean.

My hip flexors burned. My stomach churned. Fatigue gripped my muscles.

I battled against the waves, my depleted limbs spinning as they attempted to propel me against the ocean's merciless current.

The seafloor was long gone, only infinite cobalt glimmering beneath me. I was so far from land that there was no way to check my progress.

Am I even moving?

Each stroke clawed me an inch closer to land—and another mile away from any rational explanation for my presence here.

A wave crashed over my salt-swollen face as I breathed water into my lungs. I sputtered, coughing as I struggled to find air.

Am I going to die?

This was my own fault. I'd decided I was going to be one of the best swimmers in the world at the ripe old age of ten, and I let anyone who would listen—and everyone who wouldn't—know it.

I hadn't conceptualized that three hours into swimming the fifteen kilometers between the Hawaiian Islands of Lanai and Maui, I'd wish I was on solid ground.

I'd thought this swim across the Au'au Channel was going to be easy. That was just how my ten-year-old brain worked.

The longer I was in the water—the wilder the water was—the happier *I* was. It didn't matter if I was practicing in the pool or bodysurfing giant waves in the ocean with my sisters. And the perfect combination of those was a fifteen-kilometer channel crossing. So may as well do that, right?

I joined the local Chicago suburb team at five, when my aquatic skills could more accurately be described as *survival* rather than *swimming*.

My older sister Rachel was doing it, and as someone who worshiped the ground she walked on, I had to do everything she did.

I was told that Rachel was one year and nine months older than me, but I was convinced we were twins—we have the same ocean-blue eyes that disappear when we smile, the same upturned Cindy Lou Who nose. And, of course, I "manifested" growing to exactly the same height as her.

I was *also* told that I needed to learn how to do freestyle before I could join the team. I disagreed. So, when we went to drop Rachel off at the pool, I packed my swimsuit, snuck in behind her, and faked it until I made it.

My relationship with swimming wasn't love at first stroke.

It was born out of stubbornness and spite.

On our second day on the swim team, the coaches pulled Rachel out of the pool to move her into a faster group. I gasped, horrified. Did they intend to *separate us*?

I jumped out of the water in world-record time and hurried forward to stop this crime.

"Rachel and I have to stay together," I declared. I was only on this team because I wanted to spend every possible minute with Rachel. She was my best friend. My rock. My role model. My *twin*.

"This group is holding Rachel back," one coach explained.

"Then I'll go with her."

"You'll be able to join her when you get the basics down."

"It's okay, Becca," Rachel said as another coach led her away. "You'll be fine."

Instead of "being fine," I screamed at the top of my lungs.

The coaches formed a barricade between Rachel and me. From then on, I had one mission: *I'm going to get past all of you. I'm going to get good enough at this dumb sport to be in Rachel's lane.* I wanted the actual swim practice to be like what happened *after* practice, when Rachel, our friends, and I would put our swim caps over the drains in the showers and flood them so we could slip 'n' slide. I wanted practice to be like every swim meet when we'd write *EAT MY BUBBLES* on each other's backs, build towel forts, and eat Fun Dip until our stomachs hurt.

When I finally got into Rachel's lane, I'd be included in the fun that I was sure was happening on the other side of the deck. In the meantime, I'd have to stare at the black line on the bottom of the pool, alone.

But as I focused on improving, something magical happened.

I started looking forward to every practice. I tuned out everything except the sound of water rushing past my ears.

Somehow—at age five—I had found purpose in the pool. It wasn't just about getting to be with Rachel anymore. It was about the quest. I was Lucy from *The Lion, the Witch, and the Wardrobe*—but instead of journeying to Tumnus, I was journeying to Rachel's lane.

My imagination ran wild. I'd been imprisoned in the "slow" lane, and I had to be ready to escape when my captors opened the cell door. I had to pass my fellow prisoners until I was leading the lane. That was where I'd have the best chance of a successful prison-break.

As I broke my team's six-and-under record, I felt like the most powerful swimmer on the planet. It was intoxicating, efficiently slicing through the water like a knife.

I fell in love with jumping into the pool. With pushing my body toward Rachel's group. With playing my prison-break game.

I passed all the other five-year-olds on the team. Then the six-year-olds. At swim meets, I was the only eight-and-under entered in the mile, 200 fly, and 400 individual medley.

I was the heroine of my own swimming novel. The chosen one who loved swimming the hardest events, fueled only by her quest and dozens of Hershey bars.

I was Dorothy in *The Wizard of Oz*. I was Joan of Arc saving France.

I was Becca Mann, and I was going to be in Rachel Mann's lane soon.

Maybe this mindset was born of the hundreds of fantasy novels I'd read. Or maybe it was my Catholic upbringing, where my role models were martyred saints. Regardless, it had been determined: I was the Chosen One.

The day a coach pulled me out of my lane and walked me toward Rachel's, I felt unstoppable. This was my moment.

I hopped into the pool, grinning at Rachel as I took my place behind her. Rachel smiled right back, then pushed off the wall. I waited the assigned five seconds, then followed.

I spun my arms like a windmill, determined to prove I could keep up with the big kids. To show I belonged. To have more fun.

I made the interval, getting several seconds of rest before I had to do it all over again.

And I did. I made the entire practice.

On the way home, I watched the suburban Midwestern houses pass by through the car window, on cloud nine with an excellent view of a seemingly limitless horizon. The world was my sandbox, and I had only played in a corner.

What else can I do? The idea was addictive.

What else do I want to do?

I was proud of myself—I wanted to hold on to who I was in that moment. I knew exactly who I was. Driven. Passionate. Good. A heroine.

I was going to be that person—my eight-year-old self—forever. It didn't—*I didn't*—get any better than that.

A few years later, the 2008 Olympics played out on my family's TV. I didn't care to watch—I was too busy pretending to be a demigod in the forest in our backyard, writing stories in my mind. The Greek Olympians had *real* powers, unlike the athletes on the screen. But I hated being left out, so my imaginary adventures brought me back to the TV.

I rushed back into the living room just as Michael Phelps won his eighth medal. My family was loving it. Me?—I wasn't sure. A myriad of emotions burst within my chest, the most prominent of which resembled jealousy.

If someone had told me that Michael Phelps and I would be training together five years later, I would have thought, *Makes sense.*

"You missed it, Becca!" my mom exclaimed.

"So?"

"So you should watch," my dad said.

"Why?" Why watch swimming when I could just swim? "I'm going to have more than that one day. I'll get nine."

Maybe *this* was my next big quest.

"Okay. But just so you know, it'll be a lot of work," my mom said.

"I know," I replied with a shrug. "I gotta go—Poseidon needs me."

I loved swimming more than anyone, so I would be the best at it. It was simple kid math. The person who likes something the most is the person who gets the glory. I'd gotten into Rachel's lane. If I could complete that challenge, I could get more Olympic medals than Michael Phelps.

But there would be other challenges first—the next of which presented itself on a family vacation in Hawaii while crossing from Maui to Lanai on a ferry. My mom wondered if a swim was done between the islands. "It's so beautiful. I think I'll have to get in shape and swim across it."

"You can't," I interrupted. "*I'm* the swimmer of the family. *I* have to do it. You can't do it before me. I like swimming more than you do."

I wasn't *supposed* to have been a swimmer. I was born and bred into a family of triathletes—that was the only reason Rachel had joined the swim team in the first place. I couldn't let it be taken from me. I knew I could cross the Au'au Channel. I thrived in the Hawaiian waters. The bigger the waves, the more fun I had.

I was the Chosen One, and I'd found my next quest.

"Promise me," I said to my mom. "Promise me you'll let me do it before you do."

"You really want to swim it?"

"Yes. I *have* to."

My mom took in the determined glint in my eyes. I wondered if she could see what I felt—that I absolutely *had* to swim across the channel.

"Okay," she agreed.

She knew—it was the same look I'd given her over a year before when I told her I wanted to swim my first 10k in Miami. It didn't matter that I would be the youngest competitor by years—a *lot* of years if I didn't include Rachel. If there was something *harder* to do, I was going to do it.

My parents weren't going to stop me. They told me I could do whatever I set my mind to, and they made sure those weren't just words. If I wanted to swim across the ocean, they'd help me make it happen.

I craved the adventure. I wanted to look down and not be able to see the bottom of the ocean. Crossing the Au'au Channel was so alluring that I was surprised I hadn't thought of it before the horrifying idea of my mom being a better swimmer than me was presented.

My mom found a boat captain who was an official Hawaiian Channel Crossing Certifier, and I got ready to embark on the longest swim I—or anyone my age—had ever done.

The preparation wasn't theatrical. There was no training montage. I didn't change my routine. I just figured I would be fine, as I had a strong enough base.

A twinge of nervousness coursed through my gut as I watched the support boat, which looked like a floating bathtub, drift toward where I stood with my parents on the dock. The perfect boat for tiny me.

My dad gets seasick, so he stayed on Lanai to have a nerve-racking beach day with my sisters. He wasn't the biggest fan of this adventure, but he knew better than to try to stop it. My mom would be my feeder, responsible for keeping my energy up throughout the swim—and watching me to make sure nothing bad happened.

We didn't have much of a feeding plan. I was too naive for that.

The crossing began at Club Lanai, a beach only accessible via a dirt road. The boat dropped me off about a kilometer away since it couldn't get over the reef to take me closer. I'd have to swim to shore before I could turn right around and start my adventure.

I jumped into the water, letting the cool waves dissipate my underlying anxiety the moment I was submerged, the colorful fish calming my mind.

Ten minutes later, I climbed onto the deserted beach. I stood alone, a ten-year-old girl with nothing but her cap, goggles, suit, and smile. It felt right. I didn't need cheerleaders—I only needed myself and the ocean to cooperate with me.

I took in the landmass on the horizon. It didn't look very far. Five hours tops.

I grinned, no longer nervous. I shook out my muscles. Did the sign of the cross.

Then I waded back into the Au'au and swam toward my potential.

This was it. The clear water sparkled, sunlight reflecting off the reef below.

I was the coolest ten-year-old on the planet, the cobalt blue as endless as my joy. As I swam over the fish, I wondered if they, too, had made the commute to Maui at one point or another.

I plowed through the waves like a warrior. I was free, powerful, grown up. The sun shone and the water rushed through my ears.

And as I passed the idling boat, the bottom of the ocean disappeared.

The first few hours passed like a daydream. Hundreds of jellyfish glowed beneath me, and I laid eyes on the first sea turtle I'd ever seen. I sang to myself. I watched the details of Lanai fade into the distance.

I don't know why more kids haven't done this, I thought, *It's so fun!*

Despite the endless depths, I felt safe in the ocean—more comfortable, more aware, more in tune with my body and my surroundings. The water was an extension of me.

I belonged there.

I hadn't even conceptualized that this swim was going to be hard. I'd thought I was just going for a very long, fun swim across the ocean.

The first half is *always* fun. The second half is when my inner demon emerges.

Around hour three, with four miles to go, that's exactly what happened.

The current picked up. Maui, which had been getting consistently larger, stayed just out of reach. As I struggled toward Maui, I began chanting, *You are Becca Mann. You can cross this ocean. You will cross this ocean. You are the toughest ten-year-old on this planet. You love swimming. You are awesome.*

You love a challenge. I spat the salty water of the Au'au Channel out of my mouth.

You love swimming. I got stung by the dozenth jellyfish.

This was a different beast from the calm ten-kilometer race in Miami a year and a half before. Rachel had been forced to swim with me through every loop of that course. Now, I was alone in the wild, untamed ocean.

A shout from the boat made me lift my head. "You need to feed!"

I reluctantly treaded water and glanced up at my mom, giving up hard-fought meters to the current. "I don't want to."

"Too bad."

Touching the boat meant disqualification, so our feeding system was simple. She threw me a Gatorade. I glared, chugged it, and threw the empty bottle back.

I kept stroking. Was Maui getting closer . . . ?

You love swimming. You love a challenge.

"Why am I going so slow?" I demanded when my mom threw another Gatorade into the water beside me.

"You're almost there."

I didn't believe her. I only believed the pain. But the only way to get the glory was forward. No matter how frustrated, tired, and over this crossing I was, I had to keep going.

Ow, ow, ow. I winced with every stroke.

I was swimming in place. Everything hurt. I was angry with my mom for no reason. I was angry with the captain. I cried into my goggles because I knew that the rest of the channel was going to be miserable. Why couldn't my body do this as efficiently as I thought?

Everything comes to an end. I'll get to Maui at some point.

It didn't calm me.

Quests aren't supposed to be easy, I reminded myself. *That would make a really boring book.*

It didn't soothe me.

Hour four passed with hardly any progress. I stopped feeding. If I treaded water to feed, I would lose ground, and I would be in the water longer.

For the first time in my life, that sounded like a bad thing.

I tried to think about how good it would feel when I was done. I was going to eat so much food. I was going to lounge around for a week. I was going to brag to Rachel and Julia—my blonde, curly-haired younger sister who used her cuteness to get whatever she wanted—and tell them that I couldn't take the garbage out for the next year because I was "still recovering."

I sang *Wicked the Musical,* reminding myself that I was Elphaba. *Loathing, unadulterated loathing . . .*

I want to get out. I don't want to do this anymore.

Another hour.

I was going to look up. If I was still in the middle of the channel, I was going to have to come up with a new plan for getting there.

My thoughts must have gone right to God's ears, because Maui was closer.

Significantly closer.

Adrenaline surged through me.

The closer I got to the island, the more the current died down. The more I sped up. The effects of pure adrenaline pumped through my blood—my soul—and rejuvenated my tired body. By hour six, I could make out individual palm trees.

The closest beach was more a collection of rocks than sand, just south of Lahaina. I sprinted for it, invigorated by the nearness of victory.

The bottom of the ocean reappeared. I was doing it. I was almost—

There. I made it. I was finished. I climbed onto the rocks, almost falling as I hauled myself out of the water.

I squatted on a rock and looked back at Lanai, catching my breath.

The crossing took me six hours, twenty-six minutes, and forty-six seconds.

It was the hardest thing I'd ever done. My face was swollen. My muscles ached. I never wanted to move again.

And yet, finished with that seemingly Sisyphean task, I was proud. No—I was *impressed*. I'd powered through almost four hours of challenge to get to the other side, pushing myself past my limits and proving that I was just like the characters in the books.

No one is proud of doing something easy. Nothing was off the table.

So you swam across that channel? What else can you do? What other dreams do you have? a voice in my head taunted.

No. It *tempted*. I became the youngest person ever to swim across the Au'au. My name ended up in the Oahu airport, joining a list of other Hawaiian Channel swimmers. I'd gotten so sunburned that my arms were covered in quarter-sized blisters that I was so excited to show off to my sisters.

I wanted the next quest. I *needed* it to satiate the competitive voice within myself. How good could I be at doing the thing that I loved? What could I accomplish? How far could I go if I *really* tried?

Anything. I can do anything.

That was what being a swimmer meant to me. I wore the identity like a badge of honor, ready to take on the world. Ready to chase things I wasn't even sure were possible to catch.

The moment I saw my mom, I smiled smugly. "I did it before you did."

"*Res ipsa loquitur*," she replied.

It was a Latin phrase we used in our family. *The thing speaks for itself*. Let your actions be your words.

And they were.

2

WHAT IF, WHAT IF, WHAT IF?

I was wearing a tank top with a whale on it the first day I walked onto Herbert's pool deck in Austin, Texas. A thousand miles from the kids I'd swum with in the Chicago suburbs. Everything was bigger in Texas, including the teens who were about to become my training partners.

I trailed behind my mom, trying not to glance up into the faces of the older, more muscular swimmers.

Herbert was in his late sixties, his hair and mustache snow white. He wore a rusty Texas Longhorns T-shirt, his brow furrowing as I stood in front of him and met his glinting eyes.

Clearly, he'd been expecting someone older. Or bigger. Probably both. Not a newly homeschooled ten-year-old.

"Glad to see you dressed for the occasion," he said, nodding at the whale. Heat rose into my face, but I would soon discover that he wore the same shirt every day.

I decided I liked him. He rarely smiled, so I knew that when he did, I'd earned it.

My sisters' triathlon coach had swum for Herbert in college and had recommended I try him out after I'd climbed through the clubs of Illinois and found none of them challenging enough. I needed better athletes to train with. Better coaching.

Herbert gave it to me.

★ ★ ★

Three years after my first training trip with Herbert, he moved to Clearwater, Florida. I convinced my parents to let me move there too. Permanently.

It was December 2010. I had just turned thirteen and cemented myself as the all-time fastest eleven-to-twelve-year-old distance swimmer in the nation with two National Age Group Records.

My plan was to make the 2012 Olympic Team a year and a half later, get gold, and then move back to Illinois and start my freshman year at regular high school to be reunited with my sisters and cats. Those eighteen months would be completely consumed by swimming. The days of jet skiing between morning and afternoon practice on my Texas training trips were long gone, replaced with compression wear and long naps.

I believed. As my mom once told me, *Doubt is the first step to failure.* So I was going all-in on myself. No doubts.

I brought my Elphaba hat. My crucifix. All my favorite books. The map I'd created of Quanx, the imaginary land modeled after the forest in my Illinois backyard. My mind spent half its time there, and I was beginning to write it into a fantasy novel.

My mom stayed with me the first week in my new Florida Airbnb.

After moving me in, she'd leave for a month to return to mothering my sisters and running her law office. She was replaced with a family friend, who would be followed by my dad, my grandma, and finally, another family friend. I'd never been away from my mom for so long, but I told myself it would be fine. I'd talk to her on the phone every day. There was nothing to worry about.

But a tightness grew in my chest with every passing day when I realized *I* was the one running my life. Rachel wasn't around to make me food. My dad didn't do my laundry. My mom didn't unpack my swim bag if I was too exhausted to do it. Julia wasn't bossing me around, making me co-star in her music videos.

The gates to hell broke loose three days after my mom left.

It was a Thursday. A teammate said something random after practice that convinced me something terrible was going to happen to my family.

I had no idea what was happening as the world faded away. All I could perceive was fear. Terror.

Everything else was hidden behind glass.

I just need to sleep, I decided. *Tomorrow, I'll wake up, and everything will be fine.*

I didn't sleep that night. And I couldn't force down breakfast the next day. I didn't even belt *Wicked* on the drive to practice.

When I finished morning practice in tears and Herbert approached, I rubbed at my eyes and said, "Sorry, there's something in my eye." But my voice sounded as if it came from someone else.

Herbert attempted to lighten the mood. "Yeah, your finger."

I offered a half-hearted grin. Everything felt far away, as if behind a glass door.

I found myself back in that cloud of intense fear several times a day.

My thoughts were spiraling out of control, though I did my best to hide it. Frequent episodes of fear about irrational things plagued me, making me feel as though I were living behind a veil, occasionally taking away my appetite for days.

Sometimes, I would spiral during practice, obsessing that my entire family *wasn't* just 2,000 miles away—they were dead. On those days, the black line became a prison, dark and foreboding. My mind ached for something else to latch onto, and the fantastical imaginations I had summoned when I was younger turned sour. Scary. Disturbing.

What if I think about the devil so much that I start doing his bidding?

Even positive affirmations about swimming became tainted with poison. "Anything is possible if you *believe*," person after person told me.

What if that means that thinking my family's dead actually kills them?

Not possible. Not true.

What if reality is broken and that is true? asked my brain.

My stomach always plummeted first.

Calm down, calm down, calm down.

What if? What if? What if?

The pit of dread would fill until it overflowed, seeping into my ribs, my heart, and my mind, until it consumed me like a storm. Until I felt as if I were no longer in my body.

What if I'm stuck in this feeling, and then it makes me go crazy, and I do something terrible? What if it makes me kill my family or myself, and then I go to hell, and I actually am stuck in the fear forever?

What if I'm going crazy?

What if I am crazy?

My dad accidentally called me *Rachel* one day.

He has Alzheimer's, my brain convinced me. *He's forgetting things. He's dying, he barely has any time left before his brain is gone, and you're living in Florida, trying to see how fast you can swim across the pool.*

I traveled for a swim meet the next week and woke up with no clue where I was.

You have Alzheimer's. You inherited it from Dad. You're the youngest person to ever have it. You've always known you're special—you're so special that you can give yourself Alzheimer's.

Logic and rationality didn't exist in the darkest corners of my mind.

You believe your mind has the power to do anything? You have the power to do terrible things too. You could break reality, send everyone to hell, and make everyone feel the fear.

I needed to believe I could do anything to swim fast. But if I could do *anything* . . .

I could do something terrible.

When my mind managed to distract itself from the anxiety, and I found myself reverting to my happy self—daydreaming about Quanx, playing in the ocean's waves, fishing on the pier—my amygdala began to prod at the rest of my brain. *You're forgetting something. You need to be prepared.* Prepared to loop through my thoughts again, to comb through them in hopes that I missed something. That my brain was wrong. That if I went through them just one more time, I would find something in there that would prove them wrong.

The remnants of my fears lived in the corners of my mind. My fear was like eye floaters—always there but ignorable until something reminded me of their presence.

One night, just before finals of a swim meet, my mom finally back with me, I read an article about a murder—and then couldn't stop thinking about what differentiated *me* from the killer. Weren't we the same? What was keeping *me* from doing the same?

My thoughts overflowed into my body, transforming into cortisol and adrenaline until I couldn't separate myself from the terror.

I could do nothing to hide it from my mom. I burst into tears.

"What's wrong?" my mom asked, alarmed.

"I—I don't know! I'm—what if I'm evil?!"

"What?"

"What makes people evil? What if *I'm* evil?"

"You're not evil."

"How do you *know*?"

My brain was spiraling. If I was evil, then—

My mind was back on hell. I couldn't go to hell if hell was even *worse* than my thoughts. I could never do anything even marginally morally ambiguous. I would have to be perfect. Because what if I did something bad, and God decided that, as punishment, all my evil thoughts would come true?

"Do you need to come back home with me?" my mom asked.

"No!" A part of me wanted to, but that would mean giving up on my dreams. I didn't want to do that. Not when I had already given so much. Gained so much. Not when I still loved swimming and was still making great improvements.

I had to make it through my thoughts. I had to push through. If I had to choose between inner peace and swimming . . .

It would be swimming.

"What about therapy?"

The fear intensified. "I'm not crazy!" *Am I?*

"It doesn't mean you're crazy."

"No. I can't. I won't." *If you go to therapy, they'll confirm there's something wrong with you.*

The more I told my thoughts to calm down, the more erratic they became. My stomach churned. Relaxation didn't help—instead, I sought distraction. Anything and everything to take my mind off it.

The best distraction was *fast* swimming. Slow swimming allowed my imagination to go wild, but fast swimming turned my brain off.

There was nothing a race couldn't fix. The excitement of diving from the block and taking off in the pool lured my thoughts away from the dark corners of my mind and into the light.

The second-best distraction came from writing my middle-grade fantasy novel, *The Stolen Dragon of Quanx*. Writing was like watching TV for me—my body recovered while my imagination roamed free. I relished when I was in the zone. I typed away, knowing I had full control of the words on the page. Knowing I was the god of this world, and if my characters could make it through their arduous quest, I could too.

My thoughts were overwhelming for a few months, then eased up a bit, coming and going in waves. The reprieves told me that there was hope that someday it could all go away. I just had to fight my way there. Things that were easy weren't worth it. Everyone would do it if it were easy, like the Au'au Channel.

I stopped telling my mom when things were going badly because I knew she would get worried—and then her thoughts would be as bad as mine, and she would feel even worse than I felt, and I didn't want anyone to feel that way—

Especially not *because* of me.

Despite hiding my rocky mental health from her, I began developing a codependent relationship. I clung to her even when she was halfway across the country, as if she were the sole being tethering me to home. I had never been away from her for so long. We'd FaceTime every day for at least an hour, and I'd gab the entire time about the exact speed I'd gone on every repeat of every set. I was desperate to prove to her that this move had been worth it.

I *needed* her at every swim meet. After swimming poorly at the first swim meet she wasn't able to attend, I convinced myself that if she wasn't there watching, I wouldn't swim fast. I demanded she attend every competition.

I gave her homework—to look at USA Swimming's age group lists and warn me if any other thirteen-year-olds were rising behind me.

There weren't, so I made her track the fourteen-year-olds.

The answer was always *no*, until one day, on the way to swim practice, she said, "There's a fourteen-year-old who went faster than you."

"How much?"

"A few seconds in the 800."

I shrugged, unconcerned. I was rapidly improving—I always surpassed the names my mom read.

"What's her name?"

"Katie Ledecky."

"I'm not worried about it."

"She also has a faster 400—"

I waved my hand dismissively. "I'll be faster in a month."

Whenever someone who wasn't my mom stayed with me, I was angry that they didn't do things the way she did. I counted down the days until she came back. I wanted to look for shark teeth with her on the beach. I wanted her to watch me swim and tell me how much faster I'd gotten since she'd last seen me.

I asked her advice on every small drama that unfolded in my life—and I always took it, never even thinking about whether I agreed with it. She knew better than I did, and I was alone, halfway across the country, surrounded by a sea of people I didn't know well.

While I brought my mom closer, I distanced my dad. Any time he hesitated a moment too long, I reconvinced myself of the Alzheimer's, so it was best if I didn't let him trigger the thought at all. It was easier for me to push him away. Though painful, at least I was in control.

Being on the receiving end, I found, was much worse.

Rachel couldn't visit as often now that she was in high school back home and on the USA Triathlon National Junior Team. Whenever Julia came to visit, we would have *so* much fun—we'd make music videos, go boating on the dinghy we'd bought, pull a hose down to the water to attract the manatees, and bike around the neighborhood. It was like I was back home, but an upgraded home because the ocean was my new playground.

When she left, both of us would cry. Until one trip, instead of being sad, she was distant.

The worst part was that I understood.

She'd put her walls up, just like I'd done for my dad. It was easier for her that way.

The guilt meant that I tried harder to hide anything that wasn't happiness from my parents. I couldn't have them flying out and leaving my sisters more than they already were. I had to become independent—and quickly. I had to be titanium. If I could swim across the ocean, I could internalize my negative feelings and overcome them, right?

You moved out, which means you're an adult now. You have to behave like one.

The rest of the family started going on ski trips, but I couldn't join—it was too dangerous, and I was too injury-prone and clumsy. I could only come home for a few days during the holidays so I didn't miss training.

I'm alone.

My friends became the characters in the books I read and the one I wrote. They couldn't hurt me.

But the path to greatness is lonely.

That was what every young adult dystopian story confirmed—the Chosen One had to do it alone. They had to sacrifice.

Like me, even if it was more than I'd realized or even had been able to conceive. But I'd chosen this. To chase that feeling I felt after the Au'au—to chase a dream. That had to be worth something. Swimming fulfilled me. It made me *better* than other kids my age. It was a beautiful experience, one that needed to be nourished. *And* protected.

I didn't know enough to do it any differently. I didn't know I could ask for help.

I was terrified that if people in the swimming world knew *how* to hurt me, they would—because maiming me would make it easier for them to beat me.

And people liked to talk. One day after practice, before I turned the corner into the locker room, I heard the echo of a fellow teammate's voice. "Becca's family is, like, psycho for making her move here for swimming."

Rage struck like a bullet. Before I could make my appearance known, another girl added, "I would never be able to leave my brother."

No one understood—they couldn't see that *I* was the driving force behind my dreams. It always came back to my parents, as if I were a doll they'd decided to play pretend with, shipping me off to Florida for a chance to vicariously go to the Olympics.

What if, what if, what if?

Stop.

What if they're right? What if I'm already messed up? What if I have to move back to Chicago? What if I never make the Olympics, and then never have a career, and then become a drug addict, and then my family disowns me, and then I—

Seeing my mom in the stands halted my spiral. *She wouldn't do that*, I told myself, though I was suddenly questioning whose decision the move had been.

Mine, I reminded myself. Other people didn't know me or my family. I just had to keep it that way. *Res ipsa loquitur.* My swimming would do the talking.

I loved walking onto the pool deck and making the conversation stop. I decided they must have been discussing the only two things I'd given them to talk about: my choice of footwear—always crazy-looking UGGs—or my swimming.

I loved how, sometimes, when I went into the stands to find my mom, I would overhear someone talking about how much time I'd dropped. Or how I could swim any non-sprint event.

That was all I let people see—the surface level. I became a complete enigma, closing myself off entirely and sacrificing the opportunity for meaningful connections. People on my swim team were my coworkers—not my friends.

No one understood how serious I was about qualifying for the Olympics in a short year and a half. I had a vision and I was going to see it through. I knew where I wanted to be, and I was going to get there, even if I had to walk through hell. My very sense of self was built on a hunger to see how far I could go. It was *all* I wanted, so much so that swimming became who I was.

I didn't meet another teenage swimmer who understood until I went to 2011 Junior Nationals.

I was in the lane next to Katie Ledecky, the swimmer ahead of me on my precious age group list.

I studied her as we prepared behind our blocks. Her gaze held the same intensity as mine, which I'd never seen reflected in another young athlete.

I was wrong about her.

"Good luck," I called.

She looked up from the water and flashed a smile. "You too."

I immediately liked her.

She beat me, taking the Junior National title. I was the runner-up, but it had been such a fun race that I didn't care.

As we caught our breath after the race, I felt the need to acknowledge the obvious. "You're so good. And you're only fourteen."

"Well, you're thirteen."

And I had work to do.

Improvement came by showing up daily and making hard work a habit. It was hard, gritty, and painful. Herbert was the kind of coach who *made* swimmers. He was great at technique and wrote challenging, focused practices.

We swam around seven kilometers per practice—which I would later discover was my magic distance—nine times a week. Twice a week, I'd come early and Herbert would give me a brutally challenging distance set, putting the practice distance around ten kilometers.

On Sundays, I swam in the Gulf of Mexico. Manatees and stingrays swam alongside me. Some days, it took me almost an hour to get down to the nearby lighthouse because the current was so strong, then I'd speed back home in twenty.

I loved that something unexpected always happened in the Gulf.

Working hard became a habit. *Make every stroke count*, I told myself every time I jumped into the water. *Make this worth it. Make the sacrifice worth it.*

What if, what if—

I did make it worth it, occasionally to the point of migraine. Even so, I was satisfied after each practice, knowing I was doing what Herbert told me needed to be done.

I trusted Herbert.

I had gained a grandfather through him. When my mom and I went boating on the weekend, I demanded we stop at his house and invite him on the water.

Herbert would occasionally come over for dinner with my family, and if Julia was visiting, we'd put on a musical for him and his wife. He put up with all of it with a good sense of humor.

I knew he could sometimes be difficult toward the other swimmers, but I was his favorite, and he was all-in on my swimming career, believing in it as much as I did. Which was *wholeheartedly*. That was all I needed. I put my head down and trained, keeping my mind on the 2012 Olympic Team as the months ticked by. I got my Trials cuts, but I knew I had a *lot* of work to do. If it would help me swim faster, I would do it. If it wouldn't, I would sacrifice it.

The first thing I applied that mindset to was my diet.

I would eat five eggs with grapes before my 4:45 a.m. practice, followed by chocolate milk and strawberries. Next came the biggest bowl of homemade oatmeal ever seen. After a three-hour nap and exactly two hours before afternoon practice—to avoid reflux in the pool during hard sets—I ate two chicken breasts with vegetables and mashed potatoes. During practice, I drank a 400-calorie carb concoction so I wouldn't get hungry while I swam.

After practice, I had another chocolate milk, then cooked either fish or steak on my George Foreman grill, with broccoli and either quinoa or wild rice. I'd eat more strawberries at night and potentially scramble more eggs or eat leftover quinoa if I got hungry before bed.

All my meals were scheduled. I claimed it was to combat my regurgitation, but I really found quiet comfort in eating the same thing at the same minute every single day.

I went to sleep at 10 p.m. every night and napped for two to four hours every day.

I started acupuncture, though that was mostly because I was trying to find a solution for my bimonthly incapacitating migraines that followed challenging practices.

My Lithuanian family friend had a son who was an elite athlete, and she taught me about the superfoods he ate leading up to big competitions. Açaí juice. Beet juice. Chia seeds. Caviar. If it had a chance of making me swim faster, even if it was just a placebo, I was going to do it.

Ten days before a competition, I'd buy ten cheap bottles of caviar. Every day, I scooped the fish eggs onto a spoon and stared at them until I summoned the bravery to shove them down my throat. The açaí juice, which also wasn't the tastiest of drinks, served as my chaser.

I was going all-in. If the difference between being the fastest and second fastest was a jar of caviar every day, I was going to force that caviar past my gag reflex.

If I didn't swim well on a day I accidentally skipped my caviar, I blamed the bad swim on that. Even though the caviar certainly had nothing to do with it.

What if I can't eat caviar anymore? What if I forget it before the Trials? What if—

I would just sacrifice more, knowing I was trading a "normal" life for something more meaningful: my dreams.

3

LEARNING

The open water Olympic distance is ten kilometers, the race consisting of multiple loops. It's something like a chess game—only instead of just one opponent, there are between twenty-five and seventy.

You have to know how to navigate and stay on course when the next buoy is over a kilometer away. You have to maneuver within a pack of bloodthirsty swimmers, all of whom are trying to get to the same place as you, in a race where punching someone *once* only gets you a warning.

Currents. Weather. Drafting. Violence. Feeding. Strategy. Extreme temperatures. Wildlife—jellyfish, dolphins, turtles, sea lions, the occasional shark.

It's a true adventure and a sport where there's no such thing as *bad* conditions.

But the best part is the strategy—you have to have a plan that is unpredictable so your competitors can't thwart it, and have a backup plan and a backup plan for the backup plan, because something is *always* going wrong.

Herbert just wanted me to focus on the pool, but open water was still drawing me in. My personality was much more suited for it.

A pool was a container. It was too predictable. Too boring.

The same could not be said for open water. I wanted to face the untamed waves again.

Danger was whispering my name.

One of the first competitions that made the swimming community really start paying attention to me was the 2011 Open Water National Championships.

Herbert shook his head when I told him I wanted to go. "That's going to ruin your stroke."

"How?"

"It's too long. Technique falls apart at 7k. That's how you get injured."
I didn't believe that.

"You need to focus on the pool. On the 800 and butterfly. Open water will get in the way of that."

I'd never had an argument with Herbert before. We had been vehemently on the same page since I'd started training with him. A future flashed before my eyes, one where Herbert ended up like every other coach I'd had in Illinois, discarded the moment our visions for my future didn't align. Discomfort crept into my gut—a feeling I wasn't used to experiencing with him.

"But I *want* to do it."

Herbert huffed. I held my breath, praying that he would tell me that I should follow the fun—and my heart.

Instead, he turned and . . . walked away. I blinked, taken aback by the lack of a solution.

I told my mom about the exchange over FaceTime. "You love open water," she told me. "You can't just give that up. I'll talk to Herbert."

The next day at practice, Herbert scowled as he approached me. "I signed you up," he grumbled. "We're doing IM today."

My heart fell into my stomach. I felt like a misbehaving, chastised child.

You're going. You got what you wanted.

But at what price?

Our relationship over the next few weeks was strained.

What if Herbert's right? a voice whispered in the back of my mind. *What if you have to choose?*

My open water potential was untapped. I had almost no race experience and no ranking, with no clear path to improvement. My pool abilities were objectively strong. I knew exactly what I needed to do to be the best and how far I was from getting there.

You like the unknown. It's like the Auʻau Channel.

It was a relief to get a break from Herbert at Open Water Nationals, though. I had no idea what I was doing going in. I didn't understand that this wasn't just a long pool race with some contact or something that simply needed completion, such as a channel crossing. I just knew that I was as fast in the pool as the best open water swimmers in the country, which I decided meant I would be as good at open water as they were.

I knew nothing, but I knew *who* knew everything. Eva Fabian was the best American at the time. Standing at only 5'3", she was short for a swimmer, earning her the nickname "the Mighty Mouse," from the swimming community. Like me, she still had a baby face. Like me, she was homeschooled. Like me, she seemed to prefer comfort over fashion. Like me, she was a student of the sport.

I hated her.

Eva was seventeen. *Ancient* to thirteen-year-old me. She was a world champion, having won the 5k at Worlds the year before. She wasn't the fastest swimmer in the bunch—she was just the most experienced. She raced the smartest and had the most endurance.

In the sport of marathon swimming, that makes you *the best*.

I had the least experience and was the least knowledgeable, which made me . . . *not* the best.

Open water is reflective of life. Racing requires adaptability, intellect, physical and mental resilience, and just a hint of insanity.

I decided I would just do everything Eva did. I would start next to her and swim on her feet, in her draft, the whole race. It was the only move I had.

My pre-race strategies in open water almost *never* went according to plan. This time was no different.

I waded into the Atlantic Ocean for the start of the race, the sand squishing beneath my feet.

It was an in-water start. Every competitor gripped a rope that stretched between two boats until a horn set us off.

I tracked down Eva and squeezed into the spot beside her, just a little too close. She glared at me. I stared ahead, pretending that I wasn't attaching myself to her like a leech. Pretending I wasn't about to steal all her knowledge.

Someone shoved me and my shoulder bumped against hers.

"I—sorry," I mumbled.

Eva scowled and swam behind the other women to the other side of the line.

I panicked for half a second, then followed her. *I can't be deterred so easily,* I thought, staring at Eva's back as I returned to her side.

The moment I got back in place, she glowered and kicked back to her original spot.

I followed again.

At this point, Eva seemed to realize there was no getting rid of me. And there was no time left to move.

The countdown was on.

I made sure not to touch her again. I didn't need the best open water swimmer in the nation angry at me before the race even started, especially after hearing about how violent the races got.

The blowhorn went off, and I sprinted into place in Eva's draft.

Massive waves rolled over and under me, crashing into my mouth as I breathed. Salty water flooded my lungs. I breathed to the other side to avoid the waves. I willed myself to stay focused and enjoy the adventure of fighting through the water.

For the first five kilometers, all went well, with the exception of a few punches thrown by other swimmers. Every time we passed the feeding station, I squeezed one of the GUs I'd stored in the back of my tight suit into my mouth, since I'd stupidly decided I didn't need a feeder to throw me a Gatorade at the end of each loop. I stayed with the pack, despite the boat being off course, terrified of losing the draft.

I managed to stay on Eva's feet until we reached that halfway point.

Then Eva picked up the pace.

I was tired. Thirsty. I didn't have another gear to change into.

She dropped me in the next thirty seconds.

The next 5k was *brutal*. I swam by myself, battling through the waves. My mouth was parched—I felt like I was back in Hawaiian waters, the end in sight but never growing closer. I wanted to be *done*.

I finished ten minutes behind Eva.

I couldn't even consider my performance *bad*. It was my first 10k at Nationals. The result annoyed me, but I didn't have time to brood. The 5k was in two days, and I had learned a few things about navigating within a tight pack of swimmers that I could implement into the next race. Plus, I had stayed with the leaders for the first 5k of the 10k.

This was my time to shine. I could make a comeback. I would.

You know what would ruin this? my mind asked. *If you went back down the rabbit hole.*

The familiar dread washed the confidence away like a rising tide.

It took me a few hours to calm down. Focusing on Eva's race helped. She had conserved for the first 5k—not getting distracted by what was around her, as I had—then she'd made a move.

I'll do that in the 5k, I decided. *Conserve for as long as I can.*

A lot of the main contenders, like Eva, wouldn't be competing in the 5k since it didn't qualify for anything. It was purely for fun, race experience, and bragging rights.

My main competition would be Ashley Twichell, who was new to the open water scene. She'd just graduated from Duke and was now training with the best open water coach in the nation, Bill Rose. She'd gotten third in the 10k.

I took in Ashley. She was 5'9" and several inches taller than me. Narrow torso, defined muscles. She tied her long blonde hair into a bun, throwing a cap over it. Her hazel-green eyes were bright and focused as she took in the course.

Her Swedish goggles obscured her eyes before I could figure out what she was thinking. Beating her would be a challenge. Thankfully, I was up for it.

The ocean, which had been untamed during the 10k, was as calm as a pool on the day of the 5k.

Conserve, I reminded myself as the race commenced. *Be smart like Eva Fabian.*

Ashley started strong, and I got right into her draft. I let her sight for the next buoy and just focused on staying on her feet.

This was a smaller field, so there was less to think about. Less strategy.

It was the perfect race to focus on the singular task of conserving.

The first loop went according to plan. Ashley, another National Teamer, and I broke away from the rest of the field.

When Ashley picked up the pace, I was ready. I watched the bottom of the ocean blur by as I changed into a faster gear. I was *moving*.

Ashley and I dropped the other girl as we turned the last buoy. My muscles managed another burst of speed as I converted the excitement of a fantastic performance into fuel.

Ashley broke away with a few hundred meters left. But I didn't care. I was more than happy with silver.

I grinned as Ashley and I treaded water behind the finish structure. I'd managed to defeat a current National Team athlete.

I'd tasted what it was like to be near the top of the national stage. It was addictive. I needed more of it.

Open water *was* for me, regardless of what Herbert said.

I didn't know what I was doing, but I'd found people who did, and I studied them until I knew why and how they were better than I was. With giddy anticipation, I could absorb various philosophies and implement them as I continued swimming toward the Olympic Trials.

The high was only damped by Herbert when I returned to Clearwater. "The 10k is too long for you, and 5k isn't an Olympic event."

I opened my mouth, then closed it, even as anger erupted in my chest. But pool Olympic Trials were fast approaching, only a year away, and the Open Water Olympic Team opportunity had already passed. So I calmed myself and focused on the pool. Herbert's harsh words were final, and he returned to his normal self now that I was safely returned to the black line on the bottom of the pool.

4

EVERYTHING IN MY BRAIN IS SWIMMING

I visualized my races every day leading up to Olympic Trials—the length of my strokes, the feeling of the water, hitting every turn in just the right spot. I prepared my mind. When I saw the pool, my mind would believe that it had competed at Trials hundreds of times before. It wouldn't get overwhelmed by the newness of it all—it would remember that both my mind *and* my body were prepared.

I turned fourteen—the age I would qualify for my first Olympics—and 2011 faded into 2012, the Olympic year.

Beginning at thirty-three days out—my lucky number—my phone background became a countdown. It ticked down the number of days I had left to make progress.

I was practicing well. *Better* than well. Every Saturday, I did a broken 800—a set of 8x100s, holding the pace of the time I wanted to hit at Trials. I sang Don McLean's song *American Pie* every time, pushing myself as hard as humanly possible. It was painful, but it would be over by the time *American Pie* was over in my head. I could make it hurt for the length of one song.

That was what I would use for my 800 at Trials.

I danced around my house, my excitement uncontainable.

A family friend stayed with me the week before I left for Trials. I talked to my mom on the phone for an hour every day, chatting her ear off about how pumped I was. Everything was ready. *I* was ready.

But a few days before Trials, my mom came back to Florida. Before I could start repeating my loop, she said, "Rachel got into a biking accident."

My heart dropped into my chest. Time froze. I both dreaded and needed to hear the next words.

Rachel had been cycling in a draft line at thirty miles per hour with her tires an inch away from the person ahead. On those rides, if one person made a mistake, everyone went down. Friends of ours had been in accidents resulting in fractured spines and terrible concussions—and they'd been considered *lucky* to come out alive.

This wasn't something I'd prepared for.

"I—Is she . . . ?"

My mom must have seen the horror on my face. "She's fine."

My blood started pumping again, diluting the adrenaline the news had created.

Rachel had been staying with my aunt and uncle in San Diego, training for the triathlon at the Pan American Games.

"She shattered her elbow and had surgery two days ago."

"*Two days* ago?" I'd FaceTimed with my mom, like, three times since then. She'd seemed *totally* normal. "Why didn't you—?"

"I didn't want you worrying while I wasn't here."

My head spun as the ramifications of this secret-keeping nestled into my mind. I was already worried that my family was in danger. That something would happen to them, and I'd be the only one remaining.

What if something actually does *happen, and no one tells me until Mom comes to stay with me next? What if she's lying now, and something worse actually did happen to Rachel?*

My mom didn't realize that this would mean I would worry *all* the time. That if someone texted me in a style that wasn't typical, I would convince myself that someone else in the family was texting *as* them in order to soothe me. That my mind wouldn't be satisfied regarding my family's safety unless I was with them myself.

What if Mom is keeping more from me? What if I show up at Trials and Rachel isn't there, and Mom and Dad tell me that she's just recovering, but afterward, they tell me she actually didn't make it?

"Rachel's still coming to watch, right?" I asked.

"Yeah, of course."

I exhaled, willing myself to trust my mom's words. I anchored my mind to swimming. I'd already done all the work—now it was time to prove that the sacrifices had been worth it. I would make the Olympic Team.

I hadn't conceptualized how hard this move had been on my parents. How, sometimes, they had to choose between two bad options and just hope they made the right decision.

And then maybe it's time to move back home, I realized. *Maybe I get gold and then move back to Illinois and go to real high school and live with my sisters again.*

It was a tantalizing dream.

If I make the team and get a medal in London, I'm moving back home.

What if you don't make it? my thoughts whispered.

Doubt is the first step to failure. I will make it. I will make it. I will make it. I will make it.

5

2012 OLYMPIC TRIALS

When I laid eyes on the pool at the CenturyLink Center in Omaha, I thought I may have died and gone to heaven.

It had the rubbery "new pool" smell. The water was cold, and a scoreboard hung from the ceiling directly over the center of Lanes 4 and 5. I had to crane my neck to see the top rows of the spectator seating. The sold-out venue sat almost 20,000. I pictured all those empty chairs filled with people, and my mind was silently blown. They would all be watching *me* doing the thing I loved most.

It was the perfect place to become an Olympian.

I warmed up next to swimmers whose careers I'd been following for years, knowing I was more than capable of beating them.

I was swimming just as fast as they were in the warm-up pool. It didn't matter that they weren't doing the same set or that they may have been putting in little effort while I put in far more. All that mattered was that my dream wasn't just a shape on the distant horizon. Now, it was right in front of me, close enough to reach out and touch, if not grab.

Rachel and Julia arrived with my dad, and I breathed a small sigh of relief. Rachel's arm was a mosaic of purples, blues, and greens, so swollen that it was bigger than her thigh.

But my whole family was there in the flesh, so I didn't have to worry about them.

I was ready to perform. I was ready to show the world what I was capable of. I was ready to prove wrong everyone who had doubted me.

All the work had been done. My first event was on the first day. The 400 IM.

I was the last one to the ready room, as I liked to have a second warm-up less than seven minutes before I raced. It was a holding pen where the swimmers waited to be paraded onto the deck in lane order until we reached our starting blocks.

I alternated between sitting and standing, unable to sit still with my restless energy.

Weird.

I was never nervous.

I took in the feeling, allowing it to make its way through my body. It wasn't overwhelming—just an underlying hum.

Elizabeth Beisel, the fastest 400 IMer in the world, was keeping to herself, something I would later learn was unlike her. I kept to myself as well, something that I would later learn was *very much* like me.

I put on my cap, fiddled with my goggles, shook out my muscles, and prayed about a dozen times.

Everyone had bizarre pre-race rituals. Clapping. Arm swings. Slapping. Spitting. Bicep-kissing. Jumping. Goggle-adjusting. Fidgeting. Waving. Dancing. If you could imagine it, someone was doing it.

Mine always consisted of praying. I was 100 percent certain that if I didn't do it, I would swim poorly. The ritual had been born when I was five years old, and I had never *not* done it before a race.

I went all out to make sure God knew I was doing everything in my power to be a good Catholic. If I didn't get down on my knees where *everyone* could see me, God would not show favor on my swim. And I obviously would go to hell.

I was embarrassed, but I was more afraid of what might happen if I didn't do it.

Mine was certainly one of the weirder rituals. My mom said the people in the stands called me *Hail Mary*, though no one ever commented to me about it—probably because that meant their own routine was open to fire, and I would not be shy in defending myself.

But it did cue my body that I was about to perform, like Pavlov's bell. My muscles understood on a subconscious level that they were going to have to *work* in a few minutes—or seconds.

We lined up as the heat before us finished the freestyle leg. My nerves were fading, replaced with the usual calm that always settled over me before showtime. It was just another 400 IM—another two lengths of each of the four strokes.

A few moments later, we were parading out behind the blocks. No one in the previous heats had done anything too impressive, and I was in the last group. I memorized everyone's times so I knew how fast I had to swim to be one of the eight swimmers who got into *finals* to race for the two Olympic spots.

I grinned. This was what I had been training for.

I didn't notice the 20,000 people staring down at me, all wondering about the fourteen-year-old who had gotten Olympic Trials cuts in over half the events.

A primal instinct took over. I felt like a cheetah about to be released from its cage.

Nothing stood out about this race. I went into the zone, focusing on making every stroke perfect. Racing as I always did.

Until the freestyle.

That was when the hunt commenced.

Adrenaline rushed through my body as I turned from breaststroke to freestyle. My imagination took over, like how it did when I was a child. I was racing to save Quanx—the land of the novel I was writing—and each swimmer was from an enemy tribe.

I touched the wall after Beisel and looked for my name on the scoreboard . . .

My stomach leaped. I'd placed sixth out of everyone in the preliminaries, qualifying me for finals.

I only had to improve *four* places to make the Olympic Team that night.

I was doing it. I was *here* at the meet, doing what I'd been telling everyone I was going to do from the moment I'd learned how to swim.

After the race, I warmed down for twenty minutes to flush the lactic acid out of my bloodstream. I grinned into the water, already looking forward to studying my competitors' splits to find ways to beat them.

When I got out of the pool, Herbert was waiting. "You need to take your butterfly out faster and the first fifty of backstroke."

"Yes," I agreed.

"Your free will be fast no matter what. Don't be afraid of speed at the beginning."

I would need a big drop to make it. It would be hard, but that's what made it fun. I trusted Herbert and myself. I believed.

"Okay."

"Go rest up. Be back at four."

I went back to my hotel while my family picked up food. I showered, shaving all my body hair off, leaving my hair unconditioned so my cap wouldn't fall off, as it notoriously did whenever I washed it.

I caught the droplets of water from the shower and stared at them, thinking about how this was the same substance that occupied the pool. *It's moving through water. That's all. You understand the water. You can move through it the fastest.*

I put on my compression suit—shirt, pants, and socks—and sat down to check SwimSwam.com, the main swim news site, just as my family got back with my salmon, potatoes, and vegetables.

SwimSwam wrote, "But it would be remiss not to mention the 4:42.31 from fourteen-year-old Becca Mann out of Clearwater, Florida. She is the latest budding superstar prodigy of Coach Herbert, and this was her explosion" (Keith, 2012b).

I showed my family, grinning. I wasn't worried about not getting a best time in prelims—I always swam faster at night when my body was more awake. I told them Herbert's plan for the evening, visualized it, and then took a three-hour nap.

I woke up and ate a meal before my mom drove me to the pool.

Finals were a completely different atmosphere. The swimmers in the warm-up pool were serious and focused, myself included.

I was the last in the ready room again. I hadn't watched any of the previous events, so I was in the dark as to what I was walking out to—figuratively *and* literally.

Spotlights danced across the water as we marched to our lanes, the rest of the stadium in shadow. The pool was a stage, and I the performer. The entertainment. People had paid hundreds of dollars to watch me do what I did best—swim across a pool.

And I was happy to give them a show.

I allowed myself to bask in it for a moment before going back into race mode. The flashing lights were for the fans, not for me.

The arena was silent as we stepped onto the blocks.

"Take your mark . . ." the starter said. I bent down, gripping the block with all my strength.

The *beep* sounded, and I dove in.

I took the butterfly out faster, turning with the leaders. The first fifty meters of backstroke hurt—I knew as I was swimming that it would *not* be a good split. I tried to make it up on the second fifty, but when I turned for the breast, I was behind. Breaststroke was what I called my fourth best since I didn't want my brain to subconsciously think I was *bad* at it by calling it my *worst*.

Breaststroke was about *timing*, requiring patience.

A virtue I did not have.

But I managed to keep the timing right, despite my brain telling my body, *Hurry, hurry, hurry!*

I didn't make progress, but I didn't fall behind, which was a win.

I would have the best freestyle in the field—I just needed to make sure I wasn't too far to catch them.

Beisel was long gone. She was already blasting through the freestyle when I was at the flags, finishing my breaststroke.

I always felt rested going into the freestyle leg. I craved the thrill of going from the slowness of breaststroke to the pure speed of freestyle.

I thundered into the final two laps and started doing what I did best—hunting people down. I passed one competitor. Another. I was closing in on the others . . .

I touched fifth. Best time.

I nodded at the scoreboard as I caught my breath, content. The 800 was my best chance of making the team. Starting off with a best time meant that more best times were going to follow.

It meant I was the best I'd ever been.

SwimSwam reported, though I didn't read it, "The youngest finalist we saw on this first day of competition had a huge swim for fifth in 4:41.61. . . . the second-fastest time ever swum by a fourteen-and-under. If she can avoid a burnout, she's got a bright future in a huge number of races" (Keith, 2012a).

I was living *res ipsa loquitur*, and I was loving it.

The next morning was the day of the 400 freestyle, where I would be up against Allison Schmitt, USA Swimming's best female swimmer. Best friends with Michael Phelps. Was expected to break the world record in the 200 freestyle.

Allison was in the heat after me, but she was already in the ready room when I arrived, her curly brown hair tucked into her cap, laughing with some fellow competitors.

I'm not one to get starstruck, but in that moment, though it took me years to admit it, I was. A little, teensy, tiny, *microscopic* bit.

I had a heat to win, so I didn't acknowledge Allison. I rummaged in my parka pocket for my second cap.

I pressed the latex against my forehead and attempted to pull it over my goggles. It refused, the cap slipping through my fingers and snapping upward off my head. I tried again, but I once again lost my grip, and the cap flew over the back.

Why was this cap so hard to put on? I scowled in frustration, then tried again. Again. Again. This *never* happened. Why was it happening now, in front of the best swimmers in the country?

On about my sixth try getting my cap to stay on my head, I felt someone approach.

I looked up. Allison Schmitt stood over me, her narrow face turned upward in a way that made me know she was holding back a laugh. Her almond-shaped eyes were a brown so dark that they reflected light, constantly glinting.

"Do you need help?"

My face warmed. For the first time at that meet, I felt *young*.

"*No.*" I could hear the defensiveness in my voice, though I wasn't exactly sure *why* I felt defensive.

This answer had been a mistake.

"It helps if you wear the latex one below the silicone," Allison continued. "And there's less drag."

"I'm allergic to latex."

Allison's head was slightly tilted, her expression something between amusement and confusion. "Are you sure you don't want help?"

"Yes."

Allison stared at me for what may have been eons. I wondered if she was going to demand that I accept. I *obviously* couldn't get my cap on.

"Okay," Allison finally said. "Good luck."

With the swim or with my cap?

She walked away, and I released a breath I hadn't realized I'd been holding.

Accepting help would have been a display of weakness. I wanted to be treated like all the other elite athletes.

But maybe she wasn't asking if I needed help because I'm young. Maybe it was because I actually do need help.

I'd have rather eaten a pint of caviar than call her back. I had something to prove, and I didn't want to seem inexperienced. I *belonged* there, and athletes who belonged could put on their own caps.

Allison smirked from the corner. Everyone's eyes were on me. After the longest thirty seconds of my life, my cap finally fell into place on my head.

Thank goodness. I wiped the memory from my mind, shaking the embarrassment off as I shook my muscles. It was go time. I just had to make finals.

I had an outside lane—Lane 1. Clean water on one side, though I wouldn't be able to see the far half of the pool.

Take your mark . . .

BEEP!

I dived in, surfacing last, half a body length behind everyone, per usual. The nonswimming parts—the dive and the turn—were my weaknesses.

The race got off to a rough start. I felt sluggish in the water, like my arms were moving at half speed.

I was behind at the halfway point, but my body felt more warmed up. More awake.

You have to go, I told myself. *You can catch these old people.*

The hunt began. I shifted into a gear that I didn't even know I had, one discovered through pure desperation.

I passed a few women on the third 100, but it still wasn't enough.

I was going to have to swim the fastest 100 of my life if I wanted to make finals.

I set my eyes on the girl in Lane 3. She was a second and a half ahead of me, an almost impossible amount of time to make up.

Almost.

Bring it on. The end of the race was when I came alive. I was fourteen. I never died. I could hunt down the old ladies.

The gap tightened. And tightened. We flipped. The final stretch.

I stopped breathing, putting my head down, and fighting with everything in my being. My lungs burned. My arms spun. I stopped looking for Lane 3 and swam my own race, staring down at the black line as I sped over it.

I rammed into the touchpad, my eyes shooting up to the clock. Lane 3 had touched me out. There were still two heats left, but I had gotten second in the first of the fast heats.

I felt eyes on me when I finished. People were noticing me after the 400 IM, and now I was on the verge of making finals. I just had to wait eight more minutes to find out if I'd done it.

I exited the pool and went to the Mixed Zone, the area where the media waited to interview the athletes, and where the swimmers had to walk through in order to get to the warm-down pool.

SwimSwam stopped me as I walked by, still struggling to catch my breath.

"Do you realize what kind of meet you're putting together right now, or are you just kinda going through it as it comes to you?" the interviewer asked.

"Uh . . . I don't know, I'm just kinda going through it. It's just a lot of fun! I've just always really enjoyed swimming, and then, I don't know, it just makes me go really fast."

That, plus the blood, sweat, and tears I had mixed into the chlorine.

I didn't need anyone to know *how* obsessed with swimming I was. I didn't need them to realize that I was constantly thinking about swimming and how to get faster. Yes, conflicting perspectives could—and did—coexist, but I only chose to show one part.

The love. Not the obsession. Loving it was what *made* me obsessed, after all.

I placed eighth in prelims, sliding into the final by .04 seconds. I owed that time to barely breathing for the last fifty meters. If I'd taken one more breath, I would have been ninth.

The interview came out, titled *Becca Mann Just Loves Swimming*. I watched it five times.

I went about the same routine that I'd done for the 400 IM the day before. Warm down, food, shave, compression wear, visualization, nap, more food, stretch, warm up, suit up. No thought required. I instead focused on finals. I would be next to a swimmer with a fantastic back half—even better than mine, which was a rare occurrence—but a *terrible* front half. I needed to be ahead at the 200.

Allison had her goggles on in the ready room so no one could see her eyes glint. Her mood was the opposite of prelims. She acknowledged no one. Her game face was on.

As a matter of fact, *no one* was speaking.

I sat down, put my goggles on like Allison, and did my ritual.

We paraded out. I was in Lane 8, the lane reserved for the slowest qualifier. I didn't mind—it meant I could only move up.

Outside smoke.

"Take your mark . . ."

The *beep* sounded. I executed my plan. I got ahead of the slow front-halfer beside me.

I could see Allison in my periphery. She'd broken away from the rest of the field. The announcer was shouting so loud I could hear him beneath the water.

Even though I was ahead of Lane 7, I could see that I was not in the running for second place.

Go, I told myself as we flipped at the 200. *Work your magic.*

The swimmer in Lane 7 began crawling up my body, catching me. I spun my arms faster.

The rest of the pool was blocked by Lane 7's swimmer's body. It became a race between the two of us. I had no idea where anyone else was.

I fought with all my strength. We turned into the last fifty meters.

Flames shot out from the side of the pool deck when I had five meters left of the race. The heat warmed my skin as I lunged for the wall.

I smashed into the touchpad, my face beet red with exertion.

I'd placed sixth, dropping two seconds and just missing the thirteen-to-fourteen National Age Group Record.

Once again, I was content. I was still proving that I was better than I'd ever been.

It was going to come down to the 800, my final event of the meet. I felt no pressure, just a building anticipation.

As we climbed out of the pool, I found myself walking beside Allison.

"Go get gold."

"Thanks," she breathed back, glowing.

The 200 butterfly was next. For events that were 200 meters or shorter, there were three races instead of two—sixteen athletes from the preliminary qualified for the semifinal, and the Top 8 in the semifinal qualified for the final the next day.

For the 200 fly, I decided to wear two silicone caps, so the "slower" latex wouldn't be on top.

I swam a best time and qualified for the semifinal.

When I paraded out for the semifinal that night and my name was announced, I received the loudest cheer of the heat. Everyone wanted the fourteen-year-old kid with the UGGs to make it.

But I was tenth in the semi, missing finals by .48 seconds.

I *should* have made finals, but I wasn't upset. The 200 fly was my weakest event anyway. It was too short.

"I would have had you scratch out of the final anyway," Herbert said. "You need to rest for the 800. That's what matters."

The event I had been waiting for.

For the 800, I would go back to wearing my latex cap on top. The competition wasn't the time to make changes, even when Allison Schmitt was the one suggesting them.

"Control the prelim," said Herbert. "Get a good lane for tomorrow night."

Herbert was telling me I was good enough to not even have to give my all to make the Top 8.

I qualified for finals in the 800 preliminary, touching fifth, going a best time even with my *controlled pace*, and only 3.92 seconds behind the top qualifier. That was *nothing* in a race over eight minutes.

I had another five seconds in me. There was no favorite. It was anyone's race.

Which meant it was *my* race.

More interviews came as I walked through the Mixed Zone. "Are you going to be a sophomore in high school?"

"No, I just finished eighth grade, but I'm homeschooled, so . . ."

"Do you think you have a sub-8:30 in you?"

"Uh, yeah, definitely." It was interesting to me how, since people had been caught off guard by my meet, they assumed that I, too, must have been caught off guard. No one realized that I had wholeheartedly dedicated the past eighteen months of my life to making the Olympic Team.

As I exited the pool, kids—a.k.a. people born in the same year as me—asked for autographs. Shirts, notebooks, limbs. I was on cloud nine, and I didn't look down. *This* was my destiny. All the competitors and coaches that I'd ever disagreed with would be proven wrong tomorrow.

The next day, I felt fantastic as I walked into the pool to warm up.

Fellow athletes double my age and half my speed watched as I sauntered onto the pool deck with my furry UGGs.

People were noticing what I had known all along: that I was going to be—and already was—one of the greatest swimmers in the world. I felt like a living legend, an intimidating force. Not knowing or caring that everyone else just saw a baby-faced kid half their size with big zits, a bigger smile, and the biggest personality.

I warmed up in the morning, my pace 100s telling me I was about to go an 8:24. Two hours before my event, I packed my bag, put on my UGGs, picked up my parka, and had my mom drive me to the pool.

This was it. I knew what to expect.

I did my pre-race routine. Warmed up. Texted my mom that I was *"SOOOO READY!"* Changed into my race suit. Sat down and visualized one final time.

Herbert approached when I opened my eyes. "You've done all the work. Go get it."

"I will. I'm going to."

I didn't even notice my competitors when I entered the ready room, even as I gave them each a customary "Good luck." I could only see the race ahead.

We lined up before parading out.

I was in Lane 2. The perfect lane to win from, I decided. My pre-race calm had settled over me.

You're ready. You're prepared. You're awesome.

When my name was announced, the crowd roared. I inhaled, physically harnessing the energy. The crowd had decided that *I* was the favorite.

I did my pre-race praying and stepped onto the block.

Sign of the cross. Shook out my muscles.

The arena fell silent. I stared into the water, though the image didn't make its way into my mind. My arms drooped over the edge of the block, loose and rested. The silence was thick as the entire stadium waited.

I embraced the calm.

Take your mark . . .

BEEP!

A long, long time ago, I can still remember how that music used to make me smile.

This was going to hurt, so I gave my brain something to focus on other than the pain. I had to finish twenty seconds before *American Pie* was over.

The first 100 went as it usually did. I was off to a disadvantage.

I caught up by the 150.

I spun my arms, taking my usual *unusually high* fifty strokes per lap.

At the 400—the halfway point—I was a few seconds behind second. But this was where I thrived. Katie Ledecky had broken away, but the second spot was still up for grabs.

I was going to get it.

I was still in the race—if the race was still going, I had a chance.

My favorite thing about being a "back-halfer" was the mindset it came with. When going got tough and my competitors got tired, I got going.

You can get this, I told myself. *Pretend every 100 is the last 100. You don't get tired.*

But this was a harder field to catch. We were all distance swimmers—and there were several open water swimmers in the pool as well, including Haley Anderson, who had already qualified for the Olympics in the 10k. All of them had endurance that rivaled my own.

I turned at the 500. I was catching up too slowly. Yes—I *was* catching them, but I was running out of pool as the end of the race loomed closer.

My stomach churned. My heart was in my throat, reverberating through the water.

So COME ON! I yelled to myself. *Becca be nimble, Becca be quick!*

600. Only 1.5 seconds behind now. *Go, go, go!* I could only see Haley Anderson just a smidge ahead of me on the other side of the pool. That was second. It had to have been second.

I closed the gap a tiny bit going into the 700.

Last 100. I put my head down, stopped looking, and swam with everything in my being.

And the three men I admire most, the Father, Son, and the Holy Ghost . . . They caught the last train for the coast.

I rammed into the wall, pain shooting through my hand at the impact.

The day . . .

Water rushed out of my ears, allowing the roar of the crowd to seep in. I scoured the scoreboard, scanning for my name.

I dropped five seconds.

I got the thirteen-fourteen NAG.

My eyes darted for the number.

The music . . .

A large "5" was beside my name.

Died.

I'd been fighting for third. Me, Haley, and another swimmer had touched around the same time, with me coming in last. I hadn't seen Kate Ziegler, who'd touched second, break away.

The numbness of shock froze my body. I stared at the scoreboard, my jaw unhinged.

I couldn't bring myself to celebrate the NAG.

So bye, bye, Miss American Pie . . .

I forced the mournful music out of my brain. It was too cathartic. I didn't want catharsis—I wanted to be hurt.

I got my wish. When the shock subsided, the pain hit me like a truck. My chest was heaving with more than just exertion. Not even my pain-fighting adrenaline, which was still coursing through my body, could stop the tears from forming behind my goggles.

I ripped them off, dunking my head into the silence of the water. My ears rang. It was peaceful down here, in the thick water where only I existed. I opened my eyes in the chlorine to clear them, taking in the blurry bottom of the pool.

Not now. People are looking. People can't see this. Compose yourself.
My chin shook. I tried anyway, sucking on the inside of my cheek.
I lifted my head from the quiet oasis to face whatever came next.

No one in the Mixed Zone wanted to speak with me this time. I picked up my parka and my UGGs and carried them over to where Herbert waited.

Devastation painted his face. I'm sure it was on mine, too, despite my best efforts to conceal it.

"I should have done better," Herbert said. "This was my fault."

I was caught off guard. "No, it's not."

"You should have been on that team."

I opened my mouth, then closed it. I had no idea what to say. There was nothing *to* say.

You moved away from the family for nothing, my mind whispered. *You broke them apart for* nothing.

"You *deserved* to be on that team," Herbert continued. "You did everything right."

If I did everything right, why didn't I make it?

"You did everything right too," I said instead. "It's no one's fault. I wasn't good enough."

"You *are* good enough. I should have done something more. Something different with the training."

"I got the NAG," I pointed out.

"It was a good swim."

My throat was raw. "I know."

"I'm proud of you."

His words broke my heart. Was *I* even proud of myself?

No. I could've done something better. "Thank you. I'm, uh . . . gonna warm down."

This was the first and last time a coach would ever say my performance was their fault to me. Though I stood by what I told Herbert—he had done nothing wrong. I just hadn't been *good enough*.

After staring vacantly at the black line in the warm-down pool for ten minutes, I hurried into the locker room. I was relieved to find it empty.

A TV in the corner played the meet. I happened to arrive just as Katie Ledecky rose from the floor of the deck to accept her gold medal. That was when the tears started. When I was alone, watching Katie Ledecky live *my* dream.

She'd gotten what I wanted. What had *she* done that *I* hadn't? Was she just the better version of me? She was only eight months older than me. Just as guarded. Catholic. Serious.

This was salt in the wound.

Guilt nagged the abyss of my mind. She'd been nothing but kind. She was the better swimmer. And she would be the better person if I succumbed so easily to jealousy.

SwimSwam wrote, "As if a fifteen-year-old winning weren't enough, fourteen-year-old Becca Mann took fifth in 8:28.54. That breaks an epic, thirty-four-year-old National Age Group Record for thirteen-to-fourteens set by Sippy Woodhead that had been 8:29.35. That is one of the oldest records in American swimming and can't be overshadowed even by the amazing Ledecky swim. In her third final, Mann completed an outstanding meet that is one of the best we've ever seen by a swimmer that young" (Keith, 2012c).

But it *was* overshadowed.

I should have been happy. I knew that, to everyone else, it looked as though I'd just had the best meet of my life. And I had. But I couldn't be proud of myself.

It didn't matter that I'd just swum faster than I'd ever swum before. It didn't matter that I loved trying to catch someone faster than me. It didn't matter that I had become the youngest person to make three Olympic Trials finals and one semifinal in a single meet. That wasn't enough for me this time. I wanted to be an Olympian.

I wanted the label. I needed to prove that moving to Florida and betting on myself hadn't been for nothing.

I was supposed to be the Chosen One. But I'd failed my quest. The book didn't have a happy ending.

I didn't bargain with myself. There was nothing else I could have done to go faster. I'd made no mistakes. I'd just needed more time.

As I walked out of the locker room, random coaches or swimmers told me, "Once you go through puberty—"

"You're going to grow a few more inches—"

"You haven't started lifting yet. You'll put on muscle—"

I never used my age as an excuse—I used it as a weapon.

"You're going to be unstoppable in 2016."

"2016 is your year."

"You're going to qualify for five events in 2016."

The more 2016 was mentioned, the angrier I got. I wouldn't be fourteen anymore. I wouldn't be a child prodigy. I would just be like everyone else.

Why did no one understand how important it was for me to be the youngest of them all? To be *the best*?

Plus, it was a whole *third* of my lifetime away. It may as well have been a millennium.

I'm not going to be able to get eight Olympic Medals like Michael Phelps did.

The words tainted my brain like poison, even though that goal wasn't possible for a distance swimmer like me, and I couldn't sprint to save my life. The 1500, which was my best event, wasn't an Olympic event for women. That left the 800, 400 freestyle, 400 IM, 200 butterfly, and 10k for me to get medals in.

Not enough. Even if, by some miracle, I happened to make the 200 freestyle and the 4x200 freestyle relay, it wouldn't be enough.

Maybe I can also get good enough at the 200 IM?

That was what I was going to have to do. This would be my new challenge. I would have to stay in Florida another four years because I wouldn't give up on my dream this easily. My vision of going back to the Chicago suburbs, to real school, was laid to rest. I'd channel this failure into my training. I had four years to get to the top. I would make every day count.

I *had* to.

I *had* to be an Olympian, and I *couldn't* just be an average Olympian. I couldn't be mediocre.

I was too terrified of mediocrity to even admit I feared it.

6

SHE PEAKED

I refused to be Icarus after Olympic Trials. I'd flown too close to the sun? Fine. I'd make new wings out of something that didn't melt.

I wasn't going to rest on my laurels or wallow in defeat. Instead, I did the only thing I knew how to do—I got back to work. I transformed everything that I hadn't achieved at Olympic Trials into a blazing trail toward 2016.

I exploded onto the international scene in 2012, my first year on the USA Swimming National Team via being in the Top 6 in the nation.

I went to Junior Pan Pacific Championships a few months after Trials, getting three best times and winning four of my five events. I got two more thirteen-to-fourteen National Age Group Records in the 400 IM and the 1500.

I was drug tested for the first of what would be tens of dozens of times after winning the 1500 at the US Open Championships. Since I was a minor, my mom had to accompany me to watch the person who would watch me urinate. I reached a high enough world ranking that I entered the International Drug Testing Pool, meaning that I had to submit my 24/7 whereabouts. They could come and demand a blood and/or urine sample any time between the hours of 5 a.m. and 11 p.m.

Being on the National Team meant that my every whim was catered to. Something hurt? There were five doctors, an MRI machine, an ultrasound, and a PT regime waiting. Struggling with the mental game? Here are five sports psychologists to choose from. Need help with your diet? Talk to the nutritionist.

I got five vials of blood drawn monthly to test my recovery and nutrients. Competition expenses were reimbursed. A sleep monitor was delivered. Speedo representatives gave me free tech suits under the table. Race footage was available after every meet, with stats and a race analyst ready to discuss it with me.

I found myself invited to international competitions by USA Swimming, where I would train, travel, and compete with Olympians I'd had on my radar to beat for years. When the invitation came, my mom told me, "Never turn down an opportunity to see the world. Especially for free."

The first competition was in Turkey. Bill Rose, Ashley Twichell's coach, was the head coach of Team USA.

I immediately loved Coach Rose. "What are you thinking for training?" he asked. "Are you tapering? Just tell me what you need."

I did, and Coach Rose gave me everything I wanted—splits, practices, advice.

Life became a cyclone of travel and competition. I won the 800 at the Berlin World Cup and got almost a dozen medals between Berlin and the Moscow World Cups. I would have won $3,000 in one week if I were professional, though I couldn't accept the prize money since I was keeping my NCAA eligibility. I would likely be the top college recruit of my year in the nation since my best 1650 time would have won NCAAs, which meant a full ride to wherever I wanted.

As I went through puberty, I became convinced that my body had adapted into the most efficient swimming machine that it could be. I lived in the water as it changed. I was still on the short side for an elite swimmer, but the rest of my body adjusted. My shoulders broadened. My rib cage expanded to accommodate my lungs. My wingspan lengthened to six feet.

Swimming took over my life yet again. I'd been naive to think spending another four years in Florida had been anything but inevitable.

I felt on top of the world as I traveled, brushing off not making the 2012 Olympic Team and setting my sights on 2016.

The whirlwind distracted me from my spiraling, obsessive thoughts. It was hard to catastrophize amid the excitement of international competition and the thrill of being known and rooted for. If I swam fast, I couldn't fixate on disturbing what-if scenarios.

Herbert, my family, and I were no longer the only people who saw me as one of the best swimmers in the world. Since Trials, I'd become the talk of the swimming community. People were whispering—and commenting on SwimSwam—that I was "maybe the most diverse swimmer in the country" because of the number of events I could swim at an elite level.

But my mindset had shifted after Trials—I stopped trying to win medals and started to chase after the best version of my swimming. The dream was still the same, but this way, I had complete control over how I pursued it.

And that greatest version of myself wasn't in the pool. Yes, I wanted to challenge Katie in the distance events—but not as much as I wanted to master open water. No matter how much Herbert tried to make me forget about it, it continued to call to my soul.

I decided to go to an Open Water World Cup the month before Nationals to get some race experience. I wanted to make summer World Championships, also known as "the Olympics of the non-Olympic years," in open water.

The race took place on Cozumel Island, Mexico, in the clearest aqua water I'd ever seen. It was an eight-loop course, and the best of the best open water swimmers would be competing.

I had more pool speed than all of them. I figured that meant that I would be able to beat them.

But the postcard-blue water was deceiving.

The current was so strong it took double the time to swim against it.

The leaders dropped me on the second loop. I couldn't hang, and I had no idea why when everything physically, mentally, and emotionally said that I should be able to keep up.

After the race, Herbert once again texted me, *"You should focus on the pool."* It made sense. I was *better* at pool swimming and was establishing myself as one of the best in the world.

But it didn't matter. I could have been Michael Phelps and it *still* wouldn't have mattered—I would have given it all up for an unpredictable race in the ocean. Cozumel humbled me, making me even more determined to figure out how to master open water swimming.

I approached the head of the USA Open Water National Team, Bryce, after the race and asked, "What can I improve?"

"A lot."

"Good. What?"

"Let's start with your feeds." After hearing everything I'd been doing wrong with feeding, we talked about drafting. Sighting.

Bryce had never been an open water swimmer or coach. Despite telling me what was *wrong*, he didn't know how to teach me what was *right*. And I couldn't apply his advice because I knew nothing about strategy, or sighting, or conservation. Neither did Herbert, and he wasn't inclined to help.

I had a month before Open Water Nationals to figure it out. So I went back to Florida and I googled. I read articles. I studied. I hyperfixated.

I didn't have to search long before I hit the jackpot—videos of Jack Fabian, father and coach of Eva, talking open water strategy, drafting techniques, drills, and navigation, and most were accompanied by a PowerPoint.

Bingo.

I was a kid again, learning new skills, and I ate it up. I took notes. I studied the Nationals course map, memorizing the distances and turns. I made a feeding stick out of a golf ball retriever.

I couldn't rely on my pool speed. I had to have endurance.

Thankfully, Herbert's practices were long enough that I knew I could handle the distance if I swam a smart race.

2013 Open Water Nationals were in Castaic Lake, California. My mom would be my feeder. Herbert did not attend.

There's nothing quite as exhilarating as an open water race day.

I arrived at the course before sunrise. The lake was obscured by a thick layer of fog, the turn buoys hidden behind it.

At the check-in tent, a volunteer outstretched her hand for my ID, then handed me my race ticket.

"Nails?"

I showed her my toenails. She nodded. Then my fingernails.

"Clip that pinky."

She pushed a Tupperware container of nail clippers in alcohol toward me. I clipped off my pinky nail, making it short enough that I wouldn't be able to scratch my competitors.

"Suit, cap, and goggles?"

I showed her my suit, followed by my caps and goggles.

"Good luck, Becca."

Next, my numbers were stamped onto my body, my timing chips wrapped around my wrists.

I warmed up and changed into my race suit. By now, the beach was bustling. The fog had lifted—the course didn't look quite as I'd visualized it, but it didn't matter. For the first time going into an open water race, I was prepared.

I had my mom rub Vaseline all over my straps so I wouldn't chafe, then my ankles for the unlucky competitors who decided to grab them. And my cap, so anyone who tried to rip it off—as someone had attempted the year before—would have trouble getting a good grip.

"If you're with them on the last lap," my mom said as I tucked a GU into the back of my suit, "I know you're going to win."

This year, I wasn't going to be the one hanging on for dear life. *They* were going to have to hang with *me*.

I grinned. My mom believed in me perhaps even more than I did, and it was comforting to know that she would be on shore, sending all her energy my way.

I ran through everything I'd learned from Jack Fabian's videos. I remembered my training. I had to get top two to qualify for World Championships in the 10k.

It was time.

I started next to Eva again. By now, she was used to me being her shadow at the beginning of the race. She didn't move, just threw me an irritated look.

Rude.

The race commenced. I stuck to my plan through the first five of six loops, saving up for the final sprint as much as I could, using the new sighting skills I'd learned from Jack Fabian, and taking a few extra seconds at the feeding station to chug all twenty ounces of my bottle.

Sure enough, I found myself with the leaders going into the final lap. My mom's words echoed from my mind to my muscles. *I know you're going to win.*

I added more kick and surged to climb my way up to the front, passing Haley Anderson, who had won an Olympic Silver in the 10k in London the year before.

I broke away with a few others, including Eva Fabian and Ashley Twichell. I accessed my pool speed. All of us came into the finish chute together. I increased my stroke rate. I reached up for the finish structure . . .

I slammed my palm into it.

Second.

I'd done it. I'd made World Championships.

The biggest grin stretched over my face as joy spread through my exhausted body. I found my mom in the crowd—her expression mirrored mine.

I'm the second-best open water swimmer in the country.

I was happier than I'd ever been in my entire life.

I went to the drug testing tent afterward. I sat down beside Eva, who'd gotten third.

Eva didn't even look at me as she chatted up the drug testers. "I just get to play violin instead of homework."

Eva had played the national anthem at pool Nationals a few years before, and everyone *loved* talking about it.

"That's amazing," the drug tester replied.

"Yeah! I'm *loving* Yale."

I rolled my eyes behind Eva's back.

She's still mad at me for starting next to her, I decided. It was ironic that, without her dad and his open water videos, I wouldn't have beaten her.

I thought about telling her but decided against it. I figured she didn't need an even *bigger* ego.

SwimSwam wrote that the Team USA World Championship team would include "fifteen-year-old Becca Mann from the Clearwater Aquatic Team. Most of the focus on her has been around her pool swimming, but her growing reputation for a love of tough races makes her a great candidate in open water" (Keith, 2013).

★　★　★

At World Championships in Barcelona, my open water schooling continued. We arrived two weeks before the competition for a training trip in Mataró. Our pool was on the beach just a mile from the hotel, allowing for practices to consist of both pool and ocean training.

The coach was a woman named Madeline, who trained Haley Anderson at USC.

Madeline had an ageless look to her—I couldn't quite figure out if she was thirty or fifty. It extended to her personality—a youthfulness that could be considered either carefree or immature.

I loved her from the moment we met.

Madeline and I were walking behind an athlete who had a giant, overflowing swim bag, en route to our first practice. Curiosity getting the better of me, I asked, "What's in your bag?"

"Oh," he said. "It's full of sups."

Madeline and I exchanged a confused glance.

"Subs?" I asked. "Like sandwiches?"

"No, *sups*. Supplements."

"Oh. Well, that's less exciting than subs. I was going to ask for a turkey."

Madeline burst into laughter. "I wanted a ham."

"Are there different bread choices? I only eat whole wheat."

"There *must* be some sourdough in there. What about cheese?"

Madeline and I laughed the whole way to the pool about *sandwiches*.

I soon discovered that Madeline laughed at *everything* I said. She was superstitious about numbers the same way I was. And she paid attention to my swimming. She let me DJ in her car and sing as loudly as I wanted. She made *every* practice fun.

Madeline subtly planted the seeds of USC into my brain. She included me in a way that made me feel as if I were already a Trojan.

So did Haley.

Haley Anderson was calm, cool, and collected. She carried herself with impeccable posture and grace. Her eyes were clear blue—so light that I was convinced they would shatter like ice if I looked into them for too long. At practice, she wore foundation sunscreen on her face.

She was a natural athlete—she could have swum the 10k straight out of the womb. She was a master at adapting, becoming just a little bit better with every race she swam.

I'd mentally nicknamed her *Cap Twister* after she'd twisted my cap sideways at 2012 Open Water Nationals. I didn't hold a grudge over it—I hadn't known how to maneuver within a pack at the time and had probably deserved it.

Haley tolerated me at first and, eventually, found me both amusing and irritating. She wasn't afraid to tell me, either. Sometimes, she was my best friend; other times, we'd get into petty fights, and I'd go out of my way to annoy her while she tried to ignore me.

I relished being included in their group. Madeline, Haley, and I. The Trojans of present and future.

"Haley and I did a lot of ocean swims before this," Madeline told me. "And we swim outside year-round."

"That's so nice," I said, already dreaming about USC.

"*And* we let the swimmers have the aux during practice."

But Madeline wasn't who I learned the *most* from. Instead, the older swimmers—who were some of the best open water swimmers in the world—hung back to teach me tricks and strategy.

Especially Alex Meyer—a 2012 Olympian with a wicked sense of humor, a Harvard education, and a career full of experience he was more than willing to share.

The only swimmer who didn't go out of her way to help me was Eva.

I'd taken her spot as the young prodigy. She'd been the youngest person on the Open Water National Team for six years until *I* came along.

The more we interacted, the more apparent it became that there would be no easing the tension between us. I thought she was pretentious, and she thought I was cocky. We both kept our distance. Thankfully, we weren't competing in any of the same events—I was swimming the 5k and 10k while she was doing the 25k.

One night, when Eva and I were forced to eat together, I said, "The 25k is *easy*. You just have to swim—it's not like you're going fast the whole time, like in the 10k."

Eva shot daggers at me. If looks could kill, I would have fallen dead on the spot.

Thankfully, Jordan Wilimovsky, a fellow rookie who was also swimming the 25k, cackled. The tension broke, though Eva was still irked, and I internally rebuked myself for my inability to think before I spoke.

"So," Jordan said good-naturedly, "what *would* be hard for you? Crossing a 1,000-mile channel?"

"That's closer to hard, at least," I said with a mischievous smile, thinking about how challenging the Au'au crossing had been. "But there are some other things I want to do first."

"You don't want to do that," another athlete said, joining us. "Those channels sound miserable."

"Because they *are*," someone else piped up.

"Not to me." I had a feeling I would dip my toe back into channel swimming in the future, but I wanted to achieve my Olympic dream first. A channel crossing was all about grit, while Olympic events were about precision.

Eva rolled her eyes.

The races in Barcelona were held in a disgusting marina. I watched a yacht pour a chamber pot into the water just before I jumped in.

Ew.

"*Caca en el agua!*" Eva yelled before diving in. I would have been amused if I'd disliked her less.

The 2.5k course began in one inlet, went through the main area of the marina, into another inlet, then back around to the start. It was interesting and would probably be fun—but violent with all the turns.

My first Open Water World Championships went *very* well.

I was eighth in the 5k, just a few seconds away from a World Championships medal.

But the 10k was what mattered. The Olympic event.

Several of my teammates gave me tips on how to improve. I took them all to heart when, two days after the 5k, I was back on the start pontoon for the ten.

I waited for the signal, my toes wrapped over the edge of the start platform. I wanted to avoid the violence of the pack, so I was determined to be the first in the water.

I leaned forward after I heard the starter say, "Take your mark . . ."

It was an obnoxiously long wait. I teetered on the edge of the start platform—and I felt myself *falling*.

AHHHHHHH! my brain screamed, unable to think anything else.

I instinctively reached for the competitor beside me—an Olympic medalist—to hold on for dear life. But instead of pulling me back, she shoved me so I couldn't pull her down with me.

All is fair in love and open water.

The horn sounded as I was airborne, so I didn't get disqualified. I entered the water feetfirst rather than headfirst.

I was immediately at a disadvantage. Everyone else was stroking away by the time I resurfaced.

Elbows were thrown into my ribs. I was held under a buoy until I was afraid I would drown.

I tried to roll with the punches. I tried not to panic. I put all my energy into getting to—and staying—where I wanted to be.

But when we had one loop left to go, a hand landed on my cap and tore my goggles off my face.

I watched as they flew through the air and landed in the water ten feet away with an inaudible, anticlimactic *splash*.

I couldn't even see who'd done it.

The leader swam right over where my goggles had sunk. There would be no getting them back now, especially because—you know, the *murkiness* of the water.

I plowed on, opening my eyes underwater. The filth didn't matter. If I got sick, it would be after the race, and nothing *after* the race mattered.

I decided that I was happy my goggles had been ripped off my face. It was a rite of passage.

What I didn't love was that we were going into our last loop, and the feeding station—where my backup goggles would be—was off course.

No one would be stopping there. I'd have to swim off course, then go back, and hope I could make my way back up to the front.

I was in a good spot—the Top 5.

I wouldn't be after getting the goggles. Did I need them? I still had 2.5 kilometers left.

I made a calculated decision, then stopped doubting myself, broke off the side of the pack, and sprinted for the feeding dock.

Madeline had the goggles waiting on the end of the stick. I grabbed them and threw them onto my head, then sprinted back for the leaders.

I'd lost my position. By the time I caught back up to the pack, I was around thirtieth. But the adrenaline was flowing. I'd handled that *so* well. I couldn't have done it better. And there was still time to climb the ranks. I would get back to where I'd been before.

But it was going to hurt.

I started to make my way up the outside, using my competitors' hip drafts as Alex had taught me. But my progress was too slow—yes, it was progress, but I was running out of runway—we were approaching the finish, and I still wasn't where I wanted to be.

I was back in the Top 10 for the last 200 meters. I sprinted with everything in me. I passed the other American. I passed a few more people . . .

I touched eighth.

Eighth in the world. Only 4.2 seconds from gold in a one-hour, fifty-eight-minute race.

It wasn't bad. Yes, I'd wanted a medal, but I would take it. I'd learned how to adapt and maneuver within a group of swimmers. I'd learned how to think without panicking.

A loss was more valuable than a win. If it had been a smooth, easy race, it wouldn't have made me stronger, better, and wiser.

Instead of going back to training in Clearwater, I flew straight from Barcelona to Irvine, California, for the US Open.

I expected to ride the momentum into my next competitions.

Instead, I struggled through the meet. I can't remember how fast—or slow—I went, just that it was subpar.

My pool season was *not* panning out.

Thankfully, I had another meet to redeem myself at. A week later, I was on a plane to Dubai for the Junior World Championships.

Again, I was nowhere near my best times in the five events I swam in Dubai, but I did manage to snag a win in the 1,500—becoming the Junior World Champion—and a few silvers.

I was disappointed. I was all-in on being the best *me*. The medals didn't matter. I wanted best times.

"You've been traveling a lot," Herbert texted me from Florida after the meet, *"and focusing on open water. You'll put some work in when you get back."*

I *had* been on the road for months. I loved traveling—I felt less alone surrounded by other athletes from Team USA than I did alone with whoever was watching me in Clearwater. I relished competing internationally, and I loved exploring and adventuring.

I tried to brush off my slower times, but the comments on SwimSwam were . . . not ideal. Open Water was a much less popular sport than pool swimming, so people didn't really care that I was breaking out there.

Olympic Trials were a fluke.

She peaked.

She's not going to be able to go as fast when she goes through puberty.

Who's next?

It was always "Who's next?" Never "Who's here?"

Everyone wanted to know who was going to step up and destroy me. When I faltered, the world turned. When I aged, it discarded me. When I was doing well, everyone was bored.

I was furious. I was the youngest person to qualify for the USA Swimming World Championship Team! I had gotten eighth in the *whole entire freaking world* in two events!

But I needed to be better. I was fifteen—and aging out of my child prodigy label. No one saw me as a sweet, innocent ingenue they could get behind as they had at Olympic Trials.

The critics gave me the fuel I needed as I headed home to Florida. I let the anger ferment into an energy that charged me as I got back into hard training. I was excited to prove them wrong.

The closer I got to the top, the harder—and smarter—I had to work to improve. It would come in the minuscule details. In showing up every day.

This plateau was part of the process. I just had to keep at it until the incline increased again.

I wasn't sure what was causing it. Maybe it was the travel. Maybe I was broken down and about to rebuild myself into something even better. Or maybe I was mismanaging my energy and needed to figure out how much to distribute to what I was trying to achieve.

Or maybe it was because I was outgrowing my environment.

I was still climbing the mountain. That much I knew, even if I had fallen into a valley. There was a way to excel at both pool and open water—I just had to make sure I had the right tools.

7

SO LONG, FLORIDA

I went back to Clearwater with the intent of settling into some focused, uninterrupted training. I was ready to put in the work.

Except, when I got back, Herbert was a bit distracted and didn't seem to have a plan for me.

And I *needed* a plan. I'd regressed. I wasn't good enough yet to be regressing. I still needed to be *improving*.

One practice, Herbert pulled everyone aside and told us that he had decided that *underwaters*—the dolphin kicks swimmers do beneath the surface on each wall—were slowing us down.

"You're going to take one kick to the surface."

I thought this was a terrible idea. If someone's underwaters were *slow*, it was because they weren't maximizing their speed off the wall. It meant they needed to *work* on them. I snorted. The other star swimmer, Casey, who was nearly as good as I was, glared at me.

I usually agreed with Herbert when it came to swimming. He loved finding innovative ideas, but he would often drop them if the trend didn't immediately pay off. This was one that I knew wouldn't stick. In a month's time, I was sure he would realize that getting rid of underwaters was a bad idea.

When we hopped in the pool, I refused to change my underwaters.

After one hundred meters, Casey turned to me. "Herbert said we're not doing underwaters!"

"I'm not doing that."

"Herbert *said*."

"You don't need to worry about what I'm doing."

"You think you're above Herbert now too?"

"I think it's none of your business."

Casey pushed off the wall. I was thrown—Casey could be prickly, but I'd considered her a friend. As much as she could be, anyway, with me never opening up.

Maybe she's just mad I'm better than her? One of the other swimmers had asked her what it was like to always be #2 to me a week before.

But I wasn't sure.

Herbert didn't seem as invested in me, and I felt like I was on my own once again.

I didn't know how to do this alone.

I'd made the National Team in Open Water and the 200 butterfly—which was one of my weaker pool events. I needed Herbert back. He was more than capable of helping me get to the next level, but I needed more consistency.

After three months of this "training," USA Swimming invited me to more world cups in Tokyo and Beijing. The competitions were a few weeks away. I accepted the moment I got the email between morning and afternoon practice, then went back to the pool. "You're traveling *again*?" Herbert grumbled when I told him. "Did you learn *nothing* from traveling all summer?"

"I haven't traveled in three months, and I've never been to Asia."

"You need to stay here and train."

"I already accepted."

Herbert's eyes darkened. "You can go train with Saint Petersburg Aquatics if you want to travel and focus on open water."

My respect deteriorated as swiftly as the words came out of his mouth.

Herbert and I didn't speak for the rest of the week. I didn't tell him that this meet was my chance to see if my subpar 2013 pool times had just been a fluke or if I really *was* plateauing at the ripe old age of fifteen.

Maybe I should have pretended to consult him. But it was *my* life and *my* career. I wanted to compete in the Beijing Water Cube, where the 2008 Olympics were held. I wanted to see Tokyo. I wanted to walk the Great Wall of China.

Other swimmers sensed my place as "Herbert's favorite" slipping. Herbert stopped coming over for dinner. I didn't stop by his house and see if he wanted to join us on the boat.

Without Herbert's protection, my peers' attitudes shifted. Slower swimmers began claiming my lane. My training partners began skipping laps, no longer caring when I scolded them, instead moving on to the next set, leaving me with the impossible choice of doing the workout as written or having training partners to push me.

They'd never respected me—I'd only been protected because I'd been Herbert's favorite. I felt a wave of relief when I boarded my flight to Asia, knowing I needed the reprieve.

Coach Rose was once again the USA head coach. He was attentive. He gave me what I needed for warm-up. He seemed concerned about where I was mentally.

I had a subpar showing, continuing my streak of frustratingly mediocre swimming.

But I didn't regret going. I experienced my first significant earthquake in Tokyo and got to walk along the Great Wall.

On the last night of the competition, I turned to Coach Rose. "I'm worried I'm not improving."

"You had a great year in open water."

"I know." I frowned at the water, watching the Iron Lady, Katinka Hosszu, win her umpteenth race of the World Cup series, taking home around half a million dollars.

I needed to be *that* dominant. I had to be—the cost of what I had sacrificed wasn't worth being *mediocre* at swimming.

I was terrified. My confidence came from knowing that I was doing everything in my power to achieve my goals. Why was I living away from my family if I wasn't training *the best I possibly could?*

Coach Rose's eyes were kind, sensing my uncertainty. "You can come on a training trip with me if you want. If you ever want a break from Florida."

I didn't know what I wanted. I didn't know what to do. That was the problem.

"I appreciate that." I already knew that Herbert would *never* agree to it.

People weren't talking about me anymore. When I walked onto the pool deck, heads didn't turn. People didn't admire my UGG boots, which was offensive because they were *awesome*.

I went back to Clearwater with a wavering trust in Herbert.

He wasn't at the pool on the day that marked the end of my time in Florida.

His assistant, Tom, was coaching that day.

Three times a week, we trained with pulleys. This involved a giant bucket filled with somewhere between thirty and a hundred pounds of water, depending on the set, connected to a pulley system and a rope with a belt—swimmers put on the belt and swam, lifting the bucket as they crossed the pool.

It took about twenty minutes to set up.

On this particular afternoon, Herbert had written a pulley practice for Tom to administer. But instead of Tom taking the time to set up all the pulleys, he decided he was only going to do two lanes instead of the usual twelve.

Teenagers were blowing bubbles at the bottom of the pool. Half of them were skipping every other fifty meters. They had to have someone else tell them to work hard rather than simply *wanting* to work hard in order to get better.

I did every part of the practice I could do until I only had the pulley set left. There was a line.

"I'm ready for the pulleys," I announced to Tom.

"Oh, it's gonna be a minute. Just do the other part of the practice."

"I already did."

"Oh."

I waited for him to say more. He didn't.

"Are you going to set up another lane?" I asked, impatient. If Herbert were here, this wouldn't be happening.

"No, you'll have to wait."

"How long?"

"I dunno."

My blood boiled. How was I supposed to redeem myself when I couldn't even do a practice the way it was written?

I didn't move away from my family to *wait* because the coach wasn't doing his job.

So I didn't. I hopped out of the pool, scooped up my swim bag, and stormed out of the building in the most dramatic fashion I could muster.

Eyes followed me from the water. I wanted them all to see. This was *my* career. *My* passion. I would take it seriously even if everyone else didn't.

I took the rest of the day to be angry, then I decided I would brush this off. Herbert would be back the next morning, and everything would be fine.

But when I walked onto the deck at 4:40 a.m., Herbert stormed toward me. One look at his furrowed brow signaled that everything would not, in fact, *be fine.*

"Tom respected you. *I* respected you. Everyone here looks up to you, and then you disrespect us all by leaving in the middle of practice."

Shock overwhelmed me, turning off my brain.

All my thoughts could summon were Herbert's words from Olympic Trials: *"This was my fault. You did everything right."*

How odd—I hadn't wanted to hear it then. I hadn't needed to.

But I needed it *now.* I needed to hear that Herbert had my back in more than just swimming. I needed him to step up and be my grandfather and protect me.

My ability to trust hung in the balance, forever to be altered by his next words. He was one of the very few people that I had let in—and if he betrayed me when he was already in the house, I wasn't sure I'd ever unlock my doors for anyone again.

"You need to apologize to Tom."

My heart darkened as my chin began to tremble. *Not now,* I told it. *Be an adult. Don't cry like a baby.*

"I'm not doing that."

"You *have* to."

I wasn't sorry. I don't apologize when I'm not sorry.

So that's exactly what I said. "I'm not sorry."

And I didn't *have* to do anything.

My chin tremble was growing into an earthquake. *Remain stoic,* I ordered myself. *Do not give yourself away.*

"If you don't apologize, you're kicked off the team."

Ultimatums don't work on you, I reminded myself. I took a breath. "Then I'm kicked off the team."

The words were bitter on my tongue. I felt like Herbert was discarding me. *Herbert,* whom I saw as a grandfather. Who catered every workout to me. Who would come on the boat with me and my parents. Who, despite his sometimes erratic nature, I had trusted and wanted to make proud.

Now I felt like he didn't even respect me anymore.

But *I* wouldn't respect *myself* if I apologized to Tom. I wouldn't have respected myself if I'd stood for that ridiculous attempt at a practice.

Self-respect was the only thing I could control.

I needed to train, so I dove into the pool and did the practice anyway. I wasn't going to let getting kicked off a team stop me from swimming.

Tears pooled into my goggles. My five years with Herbert were coming to an end.

All because I refused to apologize. All because I wouldn't compromise myself.

I was nowhere near my full potential. My strokes needed changes that Herbert knew how to fix but couldn't express in a way I understood. My training partners couldn't provide me with the challenge I needed.

I had become stagnant, but this was an opportunity. The world was my oyster. There was nothing tying me to Florida. I could improve elsewhere. *Anywhere.*

I was eight again, sitting in the backseat of my parents' car, watching the world pass by, knowing I could do anything I wanted. *Go* anywhere I wanted. *Be* anyone I wanted. I was no longer thriving in this environment—there was no point in staying here.

The *Golden Goggle Awards*—or as I like to call them, the Oscars of swimming—were held in Los Angeles that year. I took Rachel as my plus one.

I found Madeline in the midst of the well-dressed athletes. She was easy to spot, as she was one of the shortest among the towering swimmers.

"Can I get your advice on something?"

"Of course," she said, standing just a little too close to me.

I told her I would be leaving Clearwater.

"Where do you think I should go?" I asked. I couldn't train with her—NCAA rules prohibited it. "I'm thinking about trying out Bill Rose—"

"Don't go to Coach Rose," interrupted Madeline. "You won't get any IM training there."

I deflated at her words. Coach Rose had been my top choice. But there was one other option rivaling it.

"What about Bob Bowman?"

Bob Bowman, the coach of Michael Phelps. I'd been watching a "Dream Team" assemble in Baltimore to train under him. Seven Olympic medalists had already flocked there.

Madeline nodded, though she didn't look thrilled. "That could be good."

"Where do you think I should go?"

"Let me think on it."

The moment she was gone, Rachel pulled me away from eavesdroppers, concern written on her face. "Don't trust that woman."

"Why not? She's helped me—"

"Because she wants you to go to USC."

"Well, *obviously*."

Rachel rolled her eyes. "She doesn't want what's best for you."

"How would you even know that? You've never had a conversation with her!"

I couldn't let the fantasy I had created around USC be shattered by Rachel's take on Madeline.

I went back to Clearwater to pack up my stuff.

Herbert tried to change my mind. He called my mom and told her to convince me to apologize to Tom. She refused. He said that I could stay with him until Pan Pacs, which was nine months away, while I found a new place to train.

But I was swimming in a poisoned pool. Herbert had shattered my already fragile trust.

I needed to swim with the "Dream Team." Not kids who sat on the bottom of the pool when their coach wasn't there.

So that's exactly what I did. I packed up my Florida home, including the stray cat, Dock, whom I'd found dumpster diving on the beach.

When Herbert offered an outstretched hand on my last day at the pool, I shook it, knowing it was the last time I would speak to him. Swallowing down the conflicting emotions, I tried not to remember the plays I'd put on for him when I was ten.

I was leveling up. I wasn't going to waste time trying to make it work. It was time for new environments and bigger challenges—both in and out of the water.

8

DIFFICULT PEOPLE

My unfounded reputation preceded me in the swimming community. I was a spoiled teenager who answered to no one. I'd sucked in 2013 because I'd decided to go behind Herbert's back and lift heavy weights. I didn't go to school and wouldn't go to college.

No one knew I'd never picked up a dumbbell in my entire life, or that I was excited to go to college.

That was why my new coach, Bob Bowman, along with his coaching protégé, Erik, met with my mom and me before I officially joined the North Baltimore Aquatic Club—or, as the swimming world called it, *NBAC*.

"You're going to trust me," Bob said. "All you have to do is what I tell you to do."

If only you knew.

I wasn't going to tell Bob—especially the day we met—that he was going to have to earn that. I didn't even believe that my family was fine when they told me they were over the phone. And I'd already paid the price for trusting Herbert.

Unconditional trust was a foreign concept. I doubted it was even real. If I couldn't even trust the concept of trust . . . well, it wasn't going to happen.

Swimming was a dog-eat-dog world. If it was between my career and Allison Schmitt's, there was no reason Bob wouldn't choose Allison's. I wasn't judging him for that—he had coached her to multiple Olympic golds. I was some kid he'd just met.

But how can you trust someone who isn't going to put you first?

Bob peered at me through his small rectangular glasses, waiting for my response. He had a kind face. To anyone who wasn't me, a *trustworthy* face.

I glanced at my mom. She was unreadable. She'd let me make my own decision about leaving Herbert, and she would let me make my own decision now.

You're here for the training partners, I reminded myself. *For the environment.*

"Okay," I agreed.

Unlike Florida, where I had been the only person on my team who ate, slept, and swam, I was now going to train with a group of people who did exactly that. A group of *professional athletes.*

It meant that morning practice was now at 7 a.m. instead of 4:45 a.m. since the other athletes had already been through school. It meant training trips. It meant strength training. It meant cupping, massages, and Normatec, regular recovery services I now had on top of the amenities from USA Swimming.

I was suddenly swimming with some of the best swimmers in the world. Michael Phelps. Allison Schmitt. Ous Mellouli. Chase Kalisz. Conor Dwyer. Matt McLean. Lotte Friis. Cierra Runge.

Every single one of them had an Olympic Medal by 2016.

Me? I was one of the worst in the group, which was *perfect.* It meant I would have to step up to keep up.

We all wanted to be great. That was what *made* us great. No one forced us to swim for four hours every day. We each took the steps to be the best we could be rather than just dreaming about it or not even trying because our chances were so slim.

None of us were afraid of failure. Mediocrity, maybe. Failure, no.

It was a six-lane pool with two fifty-meter lanes and four lanes with a bulkhead at twenty-five yards. All the swimmers rolled out and stretched on moldy mats in the corner of the deck. The locker rooms gave me athlete's foot.

Welcome to the training center of Michael Phelps.

None of us needed luxury to succeed. We just needed a good coach, good training partners, good practices, and good recovery.

I didn't care as long as I had access to a long course pool.

I perched on the edge of the least moldy yoga mat I could find. I got a few nods, but no one was overly friendly.

Bob came out of his office and handed out the written workouts.

Every practice had a motivational quote written at the bottom, along with a countdown to all the big competitions of the year and the rest of the four-year Olympic quad.

"*Even fools seem smart when they're quiet,*" I read. I looked at Bob—he was staring at me with something like a smirk on his face.

"Well, it's a good thing I'm not a fool—I can talk all I want."

"We'll see about that," Bob said.

I put my equipment bag behind Lane 4 and threw my cap over my head. I hadn't even started unpacking before Conor was staring me down.

"You can't be in this lane, Becca."

"Do we have assigned lanes?"

"No."

"Then why—"

"You have to know your place here."

"And where is that?" Anger flared within me, even as I realized that Conor didn't seem to be on a power trip. His voice was low, so the others couldn't hear.

He's trying to help me, I realized. But I didn't want his help.

"Becca, go to the long course lane," Bob's voice echoed from a few lanes away. He pointed toward the group of other distance swimmers gathered around Erik.

The distance swimmers and I primarily trained under Erik. He was green but a solid coach with an eye for technique.

They wanted me to fight for my right to belong, but I didn't bother. Instead, I fought for my right to be the best. I held my own in the first practice.

Immediately afterward, Erik motioned me over. "We need to fix your stroke."

That was music to my ears. "Tell me what to do."

"Your distance per stroke is *fifty* per length."

"I know."

"Allison's is thirty-seven."

"What *should* mine be?"

"No more than forty-four. Ideally, forty-one or forty-two. I mean, you have great tempo, but you're not pulling water. Everything is disconnected."

"But I have a good catch," I said, not understanding.

"Yes, but your arms and your hips aren't moving *together*. It's one movement through your core. Your body is disconnected."

In two sentences, I understood.

"Think of driving your stroke through your hips. If you—"

"Can you watch it now? I think I get it." I needed to lock in the feeling before the image left my brain.

I cut through the pool in one fluid motion, my entire body working as one. I felt as if I was working *with* the water rather than working to get myself *through* it. I had been swimming in *pieces* my entire career.

When I looked up at Erik, he flashed a pleasantly surprised grin. I sensed that he was excited to coach me.

"That's *much* better. We'll work on it more tomorrow. Go get ready for dryland."

Dryland. Swimmer lingo for *training outside the pool*. My lingo for *hell*.

Dryland occurred outside in what was known as the "dojo," a tent-like structure insulated with pool covers.

Our strength trainer, Jeremy, was *not* pleased by my somewhat late arrival.

"You'll get here when the other athletes get here."

"Okay." I didn't tell him I'd been working on my technique in the pool. I wasn't one to make excuses, and he didn't seem like he'd appreciate one anyway.

We broke into two teams of three for a "medicine ball relay." Whichever team could toss a twenty-five-pound medicine ball faster won.

Jeremy handed the medicine ball to the two starters.

I was not prepared for this. Not at all.

"Go!" he yelled.

The medicine ball came flying at my head at what must have been *at least* one hundred miles per hour, thrown by Truck, a 6'6" athlete.

There was no time to think. My body reacted before my brain could. I ducked.

The ball hit the pool-cover wall, almost ripping a hole through it.

The other team kept throwing while my team stared, all their mouths wide open.

"Stop!" Jeremy bellowed.

I stood there, not knowing what to do with my arms. Should I pick up the ball . . .? Or was I supposed to stop too?

"Pick it up, Becca!" Jeremy demanded.

I did. It was heavy, and I wasn't even throwing it.

Now everyone stared. Allison held back a laugh.

I would have been laughing too, if Jeremy didn't look like he was about to murder me.

"What was that?"

"It was coming at me really fast. *Too* fast."

"Give it."

I walked toward him, but he put out a hand to stop me. *"Throw it."*

I threw it. It barely reached him.

I knew that this was *not* about to be a pleasant experience, so I told myself, *It's pretty cool that my first day of strength training ever gets to be with the best swimmers in the world, who are probably also some of the best drylanders in the world.*

It was clear that I wasn't going to be able to do what they were doing. But Jeremy wasn't stopping there. Not yet.

Before I had time to prepare, Jeremy threw it back at me with maybe even more force than Truck had used. Once again, my body reacted before my brain, and I ducked.

"We don't have time for this. You're going to catch it next time," he said. "Get back in line."

Shoot. My eyes darted around, finally meeting Allison's. *Help,* I plead with them, hoping she would understand.

Allison looked away. My spirits dropped. I was on my own.

This was going to be *brutal.*

But then, Allison took a step toward the center of the relay, subtly changing places with Truck, so she'd be passing it to me instead.

I swallowed a sigh of relief.

When the ball flew toward me again, I could tell Allison had tossed it at half speed. I still had to brace myself, but at least I could catch it. I flashed a grateful look as I threw it back.

All in all, a solid first day of practice.

The next day at the pool, Bob approached the moldy corner with an eight-pound medicine ball.

"We're going to throw this back and forth every day until you can catch it."

Unlike the others, Bob threw it lazily to me. It was easy.

"Tomorrow, we're going to stand farther away!" Bob said merrily.

"Sounds good!" I replied, somehow putting even more cheer into my voice than he had.

There was no malice in Bob's demeanor—I took it as, *This is your weakness, and if you work on it every day, you can make it into a strength.*

But every day with Jeremy felt like a battle.

No matter what I did, I felt like I was always in trouble, sometimes for things as simple as sitting on a bench.

We started using new pull-up bars that ripped my hands open. I showed my mom over FaceTime, and she told me I needed to wear gloves until they healed.

When I waltzed into the weight room and put my gloves on for pull-ups, Jeremy practically ran toward me, furious. "What are *those*?"

"Gloves."

"Do you see Michael wearing *gloves*?"

"Michael has fifteen years of calluses."

"Because he doesn't wear—"

"I have the literal stigmata, Jeremy," I said, lifting my raw palms into the air as if I were being crucified. "I look like Jesus risen from the dead."

"You're not allowed—"

"My mom said I had to." I hated using that—hated pointing out my age—but it generally worked. No one wanted to deal with a "crazy swim mom."

Massages were first come, first served, but Jeremy sometimes made me wait until everyone else got one, once making me sit there for two hours after practice.

I don't care, I lied to myself.

But I did. Because I liked the softer side of Jeremy—the side that I saw on Sundays.

Every Sunday, Jeremy and I would set aside our differences to go to church together.

He was kind. Asked how I was doing. Talked about how I was going to win Nationals. Talked about his kid. Talked to *me* as if I were his kid.

It was bizarre—how could a man who filled me with dread every time I entered the weight room also pray in the pew beside me?

Jeremy was a complicated human with his own priorities. I wasn't a sheltered child anymore. I was in a professional environment, surrounded by egos.

This must be what high school is like.

This team had cliques, and I fit into none of them—though I knew which one I *wanted* to be in.

My first step to getting in was to earn a nickname.

Respected people got nicknames bestowed upon them by Michael or Conor. All the cool kids had nicknames. MP. Schmitty. Truck. The Danish Diva. Big E. Gingie.

Though I would never tell a soul, I desperately wanted one.

But no one paid me much attention, except when I tripped over my own feet in dryland.

★ ★ ★

Four months later, it was time to test my new training.

My first meet since the change in environment—since turning sixteen. My first chance to prove that I was better than ever.

The swimming world has a short memory. Have a bad race? Okay, maybe you're sick. Or tired. But *two* bad meets? You must be exhausted from really heavy training. That *has* to be it, otherwise you might be getting past your prime. After three bad meets, you're tossed aside. Discarded. People move on to the next shiny thing.

I'd disappeared for half a year to train. People were curious to see if I would be back to my usual self or if I was just a child prodigy who wouldn't be able to take my career into adulthood.

The first event of the Mesa Pro Swim Series was the 400 freestyle. This was an exciting one for NBAC, as all our female swimmers were exceptional at the event.

Sure enough, five of us qualified for the eight-person final—me, Allison, Lotte, Cierra included.

It was a heat of NBAC.

"Okay," Bob said. "Whichever one of you wins the final gets to pick the practice we do on Thursday."

There was nothing I loved more than a prize. It was just more incentive to show all these snobby swimmers that I was just as good—or *better*—than they were.

"We can't have Becca win," Paul, a twenty-four-year-old with an attitude as sharp as his features, whispered to the others. "She isn't going to pick recovery. She's going to pick something hard."

Duh. I still had goals to achieve.

I flashed a glare at Paul, then went about my business. I was going to *res ipsa loquitur* this race.

I raced that 400 like the Olympics were on the line.

I was the first NBAC swimmer to touch, getting an almost-best time.

I couldn't stop myself from gloating. I usually hated losing more than I loved winning . . . but playing a stupid game and winning a stupid prize? *Nothing* beat that.

I paraded over to Bob. "Thursday. The ladder set."

Bob looked amused, though I was beginning to think that amusement was just his resting face.

The ladder set was my favorite—and one of the hardest sets. It was 6400 meters of freestyle and IM stroke, all on tight intervals. I *loved* it. I was the only girl who would go on the men's times, with the occasional exception of Allison.

Most of the group *hated* this set. Especially Paul.

But I didn't care. I was showing up at this meet. Redeeming my lackluster 2013. Reminding people that I still existed and was one of the best swimmers in the world.

"I'm just so excited!" I said, putting my wet feet into my bedazzled fringe UGGs before my final event.

Conor took them in, his eyes hidden behind his blue aviator Ray-Bans. "You know what a hype beast is, Becca?"

"No."

"*You're* a hype beast."

It felt like a compliment, so I took it as one. "Because I'm excited all the time?"

Conor didn't respond, instead looking around until he found Michael. "MP, you think she's a hype beast?" He tilted his head toward me.

Michael's face was unreadable as he stretched his quad. "You a hype beast, Hype Beast?" he asked me.

"Maybe, depending on what it means."

"Alright, Hype Beast," Conor said with a grin.

Michael chuckled.

I'd done it. I'd gotten a nickname.

I googled what a hype beast was when I got home. *Someone who loves trends, especially involving footwear.* I loved it.

I had respect. I wasn't liked—but being respected was much more important to me.

It wasn't just my teammates. After the meet, Swimming World wrote, "Mann is making some strong inroads this year after falling off the radar. Mann failed to put up strong times in 2013, and I will admit to calling her breakout in 2012—which included making four finals at the Olympic Trials—a fluke. I'm happy to be wrong."

But with respect came jealousy. Thursday afternoon, I sauntered onto the pool deck, excited for my practice.

Paul glared at me as he rolled out. He'd been training with the group twice as long as I had and still had no nickname.

We spent over a third of the year training at the Olympic Training Center—or, as we all called it, the OTC—in Colorado Springs. The block of gray concrete buildings was an anti-oasis amongst the mountains and nature. It was a former military base, with the dorms in the old barracks, the rooms' cinderblock walls and carpet from the 1900s. It was the shadowy place that Mufasa forbade Simba from visiting in the Pride Lands.

Doing well in Mesa had earned me begrudging respect from the best athletes but loathing from the slower ones, who didn't like me climbing over them in the ranks.

On our second training trip at the OTC, Bob decided to shake things up a bit. Instead of the weekly practice schedule of double, double, single, double, double, single, day off, we would instead be doing triple, triple, double, triple, triple, double, day off.

On the triple days, we woke up for 5:30 a.m. practice. We'd finish around 7 a.m., then be back at the pool for 11 a.m. to 1 p.m. practice, followed by dryland from 1:15 to 2:15 p.m. Our third practice was from 5 to 7 p.m.

I loved the challenging schedule. I was beat down, but I knew that this training would make my mental game stronger than ever.

My teammates, however, were not nearly as enthused by this training trip as I was.

It was probably a lot harder on them—seeing as they were all in their twenties or thirties—than it was on me at sixteen. Even so, they were *crabby,* and they did not appreciate my constant "I'm *so* excited for this practice!"

Less than a week into the grueling schedule, I was met with my first ounce of resistance.

"Shut up, Becca." Paul sneered. "Read the room. No one else is having a good time."

My mentality was partially a shield—I sensed the negative energy festering around me, born through complete and utter exhaustion. I couldn't fall victim to that. I walked with a constant pep in my step, knowing I would talk about this training trip for the rest of my life if I made it through.

This was an environment where I had to stick up for myself because everyone was too busy watching their own backs. "Good thing everyone else doesn't need to be having a good time for me to have one!"

I dove into the pool, brushing off the exchange.

After the second practice, I changed and headed over to the massive weight room for dryland. Inside, I could only see Michael, who foam-rolled near the door.

I picked up a foam roller and sat beside him. Michael had three primary expressions: the mischievous smirk, the angry furrowed brow, and the blank neutral expression.

His face was the latter as he rolled—he was in his own world, and I relaxed into mine.

A few seconds later, Jeremy appeared from around the corner with the rest of the athletes, glaring as he marched toward me.

I internally braced myself, my spikes protruding as my protective shield activated.

"Hype Beast!" he shouted. "What do you think you're doing?"

"Rolling out."

"Do you see anyone else doing that?"

"Yeah, I see Michael doing it."

"And you thought you'd join Michael instead of *everyone else*?"

I stood up, taking my time. It didn't take much to trigger my temper after Paul's morning comment. "I didn't know where you were."

"Because you're *late*."

I looked up at the clock. I wasn't *late*—he had started early.

"So, Michael can foam roll, but I can't?"

Michael stood up at this, the neutral expression giving way to the furrowed brow. "How many Olympic Medals do you have?" Michael demanded. "Do you have twenty-three?"

"How many did you have when you were sixteen?"

Michael stared.

"That's right—none. Was I supposed to get twenty-three when I was fourteen?"

Michael's eyes widened. I prepared myself—I had no idea what for, but. . . something bad. I knew it.

I willed myself to stand firm. To not be afraid.

"Good point, Hype Beast," Michael said, the smirk appearing on his face.

I deflated, releasing a breath I hadn't realized I'd been holding.

"Start," Jeremy growled. "Now." He passed me my workout, and I scampered away before my luck changed.

The worst moments always came in the weight room when I was at my most vulnerable because the athletes who disliked me could get away with telling me how they really felt.

Things had settled down by the time we stretched on the artificial turf before dryland the next day.

Lotte, who was ten years my senior, groaned as she lifted her head from child's pose, glancing at me. "I'm too old for this. I can't be swimming six hours a day like I'm a teenager."

"C'mon, Lotte," I said, grinning. "Some grandmas swim for six hours a day too."

Another athlete overheard and scowled at me. "You need to treat Lotte with *respect*."

"I was just teasing. Lotte's my friend."

"Who would ever want to be *your* friend?" the athlete snarled. "No one here."

My heart dropped with my mouth.

I looked to the surrounding athletes to defend me, but everyone within earshot was quiet.

Don't react. Don't react. Don't react.

My chin always betrayed me first. I hated it for that. *Stop!* I ordered it as it wobbled. *Do not react!*

The instigator must have seen it. She frowned and looked decently ashamed. "I'm sorry. That was mean. I didn't mean that."

"It's fine," I said, looking away before my eyes could start watering.

Don't be a baby. This isn't worth crying over. Don't give her that power.

Yes, she'd apologized, but the damage was done.

Jeremy called the athletes over to him. I waited a moment, trying to pull myself together. I couldn't let anyone see me like this. I couldn't show weakness, especially not in the weight room, where I needed to be emotionally indestructible.

"Hype Beast!" Jeremy bellowed. "Get your mind out of Quanx and get over here!"

I swallowed, then stood.

"Hustle!"

I took a place behind the other athletes. Thankfully, no one looked my way.

This environment was just as unfitting for me—if not more so—than Clearwater. Would I have to leave here too?

Just see how you do at Open Water Nationals, I told myself. It was *good* training. It didn't get any better than this. Swimming fast was more important than being around nice people.

After dryland, I went into the laundry room and FaceTimed my mom.

"I hate these people!" I cried, my words drowned by the dryer. "I want to go home!"

I hadn't been in Baltimore long enough to call it home, and I had been away from Illinois for so long that I no longer considered that home either.

I meant I wanted my mom. I wanted someone to protect me.

I let the tears flow. My cheeks were red with the embarrassment of being so upset. It was so trivial. It didn't matter.

When I told my mom the story, she let out a string of profanity and threatened to call Bob.

"It's fine," I said, beginning to worry about the thought of my mom worrying. And horrified at the idea of Bob and my mom having a conversation about it. "She apologized."

"Still! She's a decade older than you; she should act like it."

"It doesn't matter," I said. "I'm going to win Open Water Nationals next week. Maybe then I'll be left alone."

I knew it wasn't true. It was going to make it worse with the others.

It was a strange dichotomy to love the training and despise half the people I interacted with. But it was familiar, and it confirmed what I had always known to be true: *Trust no one.*

"*Res ipsa,*" my mom said.

I nodded. "Can I see Dock?"

Before bed that night, the other athletes and I met in the common room of the barracks to play the card game *BS.*

"One 6," Cierra said, tossing a card into the middle of the pile.

"Liar," I replied.

Everyone stared at me. "What?"

"*Liar.* Pick it up."

Cierra looked bewildered, but she picked up the pile.

The next time I called someone out, I said the same single word. "Liar."

The third time, Paul snapped at me. "Just say BS!"

"No." Even though my intrusive thoughts had calmed, I still refused to break my unnecessarily strict internal code. It included not swearing, going to church every Sunday, making sure fights with my family were resolved immediately in case something happened to them, adhering to all the rules of Catholicism even if I disagreed, not consuming scary media in case it made me spiral, and doing my best to be a good person while remaining true to who I was and sticking up for myself.

I had no gauge for how fragile my inner peace was and had no desire to test it. Saying "liar" instead of "BS" was a small price to pay to avoid repeating whatever mental issues I'd had after moving to Florida.

"I don't get why you can't just say it!" Paul said.

"I don't get why you're so mean," I shot back.

"Hey." Allison stepped in. "If she doesn't want to say it, she doesn't have to say it. Put down your cards, Paul. Actually, don't bother. *Liar.*"

Appreciation swelled in my heart. An enticing thought materialized: *Was it possible I wasn't fully alone among these athletes?*

I knew Allison wasn't interested in being my best friend, but maybe I could rely on her to stand up to the bullies.

About a week and a half into the trip—and a week before 2014 Open Water Nationals—I came down with a bad cold.

Staying healthy was hard when I was physically beat down. My immune system struggled to fight off sickness when it was also working hard to recover from one brutal practice after another.

Bob and Erik decided to take me down to doubles and singles, sparking outrage among my peers.

"You shoveling, Hype Beast?" Conor asked. "Not cool. It's about the long game."

"No. *Bob* is shoveling me."

We had our own lingo on the team, the most common term of which was "shovel."

To shovel (verb): to skip practice and, therefore, dig your own grave.

"She's self-tapering," Paul accused.

"I'm going to Nationals too," another athlete said. "How come I still have to do triples?"

Whenever people talked, I put my head underwater.

I started feeling better the day before I left for California. By race day, I was close to, if not all the way back at, 100 percent health.

Nationals were in Lake Castaic for the second year in a row. Getting Top 4 in this 10k would qualify me for Pan Pacific Games, USA Swimming's biggest competition for the year.

My eyes were on the gold.

I went through the motions. Got my number stamped onto my arms. I was thirty-seven. These numbers added up to ten, and those numbers added up to one, which obviously meant I was going to win.

Calm confidence washed over me. I had been doing triples—a 10k was going to be *nothing*.

The race started at an easy pace. I didn't push it—I just conserved.

I wonder what the others are doing for practice today.

We went into the feeding station. I grinned at Erik, who had left the OTC to coach and feed me during the race. I spotted Rachel and Julia on shore and waved.

I settled back into the pack. Some amateurs started throwing elbows—incidental contact, I was sure, due to a lack of experience.

I moved positions. The amateurs continued running into me.

I can move up and get away from this. The pace was still easy, even as we passed the 5k. Had it been this easy last year?

I made a move, settling near the front.

I wonder what everyone in Colorado's gonna think when I win this.

On the last loop, I carved my own path through the water, taking an inside line toward the next buoy. I lengthened my stroke and quickly began to pass everyone in the draft. Ashley Twichell and I got caught on each other as we turned the buoy, but I didn't panic and made up the gap within twenty-five meters, leaving Ashley in the dust.

Haley and Eva led neck-and-neck. I cut in behind them, marveling at how getting to the front had taken nothing out of me.

I thought about breaking away but let Haley and Eva waste their energy instead.

With about 300 meters to go, I knew it was time. It felt like the race was just starting.

I moved out of the draft and increased my speed, kicking as hard as possible. Within three strokes, I was even with Haley and Eva.

I kept going. Bye, Eva. Bye, Haley.

I accelerated right past them, making it look easy. Because it was.

Woohoo! I sang. I was flying. I was on top of the world, powerful and elated.

When I slapped the finish structure, I turned to see where the others were.

The pack was seven seconds behind me. They hadn't even been able to keep up with my draft.

I beamed. The seven seconds were long and sweet, asserting my dominance. Next year, winning this race would be the first step toward winning an Olympic spot since the Open Water Olympic selection was at 2015 World Championships. I'd managed to win by *seven seconds* with less than six months training with Erik and Bob.

I'm going to win by minutes next year.

I watched my competitors finish the race, secretly pulling for Haley to join me on the Pan Pac team.

Haley was second. Unfortunately for me, Eva finished third. I'd be stuck traveling with her again.

The same four athletes who had gone to Worlds the previous year qualified for Pan Pacs.

I had my moment in the limelight. I was the best swimmer there.

And it was awesome.

SwimSwam interviewed me. "You've looked more composed in a race than I've seen you. Obviously, you're getting more mature. More experienced. Also, you're training now at North Baltimore. How are all these factors playing out for you?"

I looked at the water, a smirk not unlike Michael's on my face. "Seems that they're playing out pretty well," I said, and the interviewer and I shared a laugh. "I really enjoy it too. I'm really loving everything about my life right now."

It was true. I *was* loving my life, minus the mean people. I loved the hard training. I loved going to the Whole Foods in the old cotton mill across the street from the pool. I loved beginning to realize my dreams. I even kind of enjoyed not being exactly sure where I stood with my lukewarm teammates. It made life unpredictable and interesting.

"You're the most versatile out there, so keep it up."

Twenty minutes after the race, a blind spot appeared in my eyes, my pre-migraine aura setting in. I guess I'd tried harder than I thought.

When I got back to Colorado, my teammates were unimpressed with my victory. Even the lukewarm ones were too beaten down to care.

"We swam 20k the day you raced," one of them told me.

"Cool."

Cool. That was how it was going to be regardless of where I was, and I was okay with that.

9

EXPANDING HORIZONS

The best year of my life began after Nationals.

"I've never seen a swimmer hold a plank longer than four minutes," Jeremy told one of the coaches six months after I joined the team.

"I've done a twelve-minute plank before," I piped up from the water, my filterless sixteen-year-old mouth unable to stop from bragging.

It was a costly brag.

"No, you haven't," stated Jeremy.

"Yes, I have! When I was thirteen, I did one for twelve minutes."

When I was thirteen, I was all abdominals and nothing else. My body had been in prime plank shape. I had built up my endurance over twelve weeks, adding a minute per week. It hadn't been for any specific purpose—just because I was curious.

As I spoke, Michael, who was doing a different, mid-distance workout, happened to swim into the wall.

"Did I just hear Hype Beast say she can do a twelve-minute plank?" he asked, relishing the chance to stir the pot.

"I didn't say I *could* do one. I said I *did* do one."

"You can't even catch a med ball," Michael deadpanned.

"She didn't do a twelve-minute plank," said Jeremy.

"I did!"

"Make her do one after practice," Michael told Jeremy.

"I had to *train* for that! I haven't done a plank in months." The ability to hold a long plank fades quickly without training. Plus, I had grown in height and put on thirty pounds of muscle in the three years since then. It was going to be much harder to hold with the extra weight.

"It's because she hasn't done it," Jeremy said. "She can't go past two minutes."

"I can *definitely* do more than two minutes."

"I mean, I want to see a twelve-minute plank," Michael said.

"I can do six minutes today," I declared. "And if you give me three weeks, I'll do twelve."

"You're doing six minutes today," Jeremy said.

"What happened to twelve?"

"Okay," I said, ignoring Michael. "For sure. Easy."

My grin fell the moment the water concealed my face.

I wasn't even sure that I could do four minutes with no training. I was going to have to power through. I could do anything for six minutes.

By the time practice was over, everyone was excited to watch my plank. I changed slowly, allowing myself a little time to recover from the practice.

Six minutes. That's just the length of Defying Gravity.

When I got to the dojo, Jeremy was waiting.

"Ready, Hype Beast?"

"Born ready."

The first three minutes were easy. Everyone went about with their lifts.

Around four minutes, when my body began to shake, the other athletes crowded around.

Keep going, I told myself. *You're just getting started. Three minutes is nothing.*

A bead of sweat dripped from my forehead onto the concrete. Another one.

That was the only thing I would let fall.

"How you doing, Hype Beast?" Michael called.

"Great," I said, just managing to keep the strain out of my voice. "How are *you* doing?"

Five minutes passed. Allison gave a little cheer.

"Guess you've seen a swimmer do a plank longer than four minutes now," I mumbled to Jeremy. He didn't respond.

Five and a half minutes. My abs shook. *One more minute.* I had to reach the amount that I told them I could do today. I *had* to.

You can do anything for one minute. You can hold your breath for one minute.

I should've done the *American Pie* technique with *Defying Gravity.* Why hadn't I? Was it too late now?

Don't collapse, I told myself.

"Okay, Hype Beast!" someone said.

"Don't lift your hips!" Jeremy barked. I put them down.

"Too far!"

I lifted them up. My legs were shaking now too.

Six minutes.

I stayed up for about ten more seconds, then collapsed.

"Decent showing," Michael said, a hint of approval in his voice. The others nodded in agreement. I felt a shift in them. This was supposed to have put me in my place, but instead, it *made* me a place.

The next day at practice, Michael stood at the end of the distance lane with Bob, watching as I finished up an IM set.

When I got to the wall, Michael jumped in beside me.

"You're one of the best 400 IMers in the nation—why are you doing an age-grouper back-to-breast turn?"

"Because no one's taught me the faster one."

"Watch."

I watched, and I learned.

I made the National Team in four events that year, tied for the second most of any swimmer, behind only Ryan Lochte, who qualified for five.

Despite this year being all about swimming, despite the fact that I was *on top* of the swimming world, it was also when I finally glimpsed life *beyond* swimming.

A USA Swimming staff member approached me after pool Nationals and asked if I wanted to room with an infamously high-maintenance athlete or Eva Fabian in Australia.

My spirits fell. I didn't want to room with either of them.

I hesitated, hoping another option would be offered. I had roomed with the former before, and it hadn't gone well. So, in an impulsive moment of panic, I said, "Eva."

I regretted it the moment the words were out of my mouth. At least I knew what kind of bad I was getting with the other swimmer. Eva was an unknown terror.

Despite that, even before Team USA landed in Brisbane, Australia, I felt at ease—something I hadn't managed on international trips before. It may have been thanks to Michael, who fondly told a bus full of athletes as we were bickering about something stupid, "I give Hype Beast a hard time, and she gives me one right back."

The unspoken words: *Be nice to her.*

When we arrived at the hotel, I found myself in line for room keys behind Eva. I fidgeted, not looking at her—I couldn't let her know that I had anything to do with this. That would certainly just make her hate me more.

Eva turned to Haley. "I hope we're roommates, Hales."

My heart dropped into my stomach. "Becca, Eva, here are your keys."

Eva, to her credit, didn't show any sign of being upset as we dragged our suitcases into the elevator. But the anxiety in my chest was growing into fear.

This was a terrible idea. Why didn't I think this through?

We were about to be stuck together for three whole weeks. That would mean three weeks of avoiding each other. Of walking on eggshells. Of trying to keep my mouth shut.

"What floor are we?" Eva asked. I was holding the keys.

"Uh . . . four."

Eva pressed the button. She was acting normal. Too normal.

We got into the room. I cast a look at Eva, then the bathroom door.

"Oh, you can shower first!"

It's a trap, I decided.

As I turned on the shower, I played *The Confrontation* from *Les Misérables,* believing it reflective of my current predicament.

"Valjean, at last, we see each other plain. Monsieur le Maire, you'll wear a different chaaaain," I sang.

When I got out of the shower, Eva was staring at me, her mouth slightly open. "What the *hell* was that?!"

My heart skipped a beat. "Oh, I'll, uh, be quieter next time."

"No, that was *amazing*! What was it?"

"Oh! It was *The Confrontation* from *Les Mis.*"

"Play it again!"

"It's a duet," I said excitedly. "If you learn it, you can sing Jean Valjean's part, and I'll sing Javert's. Or the other way around. I know both."

"Let's do it!"

I pulled my pink flannel llama pajamas out of my suitcase and put them on, suddenly optimistic that I'd chosen correctly.

"Those are the best things I've ever seen in my entire life."

"Huh?"

"The llamas!"

After that, we became inseparable. We karaoked with Katie Ledecky and Simone Manuel. We played a game before bed where we'd guess what we were going to dream, and if any of it was in our actual dreams, we'd get a certain number of points. We discussed theories of the universe, books, and swimming, and decided that we must be the same person from different multiverses.

"You know what?" I told Eva one night. "I want to do it all. A long channel swim and get gold in the 400 IM and the 10k at the Olympics. We can tie."

"I'm so down, dude. And you totally can." It was the first time that I hadn't been told my goals were too lofty. Too far-fetched.

Having friends is so much fun!

"How did we hate each other so much last year?"

"I don't know, but I blame the patriarchy. And now that we're friends, we're going to be unstoppable."

I hesitated for a long moment, feeling uncharacteristically vulnerable, when I added, *"Best* friends."

I wanted Eva to know that I had claimed her as part of my very small team. I didn't need reciprocation—it just felt important for her to know that I was an ally in and out of the water. That I would never elbow her during a race, even if Olympic spots and tens of thousands of dollars were on the line.

"Hell, yes!" Eva said.

This felt like the real world. I was having a slumber party with my best friend. But instead of staying up late gossiping at one of our houses, we stayed up late guessing our dreams in Australia while we prepared to face off in the 10k.

★ ★ ★

Going back into training, I lived with gratitude, feeling like the luckiest person on the planet. I had a strong body and a strong mind.

I found joy in every moment. The weather made me happy. Grocery shopping made me happy. Eating breakfast made me happy. I was living my best life. I looked forward to everything I did.

I was swimming faster than ever. Any time I went a best time, I was my best. Any time I learned from a race, I was my best.

I even got some clarity.

I was watching a singing competition show with my grandma when one of the contestants began describing panic attacks.

Dread. Fear. Disassociation.

That was what happened to me when I moved out.

Those days were behind me, and it was nice to have some answers. Maybe I wasn't quite as disturbed as I'd thought.

Everything I had sacrificed was going to be worth it, and I was having the best time working toward it.

In October 2014, life got even *better*.

I got a convertible.

On October 20, my fantasy world became public when I finally self-published the novel I'd been writing since even before I moved to Florida, *The Stolen Dragon of Quanx*.

On October 31, I was *fully* accepted by the "cool" kids of my training group.

It was Halloween practice. My teammates were hanging out later that night. Naturally, Lauren, the new sixteen-year-old, and I weren't invited. We were going to find Bob's house and go trick-or-treating there instead.

"You all need eight hours of sleep," Bob kept repeating. "And you better be ready for practice tomorrow morning." He knew this "hang out" wasn't going to be over at 8 p.m.

In the locker room, Allison pulled me aside. "You can come tonight too, if you want."

"I can't. I'm hanging out with Lauren, but thanks."

Somehow, Lauren heard about the invitation. "I want to go!" she said.

The last thing I wanted to do was go with Lauren. I didn't trust that she would be discreet regarding Bob.

But Lauren *begged* and *begged* as we drove around, top down in my convertible despite the frigid air, searching for Bob's house. I didn't think the invite extended to her. Finally, after an hour of pressuring me, I agreed to call Allison.

"Hey. Is it okay if I swing by?" I swallowed, then added, "I'm with Lauren."

Please say no. I liked traveling solo. I was a lone wolf.

"Yeah! Come by!"

I lectured Lauren the entire drive about *not overstaying our welcome.* By the time we got there, even I was tired of hearing my own voice.

We rolled up, but all the parking spots were angled in the opposite direction. "Why is the street like this?" I complained to Lauren.

"No clue."

I tried to park it but couldn't, then got out of the car, leaving it on the side of the street with its hazards on.

Allison lit up when she saw me. "Hey!"

"Can you park my car for me?"

Frank, a preppy redhead mid-distancer who had recently joined the team, appeared behind her.

The two of them exchanged a glance and burst into laughter.

"Becca," Allison said, "that's a one-way street."

Frank took my keys and parked it for me.

This is good. I just had to hope that Lauren didn't ruin it.

I followed Allison in, barely breathing, still uneasy.

We didn't stay long—no more than ten minutes. Most of the older athletes did *not* want us there, but I stuck close to Allison until she got pulled away. Then I took Lauren's arm and dragged her out the door. "I need to go to bed."

It was 10 p.m. Past my bedtime. And the gathering was showing no sign of ending soon.

Before we left, Allison stopped us. "You cannot tell Bob you were here past eight thirty. Okay?"

We both looked at Lauren.

"Okay," Lauren agreed.

At Saturday morning practice the next day, Bob took in his exhausted swimmers, all of whom were laying on the moldy yoga mats like, well—like they *weren't* moldy.

"Did all of you have fun last night?" Bob asked.

"We went to bed at nine," someone lied.

Lauren looked away. Bob opened his mouth—

"It's true," I cut in. "I was there last, and I don't think I've ever stayed awake past ten in my life."

Bob stared at me for a long moment. I met his eyes, my gaze unwavering.

Finally, Bob looked away. "Get ready."

He believed me. He *actually* believed me despite me being a *terrible* liar.

I was a hero that day. Allison beamed.

That was the moment I was officially accepted. No, not only accepted, but . . . popular.

Allison realized I could be trusted. She took me under her wing. By association, I was protected within the swimming community. She was USA Swimming's most decorated female swimmer and beloved by all.

And she was in my corner. Someone who had eight years more experience than I did, who had not only survived in this environment but thrived.

"Next time Jeremy yells at you for being late to dryland," Allison told me, "tell him you'll get a yeast infection if you don't change. He'll never say anything about it again."

Allison was always right.

"Swim in my lane and Paul won't bother you."

"Tell the chef at the OTC you're on the avocado list."

"Just apologize to Lotte, and she'll let it go."

I felt lucky. Everyone wanted to be best friends with Allison. She was funny, charismatic, and it was impossible to have a bad time around her.

But, like me, she had protected herself. Everyone wanted to be the one she let in, and she'd chosen *me*. All because I could keep a secret.

I asked why it had taken us so long to get there.

"You literally said you want to live on an island with no neighbors," Allison said.

"I can get things done there!" I protested. "No one will hold me back."

"But no one would help you. Wouldn't that be lonely?"

I mulled it over. Yes, it would be—but I would never have to question my relationships with the people surrounding me.

"I'd let *you* live on my island if you wanted to," I decided, which I believed was the greatest compliment I could give to anyone at the time.

Life was good. No—it was *great*.

I added *strong friendships* to my strong mind and strong body.

I was the best open water swimmer in the whole country. I had Olympian friends whom I actually felt *close* to, who understood what I was pursuing, something I hadn't felt with people outside my family in a long time.

I was the coolest, happiest sixteen-year-old in the whole world. I knew everything there was to know about the world I inhabited. Nothing could stop me from having fun and achieving my dreams. My love of life was contagious.

After practice, Allison, Frank, and I went to Whole Foods and then to my house to make dinner. We'd put the convertible top down, not caring that it was winter, and had driven through Baltimore's inner harbor, bundled up as P!nk blasted through the speakers, the bass much too high.

Frank drove, Allison rode shotgun, and I lounged in the back. I didn't mind. I watched the skyline and looked at the water, on top of the world.

I was high on life. In my mind, it was never going to be over. I was going to stay like this forever. *This is what life is supposed to be.*

Swim, nap, swim, dryland, Whole Foods, dinner, convertible city drive. Every day was the perfect day.

It was about swimming, but it also . . . wasn't. It wasn't all I thought about. It wasn't what I talked about with my friends. Allison *hated* talking about swimming. She left swimming in the pool, which meant *I* had to leave swimming in the pool too.

It was one of the greatest blessings Allison's friendship gifted me.

For the first time ever, there was a life beyond. The people who were just as entrenched in swimming as I was were the ones who showed me that.

I was tasting the real world.

And it was sweet.

Yet, I couldn't drown out the voice in the back of my mind. *You're getting too distracted,* it whispered. *You care more about your friends than you care about swimming.*

No, I told it. *Allison has four Olympic golds, and she's doing everything exactly the same way I am.*

The voice didn't back down. *Allison has better technique than you. She's a better swimmer. She can afford to exist outside the pool. You can't.*

I ignored the voice.

My friends and I began suntanning after practice when the outdoor pool reopened. *The sun is draining the energy you need for practice,* the voice lectured me.

Allison, Frank, Michael, and I broke a moving walkway in the Denver Airport while sitting on the same handrail because we were too tired to walk.

You're getting yourself into trouble.

Shut up! Let me live my life!

2015 Open Water Nationals loomed ever closer. I wasn't worried about it—I was confident in my place at the top of the nation and that after I won Nationals, I would get Top 10 at World Championships and secure my Olympic spot.

I swam an Open Water race in Perth, beating all the Americans and placing third behind an Olympic gold and bronze medalist.

See? I told the voice. *I'm swimming better than ever. There's nothing to worry about.*

And that wasn't even the best part.

After the competition, I trained in the Indian Ocean with Eva, our strokes synchronized. The water was crystal clear as turtles encircled us. The bottom of the sea was mesmerizing, water glinting off the sand beneath a cloudless sky.

Eva and I beamed at each other as we breathed. I wondered if she felt what I felt—that this moment was special. I was overwhelmed with gratitude—that I got to be in the middle of the beautiful ocean, doing the thing I loved most with one of my best friends.

"Becca Mann!" Eva shouted. Yes, she felt it too. "Isn't it insane that *this* is our life?"

It was ecstasy. I screamed underwater, releasing my joy into the ocean. I soaked in every moment, consumed with the overwhelming sensation that *this was what life was supposed to be.*

The flames that would burn it all down began to smolder at Open Water Nationals in 2015 in Fort Meyers, Florida.

I was ready to defend my title. To win again. It was the first of the two most important competitions of my life.

I didn't fall asleep until 3 a.m. the night before. I was too excited. I couldn't wait to jump in Lake Miramar and race for ten kilometers with the best of the best.

Instead of letting myself get stressed about the lack of sleep, I reminded myself that I'd been sleeping enough leading up to the race. I would be fine.

I went through all the pre-race steps. Number 316 was tatted onto my arms and shoulders. It equaled one again, which meant I was going to win. The numbers had spoken.

I believed this would be the harder of the two steps to making the Olympic Team. Top 10 at Worlds? I'd done that when I was fifteen, even after I'd gone off course on the last loop to get my goggles.

I'd *also* gotten Top 2 at Nationals when I was fifteen. And I was a much better swimmer at seventeen than I'd been at fifteen.

Regardless, I knew better than to think any of it would be easy. Haley, Ashley, and Eva were coming for me.

I was calm and collected at the beach in Lake Miramar. The lake was glassy, the buoys large. Navigation would be easy, with no brutal conditions.

The first three of the four loops were typical. I conserved, I prayed, I fed, and I set myself up for the final loop. Ashley led most of the race. I was happy to leave it to her so I could be ready for the only loop of the race that mattered.

The final one.

When it came, I was sitting in fifth. Ashley led, another athlete on her feet. Haley was in front of me, behind Eva . . .

But Haley was letting Ashley and the others open a gap. By the time I noticed, it was more than two body lengths.

What are you doing? I internally screamed at Haley.

I knew it was time to expend some of my conserved energy. I increased my pace and climbed up in Haley's draft, then sprinted forward to close what was now about a ten-meter gap. My heart rate increased from 140 beats per minute to 190.

Haley settled behind me, allowing me to do the work. Fine. Better than both of us getting dropped.

It took me about 400 meters to catch back up. It was an arduous climb—a necessary one, but one that took a lot out of me.

Conserve.

When I finally got there, I was gassed—I allowed myself to draft for a few minutes in an attempt to recover some energy. My racing heart slowed. I drank some of the lake water. If it made me sick, I wouldn't feel it until after the race.

After the race didn't matter.

Know how much you have left in the tank. Know when to sprint. Know when to recover, I told myself. *Don't panic about your energy levels.*

I allowed myself 200 meters to recover, then reassessed. I felt good enough to claim my crown. We had about 1000 meters left of the race.

Ten minutes. *You can do anything for ten minutes.* Just like the plank. I could handle any amount of pain.

Just ten minutes of your life, I thought. *Make it hurt.*

I passed the athlete in second, making it look as easy as it had been to pass Haley and Eva the year before.

Only Ashley remained in front of me. She had been leading most of the race. She wouldn't have much of a gear change.

I lengthened my stroke, not bothering to lift my head to sight, as I caught Ashley. When I breathed, I looked at her feet. Knees. Torso. Shoulders.

We stayed even for about a hundred meters. I had the inside line, meaning that I would have the better spot going around the buoy.

That was my opportunity. I was going to seize it.

Sure enough, I left Ashley behind when I turned the buoy.

Now I just had to hold on.

You can do it, I told myself as my heart pounded in my chest, reverberating through my entire body.

I'd broken away much earlier than I had the prior year.

You're a better swimmer now than you were then.

I sprinted. I needed to secure this victory early. I tried to break away.

But I felt someone on my feet. Ashley must have pulled herself back up into my draft.

I wasn't dropping her.

Shoot.

I couldn't slow the pace. I just had to hope that she would be wiped from leading the whole time.

Then, out of nowhere, Haley was beside me, taking a narrower path. And Ashley was coming up on the outside.

Where was this energy when you let them drop us? I screeched at Haley.

I *couldn't* get stuck in the middle. That would be the end of it for me. It had lost me a race before.

I didn't panic. I couldn't afford to. I stayed calm. In the zone. Thought about how to avoid this situation. I diverted my course, trying to cut Haley off. If she was behind me, I couldn't get stuck.

I wasn't far enough ahead to cut her off as we approached a buoy. I still had the lead, but Haley had the better line.

I sprinted. Ashley fell back to my feet. *Thank goodness.* As long as I didn't get stuck in the middle, I would find a way.

I couldn't hold off Haley. She matched me stroke for stroke, directly beside me.

Beside me *and* with the better line. I had no gear change. I was sprinting as fast as I could go. My heart thundered. I felt like I was going to throw up. I could keep this up until the end, but I couldn't go any faster. It wasn't possible.

Think. Find a solution.

I couldn't, so I started reciting Hail Marys. I needed some divine intervention and enough grit to continue my pace through the end. That was all I could do.

Please stop! my body screamed.

In 300 meters, you won't have to move again, my brain promised.

The turn came. Haley, with the best line, came out with an advantage over me, but I came out with one over Ashley.

I jumped into Haley's hip draft. Within fifteen seconds, I was even with her again.

Go, Becca!

I couldn't get rid of her. Every time I got a half-second ahead, Haley found her way back up.

My stomach churned. This was hard. Very, very *hard*. My body struggled to sustain its maximum effort.

You like hard things, I reminded myself. *You* love *them. You love open water. You love this.*

We raced into the finish chute. I had a stroke lead . . .

I reached up and slapped the finish structure a moment before Haley.

A smile spread over my face. I'd done it.

I'd won.

Step one of making the Olympic Team was a *success*.

As I floated in the water, tears sprang into my eyes.

I'm going to do it, I thought. *I'm going to be an Olympian.* Just one more race and I would do it.

The hard part was over.

I let the tears fall into my goggles. I was so relieved and proud of myself for keeping a clear mind. I'd had to *fight* for that victory, and I'd done it. I'd pushed through the pain.

I'd raced like a champion.

I was in prime condition, the first step of making the 2016 Olympic Team completed, with friends and a training environment I loved. Life couldn't be better.

I only got to celebrate for about an hour.

I was waiting in my car for the award ceremony when Bob texted me.

"Great race! I'm moving to Arizona to coach at ASU. We'll discuss when you get back."

There had been rumors that Bob would be moving. I'd texted him the week before—I was training at altitude before Nationals without him—asking if it was true, and he'd told me to focus on my race.

I wasn't surprised, but I knew what this meant. My perfect world was about to come crashing down.

I mostly trained with Erik. Erik would be staying in Baltimore.

All my friends would be going to Arizona.

I was going to have to make a choice. Dread nestled into my gut.

"I'm going to Arizona," I immediately—impulsively—told my mom.

I walked back to the beach. I'd been so distracted that I'd missed the award ceremony.

Oops.

Several opportunities were presented to me as I walked the beach.

News of Bob's departure hit SwimSwam five minutes later. He'd waited till the end of my race to announce it.

For some reason, everyone at the meet decided to speak about this with my mom instead of me, as if the fact that I was seven months shy of eighteen meant I didn't have my own brain.

Coach Rose was one of the few who approached us both. "Becca, if you want to come train with me in California, you know I'm always more than happy to have you."

Before I could reply, Madeline was at my side. "Becca, let's talk about your Worlds plan." She'd already been named the head coach. Coach Rose grinned, taking that as his cue to leave.

The moment Coach Rose was out of earshot, Madeline whispered, "Coach Rose only writes freestyle workouts. You should stay with Erik."

It was the same thing she'd said two years before. I believed her—she had my back, especially because we both knew that I'd likely be swimming with her at USC in a short year and a half.

"Madeline has my best interests at heart," I told my mom. The idea of training with Coach Rose was once again tossed aside. Even though, this time, Coach Rose wasn't even on my radar. It was between Bob and Erik.

When Erik found me on the beach, he said, "I'm staying in Baltimore and taking over as NBAC's head coach."

"That's . . . exciting."

He softened at my trepidation. "It's up to you, but if you stay, I'll make sure you get everything you need. You'll be my top priority."

If I went with Bob, I would probably be priority #4.

Noise surrounded me. Everyone was asking what I was going to do. Everyone wanted to be the first to know.

"I need to talk to Bob," I told anyone who asked.

All I could think about was how my friends would be going to Arizona. I *wanted* to go to Arizona.

In a moment of perfect serendipity, my landlord called my mom and told her she could break the lease six months early—in three short months, *exactly* when Bob would be leaving for Arizona.

There was a force of some kind nudging me toward the path I was supposed to take. The universe was gently pushing me out of Baltimore.

But I don't want to go to Arizona for the right reasons. This doesn't put swimming first.

I would already be on the Open Water Olympic Team by the time I moved to Arizona, but I wouldn't be *training* for open water with Bob. I would be training for the 400 IM.

I was going to have to choose.

When I returned to Baltimore, the tension on deck was thicker than the water in the pool.

"What's happening?" I asked Allison as she enveloped me into a hug.

"Good job!" she said, before adding, "Your hair smells *really* weird."

"I got a perm. Why do they all look like someone's trying to kill them?" I asked, nodding toward the rest of the athletes.

"But your hair is already curly," Allison said with raised eyebrows.

"I wanted to see if I could get the top curly too."

"Oh. Well, tell me if it works."

How could I choose to stay here without Allison? How could I choose to return to friendlessness when I had gotten a taste of what it was like to belong?

You barely won Nationals, the voice in my head piped up. *Not like the year before.*

"Bob's only inviting a few people to Arizona to train with him."

I gaped, taking Allison in. I knew who would definitely be invited— Michael, Allison, Chase, Frank.

But I imagined none of the other distance swimmers—my training group—would be. They primarily trained under Erik, and Bob wasn't going to steal Erik's athletes from him.

Except me—I would be the only one Bob couldn't resist inviting. My 400 IM was too good for him to pass up on.

Bob and Erik pulled me into a meeting. Sure enough, I got the offer.

I knew what I was going to do. I was going to go to Arizona. I had come to Baltimore to train with Bob. I would continue training with Bob.

I still won Nationals.

I accepted it.

"Yes!" Allison exclaimed, "We're going to have *so much* fun!"

"I know!"

There were talks of Allison, Frank, Michael, Michael's fiancée, and I living together.

Life was going to get even *better*. For the next week, I looked forward to my move. It was going to be so much more enjoyable to drive with the top down in the sunny desert. I was going to get tan. I'd have people to carpool with.

Even so, the voice continued to nag in the back of my mind. *You're not going to Arizona because of swimming. You're being stupid.*

Jeremy voiced my thoughts. Out loud, they became much harder to ignore. "Why would you *ever* choose to go to Arizona? Erik is your coach. He's the reason you've gotten this far."

I didn't reply. I didn't agree . . . but I also didn't disagree.

"And your whole training group is staying here. Who's gonna train for the 10k with you? Schmitty?"

See? said the voice in my mind. *You're a fool for not staying here.*

I finally admitted it to myself—I was going to Arizona because it was going to be more fun. *Not* because it was the right move for my swimming career.

What was I doing? I'd sacrificed too much to put my dreams second to *fun* and *friendship*.

I wouldn't get the 10k training I was going to need after I made the Olympic Team in a few short months.

I was breaking my own heart. But the only thing I wanted more than to go to Arizona was an Olympic gold in open water.

Staying in Baltimore would be how I got it.

Life's not fair, I consoled myself. I was doubling down on my dreams yet again. Giving up my new family for my dreams again. But I had to. I hadn't come this far to pick *other people* when it mattered most.

I texted Bob and Erik that night. *"Can I talk to you guys before practice tomorrow?"*

I could barely look at Bob as I sat across from him in his office, but I forced myself to stare into his eyes anyway, refusing to be a coward.

"I changed my mind. I'm not moving to Arizona. I'm gonna stay here with Erik."

A heavy silence followed.

"I'm, uh, really sorry." I wasn't sure *what* exactly it was I was sorry about, but I *was*. With my whole being.

"That's okay," Bob replied. "I understand."

I was making the best choice I could have made with the information I had.

As the weather got warmer, I couldn't help but wish I could stay frozen in spring, where I had everything I wanted and everything to lose.

But summer came anyway. The days got longer, though they felt shorter to me. They were counting down until my world became lonely again. I allowed myself to get swept up in the fun. I took Sunday trips to Washington, DC, instead of resting and stayed up late watching TV with Allison and Frank.

I wondered if Baltimore would still feel like *home* when my friends left. I wasn't sure when it had happened, but it was the first place that had earned the label since I'd moved away from my family.

On Allison's last day in Baltimore, we carved our initials into a piece of wet concrete on the deck.

Maybe this forever cements our friendship, I thought. *Maybe this means that nothing will ever change, no matter where I live.*

I knew I was fooling myself. I'd learned more than once that the only person I could rely on was myself.

10

THE WORST RACE
OF MY LIFE

Team USA's pre-World Championship training trip was out of a fantasy novel.

Lake Bled, Slovenia. With a single glance, it became one of my favorite places on earth.

Lake Bled was 2.5 kilometers long and 800 meters wide. It was encircled by mountains with a palace built into one of the lakeside cliffs jutting over the water. A tiny island with a church on it stood in the center of the lake, accessible only by boat.

Or by swimming.

The first thing Team USA did after hopping off the plane was explore the lake. Giant six-foot-long catfish swam in the depths below, keeping pace with us as we swam. It was the perfect open water training course. The perfect practice. The perfect day. "This is *awesome!*" I told Haley and Ashley as we watched Alex Meyer dive down to try to pet a catfish that was bigger than him.

My imagination ran wild. I was a kid again, pretending I had to sprint to the other side of the lake to warn my kingdom about the enemy scouts searching for the best place for their army to attack.

I was training well. I was in love with open water.

"I feel like I could swim in this lake forever," I told Jordan Wilimovsky.

"Well, yeah. The 25k is too easy," Jordan said.

I laughed, remembering he'd been at the table when I'd announced the easiness of the 25k to Eva.

"You getting ready for your 1,000-mile channel?" Jordan asked.

"Why? You doing it with me? Need to know when training's starting?"

"*Nope.*"

I did want to do a long swim at some point. Maybe when I was retired. But not now. Now it was time to go to Russia to make the Olympics.

I told Erik I wanted to do one practice per day in the lake and one in the pool.

"No," Erik said. "The pool is what works for you."

"But—"

"You only trained in the pool before Nationals."

"I think some open water training would be good for me."

"Jordan is only going to be training in the pool."

"I'm not Jordan."

"Trust me, okay? You'll be ready."

Madeline stood a few paces away, listening. *Help me,* I plead with my eyes. She believed in open water training before races. I had no doubt Haley would be training primarily in the lake.

But Madeline looked away.

Maybe I *did* just need to trust Erik this time. I was staying in Baltimore to train with him, after all. He had fixed my stroke. He had coached me to two National Championships titles.

"Okay." I cast a longing look at the pristine waters of Bled and trudged toward the chlorine.

A week later, we were on a flight to Kazan.

The sky was gray, the buildings were gray, and the mood was gray.

It was quite the contrast from Lake Bled, where everything was bright and beautiful. Bled invigorated me.

Kazan drained me as if the city itself were a vampire.

I tried not to let it bother me, but there was an eeriness in the air that I couldn't shake off.

Don't do this, brain.

The men raced the day before us. Both Team USA athletes got Top 10. They were the first two athletes named to Team USA's 2016 Olympic Team in any sport.

I will be the third, and Haley the fourth.

The USA had never named four athletes to the Open Water Olympic Team—in the years prior, there had always been at least one swimmer who hadn't placed in the Top 10 at Worlds.

This was the year that would end.

Top 10 would be easy for me. Winning was the real challenge, but one I was confident I could conquer.

I hadn't heard of anyone going to Russia to make their dreams come true, but I was happy to be the first. I got my lucky UGG boots—a pair that my mom and I had bedazzled and painted an abstract American flag all over—and took a picture of them the night before. Posted it on Twitter. *"So excited to rep Team USA tomorrow!"*

Before I left my room that morning, room 309, I thought, *When I come back to this room, I'll be an Olympian.* It didn't feel real—to think that I was going to achieve my lifelong dream in four short hours.

On our way to the venue, our van got pulled over and searched by the police. We were the last athletes to arrive, which meant the check-in line was long.

Over an hour.

When Bryce checked our feeding poles, he was told they were an inch too long, which wasn't true. Athletes were allowed to cut in front of us.

I didn't worry. I let the team staff deal with it. I just visualized and stayed focused on the goal.

When I saw my number, my heart stopped.

258.

It didn't equal one.

Stop.

I pushed away the unease that was building in my chest. *The numbers need to equal one. They have to.*

I pulled out my phone and typed to my mom, *"I'm 258. The numbers don't equal one."*

My finger hovered over the send button for a moment before resting on the backspace. *"I'm 258. And SO READY!!!"*

It was irrelevant, and I had a race to win.

I barely had any time to lube up after the suit, cap, and goggle check, the tattoos, and the nail clipping. There wasn't time for warm-up, which was fine—I'd swum in the pool for a few minutes that morning, and there was plenty of time to warm up in the race.

I was one of the last numbers called to my starting spot. I looked into the Kazanka River and did the sign of the cross.

God, please, please, please let me win. And I pray for world peace, and all the souls in Purgatory, and everyone in the world who needs help. And that I win. Please. If it's your will. Please let it be your will. Amen.

When everyone was out, a loud heartbeat played over the speakers.

Thump, thump. Thump, thump.

My heart synced with the music. This was it. This was the moment I'd been waiting for my entire life.

I was calm. Ready to win.

The gun went off, and I dove in, not falling like I had at the last World Championships.

Off to a good start!

We started off at a sprint, as expected. I tried to fight my way up to the front, but several women managed to get ahead of me.

I stayed on the right side of the pack. After hours of watching technical footage, Erik and I had decided my stroke was most efficient breathing only to the left rather than breathing to both sides.

The water was so murky that I couldn't see the feet of the girl in front of me. I stayed on the outside, unable to see what was going on in the race due to my new breathing pattern.

We sprinted. And sprinted. And sprinted.

Why isn't the pace slowing? I wondered as we passed the one-kilometer mark.

Races *always* slowed down before 1k. I was already hanging on for dear life, and we still had nine kilometers left.

Anxiety flowed through my mind, though my body was working too hard to absorb it physically. Was I going to be able to hold on at this pace the whole race?

It's not worth it if it isn't hard.

Someone crept up on my right. I didn't see until it was too late.

I was boxed in. Punches were thrown at both sides, one landing on my shoulder, the other in my ribs. It was a bloodbath, and the American flag on my cap was a death warrant.

Get out, I ordered myself calmly.

I saw an opening on the other side of the pack, but I would be breathing to the wrong side. Oh well—it was better than where I was. And that was the best I could do at the moment.

I cut diagonally through the pack, infuriating countless competitors.

A French girl added a kick, keeping me boxed in. I fell back so I could roll over her legs . . .

She caught on and stopped, creating a backup. Swimmers piled onto my back.

Curses were shouted in unrecognizable languages. There was nowhere for me to go. I was trapped—moving bodies surrounded me. Before I knew it, I was underwater. Someone was on top of me, cutting me off from the surface.

My heart pounded in my ears. My lungs screamed for air.

For a moment, the race stopped. My fight-or-flight instincts kicked in as my brain realized I was drowning.

I couldn't see anything through the murk. Terror sprang through my body as the disturbed water from the other swimmers sent air bubbles into my face.

I thrashed my head into someone's stomach, my limbs flying in every direction until my head broke the surface.

I gasped for air, then got back into the rhythm.

Where the hell am I?

I had fallen to the back of the pack. I was still boxed in. I breathed to the left, spotting the Spanish flag. The Spaniard was the only thing keeping me from the outside.

I changed my direction, hoping to force her to swim wide. Then I could spring through the—

I saw the Spaniard's fist a moment too late. It swung toward my face in slow motion. I couldn't move. There was no space, no time.

Her fist slammed into my lip, and my stroke hitched. I didn't seek retribution—no. I had to get back into this race.

The metallic tang of blood flooded my mouth. My lip pressed against my front tooth. My eyes watered.

It was nothing compared to the pain my body was in.

Stay on track, I told myself. *Get out of the middle. Stay controlled.*

I was fatigued. My heart rate was maxed. My blood needed more oxygen. I had to get out. Someone had plowed into my spot when my stroke hitched. There was still nowhere for me to go. The pack was crashing in around me.

I began stroking again, making my own space on top of someone's legs. I rolled off her into someone else.

An elbow hit my goggles, embedding them into my face. More tears streamed out of my eyes. I rolled with it, beelining for the side—

I made it. I fell back into my normal stroke and assessed the damage. I was drained, swollen, shaken. But I was still in it, and that was all that mattered.

We were finishing the first of four loops. I needed to start conserving. I was still sprinting. *How* were we still sprinting? Was this going to be the pace for the rest of the race?

The next loop was just about hanging on. I made my way over to the other side of the pack so I could see everyone as I breathed, once again getting drowned on the way over.

I was running low on energy at the 5k mark. I needed to get my act together.

I didn't know how. Not when I'd been sprinting for five kilometers and still had five to go.

One of the few things I could accurately predict during a 10k was that the second half of the race would be faster than the first half.

I couldn't physically *go* faster.

I fought the urge to vomit. The endorphins had taken care of my face, but not the physical pain that came with pushing my body to its max for what had already been over an hour.

The numbers don't equal one. They don't equal—

Stop.

Were we dropping people? What place was I in? Thirtieth? I reminded myself I had made a move from thirtieth to eighth in the last World Championships. I could do it. I *had* to do it.

It was a battle between my body and my mind. *Keep going. Keep pushing. You can do this. You have energy. You've trained for this. Stay in the pack. You're almost done. You love challenges. This is fun, remember?*

I moved up the ranks, drafting and pushing. My body screamed, *Stop, stop, stop!*

My mind screamed right back, *Fight, fight, fight!*

I passed ten women. One loop left. The final thirty-minute sprint.

I passed five more. Where was I? Was I in tenth?

I didn't know. I needed to keep moving up. Someone crept up on my blind side.

I mentally chastised myself for allowing myself to change my breathing pattern. *How could I have let that happen?*

I wasn't used to breathing to the right, but I started throwing some right breaths in for visibility. But with each right breath, vertigo consumed me. I wasn't swimming in a straight line.

Twenty minutes. You can make it hurt for twenty minutes, my mind told my body. *You love this. You love making it hurt.*

No! Stop! Hurt! Pain! Help! my body screamed in response.

This is your dream! Fight for it! my brain shouted. *You HAVE to fight!* Had people broken away?

You love doing hard things, I chanted. *You love doing hard things. You love doing hard things.*

My gas meter was below empty when I turned the buoy for the final one-kilometer stretch. I was in a pack of six women, but there were definitely people in front of us. The lead boat was ahead—half a minute ahead.

Maybe it was only one person. Maybe it was fine. I had to keep moving. Keep pushing.

My body was giving up. My brain couldn't inspire it.

My heart threatened to pump out of my chest. Every time I lifted my head to sight for the end of the course, the land spun. My brain wasn't winning. My breaths were ragged, like sobs.

My body slowed. I just wanted to be out of the river. I wanted to stop. All I cared about was stopping. Not the Olympics. The finish looked so far. The kilometer may as well have been a hundred miles.

It *felt* even further.

I couldn't make any moves. I hadn't conserved any energy.

We swam into the finish structure, me touching third-to-last in my group.

Relief flooded through my veins.

It's over. Thank God it's over.

But two seconds later, when my physical pain began to fade, the emotional pain set in, far worse than anything my body could physically feel.

My competitors floated in the water. One was even climbing up the ladder out of the river. That was a bad sign. I counted them. Around ten. More than ten?

Haley was treading water next to me. She hadn't been far ahead. She'd been in the same pack as me with a kilometer to go.

There were more than ten girls. Barely.

I hadn't made it. It hadn't been enough.

I looked at Haley, but she looked as if she were behind glass. I was watching life rather than living it. Nothing was real. I was in a dream. No—a nightmare.

I'm going to wake up. I'll wake up, and I'll get to do it again, and this time I'll make it.

But the pain was too acute to have been borne of a dream.

Haley was staring at the scoreboard, her eyes wider than I'd ever seen. Places weren't showing up yet. Just "photo finish." Everything had been so close that they had to review the footage before assigning places.

Haley's name appeared in the ninth slot. She threw her arms around the girl whose name appeared in the tenth spot, practically drowning her in the Kazanka, as elation consumed them both.

I waited for my pain to become official.

A moment later, a *fourteen* appeared next to my name.

My heart fell into my chest. It was final. I didn't make the Open Water Olympic Team. I didn't even *qualify* for the event I thought I was going to be a World Champion in.

Tears sprung into my eyes. *Don't cry. Not here. Not yet.*

My body didn't listen. It couldn't. The grief was already ravaging me, beginning in my throat and spreading in every direction, making my chin shake and my heart pound.

I didn't move. I just floated. My body in the water, my consciousness somewhere above it.

What had gone wrong? I'd made huge mistakes. There had been holes in my armor. I should have breathed to both sides. I hadn't had enough race experience. I hadn't done enough open water training. I should've raced the 5k three days before so I could dust off the cobwebs.

None of it mattered. I hadn't been good enough. That was all.

Haley turned toward me. Her face fell when she took me in.

She didn't know what to say. What could she say?

I said something, my voice a thousand miles away. My tone was monotonous, and my brain on autopilot.

Haley threw her arms around my shoulders. I quickly patted her on the back and sculled toward the ladder. There was a short line. Two opposing forces pulled at my heart: the intense desire to run and the will to never get out of the Kazanka River—because once I did that, reality cemented.

I'm not an Olympian. I'm not going to swim my event *in* my year.

On the platform, the new Olympians were jumping around, cheering and hugging each other. To an outsider, their shouts of joy were contagious. To me, they sounded like bloodcurdling screams.

To exit the platform—to get to freedom—I had to go through the Mixed Zone. I rushed for it. Now that I was out of the water, I had to get out of the entire arena. The city. The country.

I was the first athlete there. The USA Swimming media rep waited to walk me through.

"A few people want to interview—"

"No."

"Do you want me to tell them to wait?"

"No. I'm not talking to anyone."

I loved an interview. I loved recapping races, even when I swam poorly. They helped me learn. But this one I just wanted to forget. I was in no state to speak to *anyone*, let alone the media.

I tried to look dignified as I braved the Mixed Zone. Dozens of reporters stared at me. Their eyes felt like needles in my skin. Goosebumps rose on my skin.

I felt like Cersei Lannister in *Game of Thrones* being paraded naked through the tent. The media rep may as well have been ringing a bell as she followed me, chanting, *Shame. Shame. Shame.*

Most ignored me. No one cared about me after that performance.

One reporter stepped up to the fence separating us and asked, "Can I please get an interview?"

"No." My voice was leaving me. I had mere moments before I would fall apart.

I wanted my mom. I *needed* my mom.

My eyes fell on a portable trailer bathroom just outside the Mixed Zone. I rushed inside before anyone could see me.

It was empty. That's when I finally released a gasp.

I stared at myself in the mirror as I sobbed, taking in every detail of my face. The wrinkle in the center of my forehead was deep. My eyes were red and puffy, the right one swollen from a punch. My hair was plastered to my head. My top lip was swollen—twice the size of my bottom one.

I looked like hell. I sounded like hell. I felt like hell. Every breath took effort, as if my body couldn't quite remember how to do it.

How am I supposed to go back out there?

What had my entire life of training been for, if not to win Olympic gold in open water? Who the hell even *was* I without my Olympic dreams?

I'd had the chance to be the best at what I loved the most.

Within a single two-hour race, it was gone.

I recognized my own face in the mirror, but she was staring back at a stranger.

You're going to be fine, I assured my reflection. *You're going to be fine at some point.*

She didn't look like she believed me.

Another girl opened the door. I turned away from the mirror, stepping into a stall. I stood there for a few minutes, waiting for my sobs to quiet.

They didn't.

You have to go back out there, I told myself. *You can't hide.*

I took a deep breath and tried to calm my breathing. It didn't work. Nothing worked. I didn't want anyone to see me like this, but I had to get my phone.

I needed my family.

That objective got me out of the bathroom. My brain could focus on a new mission instead of the grief that made my chest heave.

Other athletes were all around. Some laughed, some cried. *Most* cried.

At least I blend in.

It was the aftermath of a battlefield of broken dreams. Though none, I realized with a hint of embarrassment, cried as hard as I did.

Erik paced near the bleachers. When he spotted me, he looked at my forehead rather than in my eyes. Tears sprang into his eyes when he took in my shaking chin. Seeing him upset just made me cry harder.

"It was a good race. You fought hard."

It *wasn't* a good race. It was a messy race. A dirty race. An amateur race on my part.

"I know how hard this is," he said. "But you still have the pool. I'm going to make sure you make it in the pool."

"Yeah."

"We *will* make sure you make it in the pool."

I believed him, but I couldn't think about the pool. Not now. Not yet.

"And we're gonna get you ready for the 800 in ten days."

His words were water in my ears—in and out with every breath, every turn of my head. I didn't have the emotional capacity to care about the 800.

I went to find my phone to text my mom. I didn't want to speak with anyone, but going past the rest of Team USA was unavoidable.

A few people tried to approach me as I climbed the bleachers resting over the river. I ignored them, hurrying toward my bag. I pulled out my phone—a long string of notifications waited on my home screen, all of which I scrolled past until I saw the text from my mom. *"We're outside security."*

I gathered my belongings, trying not to look at anyone, when my phone slipped out of my hands and fell through a crack.

I watched it fall through the air in slow motion, staring until it landed in the water with a *plop*. I felt an odd twinge of satisfaction as it disappeared into the water. What was a drowned phone compared to drowned dreams? The circumference of the ripples grew as they glided away from the point of contact.

I was at war with the universe.

A dark smirk appeared on my face. It wanted to take my phone? Freaking *have it*, universe. Take my phone.

Satisfaction circulated through my body.

Until my phone resurfaced with so much force, it nearly ejected itself from the water.

Of *course* the phone case *floated*.

I scowled. I wanted it to go back under. I was too upset to appreciate the metaphor. It was much easier to be angry at the world, at God, at the universe. I had fallen into the river and was still floundering underwater. I didn't need to be reminded that I knew how to swim and that I always floated.

I pulled my gaze away from the river to find Bryce.

I finally noticed the other members of Team USA. They were talking among each other, but whenever they noticed me, they quieted. I felt so *other*. Like I was naked. Or an alien.

I felt vulnerable—like if anyone looked at me for too long, they would see the shards of my shattered heart. They would see how easy it was for it to break. They would feel what I felt and realize I wasn't as strong as I had fooled them all into believing. They would see that I cared so much about something as stupid as *swimming fast* that one bad performance had destroyed me.

"Bryce," I finally called because he also wasn't looking at me. He glanced my way, just a little too eager.

"Becca! Yes?"

"My phone is in the river," I stated monotonously. I pointed at it. It felt stupid to even be thinking about my phone. "Can you get it?"

"Yeah, yeah. Of course."

I nodded, then left them all. And the phone. I didn't need it. All I needed was my mom.

"Becca, you're so young," an athlete's mom told me on the way out. "You'll make it in 2020."

It was exactly what everyone had told me in 2012, and it infuriated me even more this time around.

Screw that, I wanted to shout. *And screw you!*

That was four years—a *fourth* of my lifetime—away. Did people think this was easy? That I didn't pour my entire life and spirit into swimming? Did she think that I could just go another four years without taking a single day off?

I didn't care that I was young. Anything could happen in four years. I wanted it *now*. I needed it now. And I had a gut feeling that if it wasn't 2016, it wouldn't be at all.

It's not going to be open water. There were too many things I wanted to do in life. I hadn't explored countless passions because of swimming. I wanted to experience them before 2020. I wasn't going to be able to if I gave my all to swimming until then. Did I really want to live and breathe swimming through college?

I won't even be able to. I doubted I'd be able to take my daily three-hour nap between morning and afternoon practice when I was in college. And the NCAA's short course yards competitions meant I wouldn't be able to train in the Olympics' long course meters.

When I spotted my family, the sobs came back, convulsing through my entire body as my mom wrapped me in her arms. Seeing me in this state made my sisters and dad tear up as well.

"I wanted it. I wanted it more than I've ever wanted anything."

"I know."

I couldn't comprehend it. How could I not get the thing that I'd wanted more than anything, ever? How could it have evaded me when I'd done everything right? Unless—

What if I did something wrong? What if I'm evil, and this is karma getting me back?

But I'd done nothing wrong—I'd stuck to my fierce moral code. I'd trained. I'd done *everything* right.

Maybe I messed up in the future, and time doesn't really *exist, so this is my punishment.*

But my thoughts didn't lead to anxiety. My body was too exhausted, my anguish too potent.

We stood for what could have been seconds or hours. The rest of the Team USA athletes walked by. I tried to pull myself together as they passed. I'd gotten so good at hiding my emotions until I was *out* of the situation that it felt shameful and embarrassing to reveal I had any at all.

Four hours later, I was no longer hysterical. I went to the pool. I had to get ready for the 800 in ten days.

When I got back to my room—309, numbers that also didn't equal one—I took it in and thought, *I didn't come back an Olympian.*

I was going to have to make the 2016 pool team. That would be my new goal since open water was off the table.

More tears sprang into my eyes. *Open water was* my *event.* It was supposed to have been my Olympic gold medal, and I'd lost it a year before the competition.

It was unlikely I was going to be able to beat Katie in the 800 and 400, or Katinka Hosszu in the 400 IM.

Doubt is the first step to failure, I thought bitterly. But eradicating doubt was impossible in the moment. That would have to come later.

I looked through my phone at all my unanswered texts as I sat alone in my hotel room. Almost all of them enraged me.

"You're so young—"

"You're going to make the pool—"

"You still have the 800—"

"You're young—"

"Your whole career is still ahead of you—"

Youngyoungyoungyoungyoung—

I internally screamed.

I'd told my family to go back to their hotel—I wanted to be alone. I didn't want to talk to anyone. I wanted to quietly wallow in misery by myself, then push this under the rug and never think about it again.

I tweeted that night, *"Hard day for me, but really excited for Haley!!! You totally deserve it, and I'm super happy for you!!!! #rio2016"*

I wondered if the others could feel my sorrow through the adverbs and multiple exclamation points. Comments told me I was a class act. That I still had *a long career ahead of me*.

I didn't feel like I had a long career ahead of me. And I sure didn't feel like a class act. Not at all. The tweet tasted sour. False.

I wished I had tweeted something else. I wished I hadn't tweeted at all. I wished it had been me and not Haley. I wished I'd tweeted *that*.

It didn't matter. I couldn't put how I felt into 140 characters. And no one cared, anyway. The only people who cared were the people who cared about me—not the fans on SwimSwam. I was a machine to them, and that was fine.

A text from Ashley Twichell came in. *"I'm here for you if you need anything. I've been there and know how hard it is. My door is always open if you want to talk!"*

Finally, a message of substance. I appreciated it, but I had no intention of taking her up on that offer.

I wasn't very close to Ashley, and she still had a race—she didn't need to deal with the heartbroken seventeen-year-old on the team.

I couldn't be a burden, letting my bad energy seep out of 309 and poison the other athletes.

I'm okay. I knew that it was about to become my slogan.

Eva texted me—she'd been here as well. Alex knocked on my door to check on me.

I wasn't alone, but I couldn't see it. I felt like the embodiment of failure. I hadn't been able to pull through the only time it mattered.

The head of the National Team was next. *"I can't imagine how you're feeling, but I know you're going to race hard in the 800. See you in a few days."*

I put down my phone. It was 8 p.m. I was cried out. I had to pull myself together.

I went into the team room, putting a pep in my step that didn't extend to my mood. Ashley was on the massage table. The massage therapist asked what I wanted to listen to on the speaker.

"Wicked," I said. My comfort music.

I gave Ashley, the massage therapist, and apparently the *entire* third floor a concert. *The Wizard and I. Defying Gravity. No One Mourns the Wicked.*

Then *No Good Deed* came on.

"One question haunts and hurts. Too much, too much to mention . . . Was I really seeking good? Or just seeking attention?"

Why did I care so much about the Olympics? Why did it matter whether I was the best?

I knew it *did* . . . but *why?*

I was scream-singing. I dared someone to come in and tell me to quiet down.

No one did. They let me have this release. This cathartic drama.

Ashley stayed through the whole thing. She sang along to the parts she knew. She tweeted about it. That I sang all of *Wicked* and it was the best thing ever. She was supporting me however she could.

My mom texted me, *"Do you want me to come stay in your room with you?"*

I wanted to be alone. To have my own emotional release. *"No. I promise I'm fine. Love u!"*

I wasn't sure I was "fine," but I knew I *would* be at some point.

"Love u more," she responded.

"Love u most."

I cried myself to sleep that night.

On the bus to the pool the next day, Madeline said, "Everything that could have gone wrong before the race went wrong."

"What?"

"The police. The line. The feeding sticks. People cutting the line."

"It doesn't matter." *That's irrelevant.* "I just wasn't good enough." I hadn't gotten fourteenth because the police had pulled us over before the race.

Madeline searched the face that I was painstakingly trying to keep from revealing my sorrow, then tentatively asked, "How are you doing?"

"It's not like someone died." But something had died inside of me. And people were treating me like it.

Madeline laughed, which I appreciated. "And there are good things ahead. You have your recruiting trip coming up, and then hopefully, you'll be moving out of the cold to sunny LA . . ."

"Yeah, I know. I'm looking forward to it," I lied. I couldn't bring myself to feel anything about life beyond 2016. My brain couldn't compute that life after the 2016 Olympics even existed.

A swimmer added, "College was the best time of my life. You're gonna love it, Becca."

"Yeah. I'm sure I will, but . . ."

"But?"

"I don't know. I feel like I was living my best life in Baltimore. I don't know if it can get better than that." I thought about the drives around the city. About every dinner I made with Allison and Frank. It all felt so far away. How had it been just over a month ago?

Maybe if you hadn't been so intent on having balance, *you would have made the team,* a thought pinballed around my head.

I dragged myself to church that Sunday, a large Russian Catholic cathedral. I didn't want to go, but I went anyway because I was a hell-fearing creature of habit.

The second I walked in, fury settled into my heart. I'd *heard* about people being pissed at God before but had never experienced it myself.

I did everything right! I screamed at God. *I worked hard! I was as good a person as I could be! I loved it! I gave up everything!*

But the more I thought about it, the less sense my anger made. If God loved everyone equally, whose side was God even on?

God probably has bigger things to worry about.

The pool team arrived in Kazan. Within two hours of their arrival, a joint meeting of both the open water and pool teams was called.

We sat on the ground in the hallway of Floor 7. I remained at the back, next to Haley.

The head of the National Team stood before us.

"We need to honor the first three members of *any* sport to qualify for the Team USA Olympic Team! Get up here, guys."

I remembered his text, *"I can't imagine how you're feeling . . ."*

He certainly *couldn't.* His words were daggers in my heart. I had to suck on my cheeks to hold my mask of stoicism. I clapped with the others, my movements robotic.

The applause of the fifty best swimmers in the United States was suffocating.

Do not cry. Do not cry. You are not allowed to cry, Rebecca Wilke Mann.

No one looked at me as he announced them. Their eyes were on Haley as she made her way to the front of the group.

I wanted them to look at me. A few days ago, I was the star. People saw me shining from miles away.

In that moment, I had never felt more invisible. Were they purposefully looking away?

I exist! I wanted to scream. *I am just as good as they are! I had one mediocre race!*

I wanted to leave. I thought about storming away. Maybe someone would notice me then.

Don't be dramatic, I told myself. *You can take it. You've taken worse. You're stronger than this. You're awesome. You know you are.*

I could be mad at God. I could be mad at the universe. But *I* would always be there for myself. I had myself. I would be okay. That was all that mattered, even if I didn't fully understand how I was *special* in the swimming world without open water.

On the third day after not making the Olympic Team, the rest of the open water team left Kazan. I still had a week before the 800.

"You'll make it in the pool," everyone told me. Random athletes. Coaches. Massage therapists. I knew they were right. I had to focus on the pool. For both the rest of the meet *and* the 2016 Olympics.

I stopped licking my wounds and looked ahead.

I am a pool swimmer now. Open water does not exist anymore.

I noticed that the sports psychologist sat next to me on the bus to the pool every day. I'm not sure if someone had assigned him to me or if he had decided himself. I never wanted to talk to him.

Instead, on each bus ride, I reread one of my favorite fantasy series from childhood. I tuned out the world, living in the pages any time I wasn't sleeping or eating chocolate.

I have to start having fun, I decided when I closed the fifth book of the week and finished my fifth chocolate bar of the day.

I thought about the things that had brought me joy in Baltimore.

I consulted Alex Meyer, the only person as wicked as I. We went to the mini-mart across the street—the place that was supplying me with my daily dose of chocolate—and bought the only other thing they sold there: dead, dried-out fish.

Bag in hand, I approached the front desk, Alex smirking by the elevator.

"May I help you?" the woman asked with a thick Russian accent.

"Yes. My name is Elizabeth Beisel. I locked myself out of my room."

Beisel has the best sense of humor, so I knew she'd find this hilarious. This was my pick-me-up. I knew it would bring me joy, and joy was what I needed.

When she was at the pool, I snuck in and put one fish under her pillow, another in her toilet, and wrapped the final in a clean towel.

"You don't tell her it's you until you're safe," Alex told me before he departed with the rest of the other open water athletes that day. "Until she doesn't have time to get you back."

I was eating with a few other athletes a few hours later when all our phones *dinged.*

Beisel had sent a picture of the fish under her pillow to the team group chat. *"WHO THE HELL DID THIS?!?!"*

I stayed quiet. I wasn't even a suspect.

I confessed right before I left. Beisel and I exploded into laughter.

The feeling was reminiscent of Baltimore. Of fun that had nothing to do with swimming.

There are other things that made me happy.

My 800 was mediocre. I got tenth. USA Swimming, for probably the first time in their history, let an athlete leave the meet early.

The whole experience was a gut punch but also a forging by fire.

When I left Kazan, I made myself a promise. *I will not let this happen again.*

11

IT'S WORKING

When I got back to Baltimore, I threw myself back into the pool like my life depended on it.

I was fast enough now that all I had to focus on was my own improvement. If I could drop a few seconds in the 800, I would medal at the Olympics.

It paid off—the next three months, I practiced better and more consistently than ever. There was no possible way to work harder than I was working.

This was my coping mechanism. Maybe I wouldn't swim my favorite event at the 2016 Olympic Games, but I would swim my next favorites: the 400 IM and the 800.

It was good that my friends had gone to Arizona. They were a distraction. This year needed to be *all* about swimming. More so than even my years in Florida had been.

The countdown phone background that I'd had in 2012 made its way back onto my phone. Only this time, it began on day 200-something. I had 400 practices left before Trials, which meant 400 chances to get better. I was determined not to waste a single one.

I raced every time I was in the pool as if I were racing in Trials.

I was not going to let Kazan happen again. I couldn't.

I counted every stroke, never letting my stroke count go above forty-one strokes per fifty meters. If it did, I made sure I only did forty on the next lap.

That was 280 fifty-meter lengths of the pool that I was counting every day, on top of thinking about my technique, going fast, and making sure that I was actually doing what was written for the set.

But *faster* than Erik told me to go, obviously.

I gave plenty of effort when it said easy. I went hard when it said moderate. I went all out when it said fast.

And it was working.

I was a senior in high school, but I brushed off my college recruiting trips since I refused to miss a practice. Madeline had reeled me into USC when I was fifteen, so that was the only recruiting trip I bothered to schedule.

The trip was catered to me. I did an ocean workout with Haley—which, Madeline reminded me, they did *all the time*—then went boogie boarding, tagged along to some art classes, and took a trip to the Writing for Screen and Television Division.

Madeline promised me hard workouts. Fun. Open water. The beach.

It was perfect. I would go to USC in the Fall of 2016. Done. Back to Baltimore to train for the Olympics.

Erik met me on the pool deck the morning of my return. "How was it?"

"Great! I'm going there."

Erik raised an eyebrow. "But that's the only place you've visited."

"I know."

"But—they're a sprint program."

"Madeline's there."

"She does what Dave tells her to do. They barely do any yardage."

I shrugged. Madeline would give me what I needed, and I *liked* USC. And none of the other schools I was considering even had a screenwriting program.

"You're not going to get what you need there."

"This isn't about swimming." College would come after the 2016 Olympics, and all that mattered was being ready for that. What came after was irrelevant.

"Where else have you been looking?" Erik asked.

"Nowhere."

"What do you mean?"

"I mean that I need to train." A hint of annoyance crept into my voice.

"Nowhere at all?"

I didn't understand why this mattered to him when I wouldn't be training with him after the Olympics anyway. It didn't cross my mind that he might just *actually* care about me and my swimming career.

"I talked to Stanford for a minute, but I don't want to go there."

"Why not?"

"Because they're not USC."

"Can you take one more? Just to make sure."

"No. I don't want to, and I'm not going to miss a practice for that."

"Becca, you're the best recruit in the nation. You can go wherever you want."

"And I *want* to go to USC." I threw my equipment bag at the end of the lane, indicating the conversation was over. I was *certain* about USC. It was *my* future. *My* decision.

When I FaceTimed my mom afterward and told her about Erik's response, she frowned. "I mean, maybe it would be good to see another school. To have something to compare it to."

"But I'm going to have to miss a practice if I do that. Two, if I go to Stanford."

"That's not that much."

"*Yes*," I insisted, an edge in my tone, "*it is*. I have to do everything *perfectly* until Trials. I can't miss any practices."

"Well, maybe take one to a school on the East Coast and make up the practice next week."

She wasn't budging, and I'd never *not* agreed with a suggestion from my mother. "*Fine*," I finally muttered, even as my brain spun, telling me it was a terrible idea.

When I showed up at practice the next morning, I told Erik, "Can you call UGA and tell them I want to take a trip there?"

Georgia's training was similar to what I did in Baltimore. They had won NCAAs in 2014 and placed second that year. The trip would only be two days, and I would only miss one practice, which I could make up the next week.

I liked UGA's team more than USC's, but it was *all* I liked better.

I wanted to explore other things. I was acutely aware that I'd spent my life in a unique dimension, one that had exposed me to things that many people my age had never—and would never—see.

But the other kids had seen things that I hadn't—and *should have*—seen at this point. Everything I knew about college came from Allison. I didn't know how to pronounce words that I read in books. I had only taken three science classes since fifth grade. I'd never drank. I only wore athleisure, so I had no sense of fashion—only that I didn't think that what my sisters told me to wear suited me. My parents had never given me any rules to follow because I didn't need them.

I had absolutely no idea how "normal" teenagers acted. I spent my entire day in a pool, surrounded by people a decade older than me. People catered to me all the time. I got massages. I had a nutritionist. I had people who booked my travel competitions and analyzed my blood. I had weekly filmed technique sessions with my coach.

I didn't know what the real world was like. And the longer I spent in my swimming bubble, the harder the transition would be. The harder it would be to break free.

So yes, Georgia would be too swim-focused. USC had the balance I needed.

When I returned to Baltimore, I said to Erik, "I'm going to USC."

He frowned. "That training isn't going to be—"

"I don't care. I like that *school* best, and this isn't a swimming decision."

I hadn't been able to move back to Illinois after 2012, but I would get my romanticized "normal" existence after 2016. I needed to set up the rest of my life. I needed some escape routes out of the swimming world.

I was admitted into the University of Southern California a month later. The more difficult challenge would be getting into the Writing for Screen and Television program at the School of Cinematic Arts.

One of the prompts of the application was to "describe your most challenging moment." Writing an essay about moving away from home and my erratic thoughts was something I was still trying very hard to repress, so I wrote about Kazan.

I was satisfied with my application. It was *good*. I was 99 percent confident I would get in. But I wasn't *fully* excited—it wasn't the Olympics, so I felt removed. It was a life I couldn't visualize, and if I couldn't picture it, I couldn't be excited about it.

I began going to church every day, covering all my bases. *Please let me make the 2016 Olympic Team, God, and go an 8:12 in the 800 and a 4:30 in the 400 IM. Sorry about yelling at you in Russia. And please bring world peace. And I pray for all the souls in Purgatory.*

I was happy and practicing faster than ever. I was proud of how well I was rebounding. Kazan began slipping from my memory like a nightmare fading with the daylight. The loss *inspired* rather than haunted me.

I took a training trip to the OTC with some other National Team athletes. My friends were there, but I prioritized rest over socialization.

"Becca," Allison asked one night, "want to Uber to Yogurtland?"

I looked at my phone. It was eight. We wouldn't get back till nine thirty, and I needed to be asleep by ten.

"No, thanks. I'm too tired."

It felt too good to be on top—better than driving around the city with Allison. And, just in case the voice in my head had been right about distractions, I refused to have a life outside of swimming.

One practice, after I beat him in a pull set, Michael turned to me and said, "Hype Beast, this is supposed to be *moderate*. Why are you *sprinting*?"

"That was my moderate," I said truthfully. I was trying as hard as I could, but it *wasn't* hard. I barely felt pain in practice anymore.

"There's no way that was your moderate."

"I think my moderate is just faster than yours," I bragged.

He huffed, having no comeback.

Res ipsa loquitur.

Of course, being in "such good shape" came with a few concerning drawbacks . . . I had lost ten pounds in two months, and I hadn't had my period in four months. But it didn't matter. Because what I was doing was *working*.

And if something is working, you keep doing it.

Right?

★ ★ ★

I went straight to a competition in Minnesota from the training camp.

This was my moment to prove to the world that I belonged on the Olympic Team. It was November 2015—just a month and a half before the start of *my year*. It was my last competition as a minor.

I knew it was going to be fantastic. There was no way it wouldn't be.

I was ready to prove it in my first event: the 400 IM.

I cruised in the preliminary heats, easily getting the top time before finals.

Yes, I thought. *This will be good.*

I was next to Katie Ledecky in finals, with Beisel and Caitlin Leverenz, the two 2012 Olympians in the 400 IM, also in the heat.

Confidence and excitement pulsed through my body as I said my prayer and shook out my muscles behind the blocks.

It didn't matter that I was behind at the start, as I always was by the time we surfaced. I turned seventh at the fifty, but that didn't matter. I had more energy than I knew what to do with.

I blazed my way into third on the second fifty of the butterfly, feeling relaxed and controlled.

I had transformed my backstroke from a weakness into a strength. While my competitors were fatigued from the butterfly, I was just waking up—I had practiced so many fly-to-back transitions in the past months that I practically *needed* the butterfly before my backstroke to make it fast. While I had fallen behind in the backstroke in 2012, now I coasted past the two swimmers in front of me, making it look easy.

Because it *was* easy. I was coming down from altitude—and I didn't feel pain for several weeks after I came back to sea level.

Breaststroke. I had improved that as well, though it was still my fourth best.

Leverenz was a breaststroker. She began sneaking up on my left. I didn't worry—I would certainly destroy her on the freestyle.

I was worried about Katie, the only person who had the potential of throwing down a faster freestyle leg than me.

Leverenz turned into the freestyle leg two seconds before me. I didn't even blink. I was a few seconds ahead of Katie.

I put my head down and sprinted.

I caught and blew past Leverenz within thirty seconds. Katie was still the same distance behind me.

My stroke felt long and strong. I grabbed the water, each stroke propelling me forward faster than a boat.

I touched the wall. 4:37.04. I won by over two seconds, getting a best time by almost three seconds.

I caught my breath at the wall, murmured a quick "Good job" to Katie, and hopped into the warm-down pool.

In the safety of the warm-down pool, with my goggles covering my face, I allowed myself to get emotional. Tears sprang into my goggles for the second time ever due to happiness.

I preferred to celebrate on my own. I had been alone in the pool for all those hours of training, and it only felt right to keep these moments to myself.

I was doing what I promised myself I'd do in Kazan.

I enjoyed the moment to myself as I slowly swam the lactic acid out of my bloodstream. I thanked God. I thanked myself. I thanked Erik.

That night, I went back to the hotel with my mom. My USC commitment paperwork had come in, but I was two weeks shy of my eighteenth birthday, so I needed a parent to cosign.

People usually made a ceremony out of this, but I just wanted it to be me and my mom.

My future looked so, so bright. I was going to be an Olympian, and then I was going to school, where I could live my life however I wanted.

I basked in the moment. I felt so grateful. Elated. I felt like I did when I was eight when I first realized the world was my oyster.

I was doing it. I had made the world mine, and victory was so close. My swimming career was going to have a happy ending.

On the last day of the Minnesota meet, I had the 800, 200 IM, and 200 back. A triple. All of them would be within a thirty-minute window.

I enjoyed doing multiple events. I liked the challenge, and I knew I could put up decent times in all of them—after all, I trained fourteen kilometers every day. I could race for twelve minutes in total. I was known for being able to swim back-to-back-to-back events, usually going best times in the second and third events. Most swimmers had trouble doing more than a single event per day, but I just got faster.

Because I was the fricking Chosen One once more.

The 800 was first and the only event I *really* cared about.

I was next to Katie again. Only this time, she was the top seed in Lane 4, and I was in Lane 5.

Leah Smith was on my other side. She would take the race out fast—I just had to keep up with her until the 300.

Then I would leave her in the dust.

We dove in. Sure enough, I caught Leah by the 300.

Katie was already three seconds ahead.

When her lead stayed the same through the 400, I realized I must be going just as fast as she was.

I picked it up, adrenaline helping me close the gap between us.

I could see the shapes of Erik and Bob jumping up and down on the side of the pool deck as I breathed. The pool was rooting for me, and I could feel it.

We turned at the 600. Katie could tell I was right there—I knew she could. The gap stopped closing. I was two seconds behind . . .

I raced my heart out. I had never beaten Katie in a freestyle event. I wanted it more than anything.

She must've wanted to keep her throne just as badly.

She touched in at 8:19.16. I touched 2.5 seconds later, with a best time of 8:21.77.

The next swimmer was seven seconds behind me, and this field had contained everyone who would be my competition at Trials.

I was cementing myself into the second Olympic spot. I was the one to beat.

For the first time ever, I thought, *Maybe I can beat Katie Ledecky. Maybe it is possible. Maybe I can get gold.*

I gave Katie a quick "Good job" before I hopped into the warm-down pool. There was no time for celebration—my mind was already on my next event.

Just seven minutes later, I was right on my best time for the 200 IM.

I added a few seconds in the 200 back ten minutes later, but it was still a phenomenal performance.

Haley approached me after the triple. "That was really impressive, Becca."

"You could've done it too." I wasn't sure why I couldn't take a compliment, even when it was true.

But the more I thought about it, the more I wondered if Haley *couldn't* have done it. I was unique in that I could swim every stroke. And an 8:21 in the 800 freestyle hadn't been done by an American other than Katie since 2012.

I went back to Baltimore with more confidence than it should have been possible for a single person to have.

12

OVERTRAINING

It was January 2016. The Olympic year. Six months until Olympic Trials. I was finally eighteen. I no longer needed an adult to supervise me during drug testing.

I could taste the USA Olympic Team. I had successfully stepped up my game, no longer needing my age to define just how good I was at swimming. I shed the label of "child prodigy" with just a hint of nostalgia and claimed my name as an adult elite athlete. I just had to keep the course, and the 800 freestyle and 400 IM were mine.

I was at the Austin Pro Swim Series when I got my first warning sign.

I'd just warmed up for my last event of the competition: the 800. Based on my training, I was expecting an 8:16, a five-second drop since Minnesota two months before.

I felt solid. Assured.

I changed into my race suit and sat down, playing UNO on my phone as I rested for a few minutes before my second warm-up. At some point, I'd decided that if I won the UNO game, I would swim fast, and if I didn't—Well . . . I was getting better at disregarding the whole game if I didn't.

My second warm-up was always fifteen minutes before my scheduled start time. The 800 was the first event of the night, kicking off at 6 p.m. on the dot.

At 5:43, I put my phone down.

I glanced at my UGGs on the ground, my brain processing slowly. I didn't want to stand up.

No, I didn't just not *want* to.

I didn't think that I *could*.

The thought of standing made me nauseous. A wave of lethargy hit me like a truck, so powerful that I didn't know if my body would be able to support me, let alone sprint 800 meters.

I weighed a million pounds—far too much to support.

Calm down, I told myself as anxiety rushed through my body. *You're fine. You just have to stand. That's all.*

I could do it. Standing was easy. It wasn't that big of a deal. Most people could stand, and, unlike *most people*, I was an athlete. Athletes could easily stand. And once I stood, I would feel fine.

One.

I readied my feet.

Two.

I braced my hamstrings like I was about to jump across a river.

Three.

I lifted my body weight. My quads burned. My heart raced. Stars flashed in my eyes.

But I did it.

A moment later, everything returned to normal.

That was really, really weird.

I swam easy twenty-fives for my second warm-up, just a little nervous the lethargy would come back. Thankfully, it didn't. The tension left my muscles, though my internal dread refused to dispel so easily.

I pushed it down. *Doubt is the first step to failure. Doubt is the first step to failure.*

I had gotten a best time in the 400 freestyle two days before. I would get my 8:16. It was time for that. My training *pointed* to that.

I felt decent in the race. I was second to Katie, adding a few seconds, but still second in the nation.

So, it's all fine. I would keep the course. There was no reason to be concerned.

★ ★ ★

Water rushed past my ears, my body rotating through Lane 5 in Baltimore. I had left Lotte in the dust. She was nowhere to be seen.

I powered ahead. I was going faster than I had ever swum before. I was superhuman. I didn't need to breathe. I felt no pain.

I lapped Lauren.

I was about to get a world record in practice.

I swam under the flags. Suddenly, I was no longer in Baltimore but . . . Clearwater? Herbert stood at the end of the pool, his entire face distorted through the water, with the exception of his mustache.

I reached for the wall, about to get my world record—

I woke with a start, heart pounding through my ribcage, sweat dripping down my brow.

For a moment, I thought I was still swimming. When I realized I wasn't, alarm clenched my body.

I have to go to the pool. I have to swim. Why am I not swimming?

It was dark. I checked my phone.

3:24 a.m.

Dock meowed at me as if to say, *Go back to sleep.*

I listened to the cat. I could wait three hours before I hopped back into the pool.

I laid back down, closing my eyes. I swallowed the urge to rotate as if I were doing freestyle. The mattress was firm beneath my hips—there would be no swimming in bed.

My practices became sporadic after that dream, though still impressive. Still on track to make the Olympic Team.

I continued to power through, swimming fast every time the practice said "easy." I continued the eleven practices per week. I continued counting every stroke. I continued thinking about everything—technique, speed, distance per stroke, the set I was doing—all at once.

The dream became a recurring nightmare.

"I told you not to do open water!" Herbert screamed.

"I'm not!" I told him, somehow able to talk during the half-second I took a breath.

"If you had only trained pool this whole time, you would be the best!"

"I *am* the best!"

Herbert waved his stopwatch in my face. "Are you sure about that?"

My usual one "bad" practice per week—where I struggled to hit my pace—turned to two. Then two turned to three.

Julia was swimming in the lane beside me. I sprinted, trying to keep up, but she still touched the wall first. "I didn't even have to break the family apart, and I'm *still* faster than you," she told me.

"I need to be swimming," I told her. "I just need to keep practicing."

Whenever I woke from the nightmares, it took all my power not to immediately head to the pool.

My best practice times continued getting faster, even as I noticed my body having delayed reactions to my brain's orders, refusing to listen. Then came the random heart palpitations, where I felt like it was skipping beats.

I kept swimming, trusting my training.

On Sundays, Erik and I analyzed my technique, replaying it in slow motion.

"Look at how much more compact that is," Erik said as we watched my freestyle flip turn.

"Yeah, but it still has so many problems. My feet are still too close together."

"You always focus on that . . . but look at how much better it is."

He searched my face, trying to get me to see what he saw. The progress. The hope.

I saw only what was wrong. "Yeah," I said. But it wasn't *good enough*. Not yet.

Everything went to hell on February 28.

It was a Sunday. I was alone in Baltimore that weekend since Saturday had been Julia's birthday. Less than four months until I qualified for the Olympic Team.

The day started out normally. I was deeply excited for Trials, cutting vegetables as I sang along to Lorde. My ringtone cut my karaoke short. Madeline. I picked it up.

"Hey!" I said, putting down my knife.

"How're you doing? Did you see the Pac-12 results?"

USC had won the collegiate conference the day before, beating favorites Cal and Stanford.

"Yes! I'm so excited to be there next year. And my IM—Madeline, I can *definitely* win next year. My training's been *insane*. I, like, honestly think I can get the US Open and American records too."

"We *need* that, Becca."

"Well, you're getting it."

I ended the call in good spirits, taking my salad to the table as Dock trailed behind me. But my stomach felt strange—my appetite was gone.

Weird.

I forced the salad down.

An hour later, I FaceTimed my mom. "I think I can go a 4:32 this week." She was meeting me in Orlando for a Pro Swim Series three days later. I was swimming some "off" events since I had been training so well in other strokes.

My mom said something in reply, but my brain couldn't process it.

One moment, I was paying attention. The next, I felt as if I were watching the scene unfold behind a glass wall.

My excitement turned to dread. My body went into fight-or-flight mode. Terror rocketed outward from my stomach.

The fog of fear, which I hadn't felt in *years*, overtook me.

It came out of nowhere, with no thoughts triggering it as all my previous episodes had in the past. It had been over three years since I'd had one.

"I'm having a panic attack," I calmly told my mom in a voice that didn't match my inner tumult.

"What?"

"It's what I had when I moved away," I explained. How could my voice sound so even when I was in my own personal hell? "I didn't know they were panic attacks until a year ago. But I'll be fine in the morning. I think I just need to sleep."

She wasn't convinced. I wasn't either, but if there was anything I was good at, it was acting fine until I actually was.

"I'm coming tomorrow."

"What about work?"

"It's fine. I'll see you tomorrow."

I tried to sleep it off, but the following morning, I felt like I was drowning. My body could barely move. My times were mediocre.

Moving took effort. Warm-up took effort. *Everything* took effort.

My mom arrived. When she walked in the door, she looked alarmed.

"How much do you weigh?"

"I don't know."

It had only been a few weeks since she'd last seen me, but apparently, I'd lost a significant enough amount of weight since then. She forced me to eat more.

"Everything's fine. I'm just, like, sick. Or something."

"When was the last time you got your blood chemistry done?"

"A few months ago."

"Schedule an appointment."

Orlando wasn't going to be good. I felt it intrinsically, but I tried to trust my training. Which, up until that Monday, had still been fantastic, despite the increasing number of bad practices.

Erik pulled me aside. "You've done all the work. Don't let the pressure of the meet get in your head."

"I'm not *under pressure!*" I insisted, frustrated. I didn't *crumble* under pressure. I *thrived*. How could Erik not understand that when he had spent the past two years standing at the end of my lane four hours a day? I had been to Olympic Trials before. I'd been to World Championships. I'd done a ten-mile channel crossing when I was ten years old!

I'm just sick.

I would be better by the time the meet started. I would just rest until then.

On Wednesday, I traveled to Orlando. I was *not* better.

I started with the 400 IM/200 freestyle back-to-back double. I out-touched Katie for third with a time of 4:40 in the 400 IM. Like the 800 freestyle in Austin, it was decent, but it wasn't the 4:32 I'd been expecting.

And it *hurt*. Far more than any 400 IM I'd ever done.

I knew as I hopped into the warm-down pool that the 200 was going to be rough.

A bus had hit me. My muscles screamed in pain. My heart rate wasn't decreasing.

It's just a 200, I told myself. *200s are easy.*

I warmed down for eight minutes, then got back behind the blocks. I didn't do my usual jumping and muscle-shaking. I just prayed, then stood there, conserving my energy.

At the flip turn that marked the halfway point, I experienced the first race in which I truly *died*. My body burned. Lactic acid raced through my blood. My arms could barely make it out of the water.

I used to make fun of the old people who didn't have the endurance to take the race home.

Maybe this is penance for that.

I swam my slowest 200 freestyle in six years. I'd gone faster in practice before.

I saw Herbert from afar—the first time I'd seen him since I left Clearwater. My heart dropped. I hurried to the other side of the pool, where he couldn't see me.

Of course he's at the one meet that I'm sucking at.

I didn't care if Herbert watched me swim—everyone on the planet could watch me swim, and I wouldn't feel intimidated—but I didn't think I was capable of having a conversation with him in my current state.

Because I *was* sick. What else could it be?

After another embarrassing race, my mom marched onto the pool deck, bounding right past the badge checkers, to find Erik. "I'm pulling Becca out of the meet."

"What?"

"I know my kid, and there's something wrong with her. I'm taking her home."

I slumped with relief. This competition was like pulling teeth.

I took the next two days off to recover so I'd be ready to go back to hard training by Monday.

If only it were that easy.

My practices were even worse the following week. I had more panic attacks. My mom decided to stay in Baltimore with me and started watching every practice, deeply concerned about my health. Could I have mono? Could it be something else?

April rolled around, but nothing changed.

My intrusive thoughts came back with a fury, though thankfully, this time, I had more control over them.

If this stoplight turns red, everyone I love is going to die in the next five years.

Panic surged through my body as the light turned red.

What have I done? Horror swept through my body. *Why did I think that? What if my mind is capable of anything?*

This isn't true, I thought. *These thoughts aren't real.*

I had enough friends in therapy now not to brush it off when my mom suggested it again.

My blood results were concerning. I had a Vitamin B12 deficiency, low glucose, and several other problems. The blood chemist at USA

Swimming asked if I had been drinking a lot of alcohol, which I would have found amusing if I hadn't been so alarmed.

I needed more recovery, but I didn't want it. Not only was I wasting precious time, but the longer my training was inconsistent, the slower I would get. My Olympic spot was slipping through my fingers. My best efforts were no longer good enough.

My love of swimming disappeared with my ability to physically function. In its place came the thought, *If I don't love it the most anymore, is it even possible to be my best?* I was losing the hunger—the passion, the dream—and began feeling that without that hunger to be my best, I was a shell of a person.

I knew I had other things going for me. In April came the news that I'd been accepted into USC's screenwriting program. I tried to feel excited about it—but I felt *nothing.* I cared about nothing except swimming, even though jumping in the pool now felt like jumping into a pit of acid.

I'd swim well one practice, then have three terrible ones. I'd take a few days off, and the cycle would repeat itself. My resting heart rate, which was in the low thirties just a month before, was suddenly in the mid-fifties. My heart rate variability—my cardiovascular recovery rate—was lower than it had ever been. My body temperature was all over the place.

I got my hormone levels tested. In the blood-drawing room, a fellow patient said to me, "Don't worry—I'm sure you'll get pregnant soon."

I opened my mouth, shocked and horrified. Nothing came out.

Finally, when thoughts returned to my brain, my horror made room for amusement. "Thank you."

"It's a marathon, not a sprint."

"Yeah, it . . . certainly is."

The second I found my mom, I said, "They think I'm trying to get *pregnant.* How old do I look?!"

My mom doubled over with laughter . . . until my hormone results came back at the levels of a prepubescent child.

I hadn't had my period since Kazan. My doctor put me on birth control for my hormones and an antidepressant for my anxiety.

I googled. I knew what it was—I was overtrained. I had every symptom, plus more. But no one in swimming really believed in overtraining. Not in 2016.

My vivid dreams continued. Some nights, I'd find myself transported into alternate realities. Better worlds.

I crouched by the forest creek in our backyard in Illinois, cool water flowing through my fingers as I imagined the water bending to my will. I was Poseidon's demigod child, and there was nothing I couldn't make the water do.

"Becca!" Rachel's voice called from the house. This was the year that Rachel and I had been homeschooled together, just before I'd moved away to Florida.

I rose and jumped across the stream. Rachel stood in the doorway, the smell of pizza wafting out from behind her.

"I made a Costco pizza, then we have to go to practice."

"I don't want to go to practice." The forest was where I belonged—not the pool.

"Why not?"

"I want to play outside." To use my imagination. To be someone else. Not a swimmer. A demigod. Yes, I could make the water do whatever I wished, but did I really want to swim in it?

I'd wake to a melancholic heart, longing for those times. But despite the occasional comforting dream, closing my eyes scared me. In the semiconscious moments before sleep, my thoughts raged. There was nothing to distract me from the *what-ifs*.

And I didn't always find myself in my old backyard. My dreams got violent, my worst fears often playing out as if they were real.

I was back in Florida, looking for shark teeth on the beach, Julia beside me.

If I don't find twenty teeth, Julia is going to be the one thinking all the bad thoughts. She's going to be the one who has to deal with them.

It was unclear who had decided the rules of the twisted game, but I knew I had to find all the teeth. I couldn't let Julia fall victim to my mind.

Ten. Twelve. Seventeen.

But time was running out. We were back on the path to our house before I could collect them all.

"Stop!" I called to Julia. "I need three more teeth!"

"Get more tomorrow," she said, retreating from the ocean. I yelled after her, but she didn't hear me. Did she know what she was condemning herself to? Did she realize what this meant?

It was over. I'd failed. A wave formed on the horizon, but before I could see what I'd done—

I jerked awake.

Some nights, I would sleep for sixteen hours, then I wouldn't sleep at all. I couldn't regulate it.

Erik and I wanted to get back into hard training, but my mom put her foot down, still concerned. She was the only one who noticed just how broken I was.

I had another meet in mid-April in Mesa just to see where I was after a disastrous month of training. Only two months till Olympic Trials.

My friends were there, but I felt even more removed from them than at the OTC.

As I watched them warm up, I knew that I had chosen wrong. I should have gone to Arizona. I had dug my own grave. Not by shoveling but with my own bare hands.

No one digs graves with Bob, I thought, *by missing* or *doing too much.*

The Mesa meet was awful. One day, I had a double—a 200 of something and the 400 IM—and after the disastrous 200, I went and found my mom, sobbing.

"What happened?"

"I can't do the 400 IM!" I cried. "I don't want to!"

"What?" The 400 IM was in fifteen minutes. I was long past the time that I would have been able to scratch without consequence, and I was the second seed behind Katinka Hosszu.

"I need to scratch. I can't do it. It's going to be horrible."

"You won't be able to swim tomorrow then."

"Not if I medically scratch."

"Did something happen?"

"I just—I can't do it."

"Then tell Erik to scratch you."

"I don't want to." I was hysterical. "You tell him."

My mom shook her head. "There's no crying in swimming. Either you tell Erik you're not doing it or swim it. But don't cry about it."

I was terrified of telling Erik to scratch me. Of disappointing him. Even more terrified than I was to swim the event. I was embarrassed. I felt *weak*.

"Okay. I'm going to do it."

"If you swim it—"

"It's going to be good. It *could* be good. Based on my training up until . . . recently."

Doubt is the first step to failure.

"Are you going to be okay?" my mom asked.

"Yeah. I have to go." I only had ten minutes before the race.

"Good luck."

I didn't do my usual second warm-up. I couldn't make myself. I went straight to the ready room, telling myself it would be over in fifteen minutes.

For the first time in my life, I was the first one there.

Katinka arrived next.

"Are you excited for USC?" she asked.

I tried to distract myself. "Yeah, yeah. Really excited." I hoped my lie sounded convincing. "Did you like going there?"

She was a USC alum herself. "Yes, very much."

"Good."

As I suspected, it didn't go well. I added over ten seconds.

I gasped for air as I approached Erik. He looked frustrated. "You need to get back into hard training. You're out of shape with the lack of consistency of the past five weeks."

Maybe I was. Maybe I just had to dive right back in.

"Resting did nothing."

"Okay," I agreed after a moment's hesitation. Because the rest *wasn't* working. Maybe I wasn't overtrained. Because then I'd be getting *better* with more rest, not worse. "Let's do it."

My mom picked me up after I warmed down and changed. I hopped into the car as she punched an address into the map app. The ETA was just under an hour away.

"Where are we going?"

"The mountains."

"Why?"

"Because you love the mountains."

We drove through the desert in silence. I watched the setting sun dye the mountain tips red as if they were bleeding from the bottom up.

"You have a lot going for you in your life," my mom said, tearing my thoughts from the internally injured mountain range.

"Yeah," I agreed, though I couldn't bring myself to care.

"You're going to the best screenwriting program in the world."

"I know."

"And you can do anything you want."

Except swim fast, apparently.

We turned onto a dirt road. My mom stopped the car so she could look at me. So I could see her sincerity. "There's so much more to life than swimming."

I didn't know that life, but I would soon. And I would enjoy exploring it. I was too curious not to.

But it still felt so far away, just like the mountains.

I wanted to run toward them, build a cabin, live a quiet life.

I created a community in my mind. One where no one knew anything about swimming. Where hunting and gathering and friendship were enough.

I snorted. I didn't belong in that world. But I would find the world that I *did* belong in, the one that wasn't swimming, when the time came.

After a long moment of trying and failing to picture my future, I let my gaze settle on the sunset. *Isn't it crazy that the sun is millions of miles away, floating in space?*

I felt no emotion for a moment until my brain stumbled into a rabbit hole. *What if the universe isn't real, and no one's living in the same reality?*

What if nothing mattered? No one mattered? What if I was in a simulation, and space didn't really exist? Because how *could* it exist? And all that existed was fear?

"Katinka really liked USC," I murmured to distract myself, even as the usual pit of dread knotted in my stomach.

"And you will too."

"Yeah, I know."

"And you still have time to get better before Trials."

We enjoyed the mountains and each other's company, driving past some mule deer. As my anxiety slowly faded, I allowed myself to be a girl on a road trip with her best friend.

The next day, I went back to reality.

I began asking for opinions from coaches I respected. "My resting heart rate is high, but it doesn't rise when I swim. I went down to singles, and it got a little better . . . when I go back to doubles, I die again—"

"My distance sets are suffering the most—"

"Even when I put more effort in, I don't go faster. I just crash—"

No one had a solution. No two cases of overtraining were the same.

I was *getting* there. I moved up to the OTC for a few months to utilize their recovery services. My resting heart rate was still elevated, but good practices came more often. I stayed at around five kilometers per practice, significantly less than my usual seven kilometers per practice, but enough that Erik and I weren't concerned about being out of shape.

But I still had bad spells. On my third practice of getting out early in a row, Michael turned to me, a lopsided grin on his face. "Shoveling again, Hype Beast?"

"Leave me alone."

"Just a little early for your self-taper to start."

A string of profanities sprang into my mind. I kept them there—I was once again terrified of doing something that would awaken the dormant *evil* my thoughts had convinced me was lying beneath the surface.

"I said *leave me alone*," I snapped. "I'm obviously *not well*."

Michael had the decency to give an apologetic smile.

SwimSwam released their 2016 Trials predictions (Anderson 2016). There was a debate surrounding my name. I hadn't been performing well since Austin, but according to my Minnesota *and* Austin performances, I *should* have been a shoo-in. *What happened to her?* the swimming world wondered.

I was training with my competition at the OTC. Women whom I had destroyed six months ago at the last training camp were now lapping me. My lower back began to ache.

People treated me as if I didn't exist. The walls that Allison and Frank had helped topple were rebuilt—only this time, instead of using bricks, I used iron.

I tried everything. Gratitude journaling. Books about inner peace. Massages and ice tubs. But nothing I did worked.

Like a gratitude journal is going to piece my body back together.

June came out of nowhere. Less than a month from Trials.

One morning, I carried groceries up the flights of stairs into my barrack. When I bent to set them down, pain coursed through my entire lower back.

I screamed. *Not now. I can't deal with this now.* I swallowed ibuprofen. *It will be better in the morning.*

Pain radiated down my leg. Sleep evaded me.

Bending hurt. Arching hurt more.

The worst part was that I couldn't even bring myself to care. I didn't have the energy anymore. I needed a miracle, regardless of whatever was wrong with my back.

I got an MRI, but I continued to practice as if I weren't falling apart at the seams. I knew what I needed was several months with no swimming. I counted down the days, anticipation laced with fear. They were passing too fast.

Erik kept repeating, "Don't worry, it'll be fine. It's just a meet. And you've been training well enough this year that it'll be fine."

His words did nothing more than irk me. I wasn't *worried*.

I was broken.

When the results of my MRI got back, I discovered I'd herniated my L5-S1 disc and had budging discs at my L3-4 and L4-5.

Erik seemed relieved there was something he could blame my falling apart on. A part of me was too.

I got a Toradol injection. I knew it wouldn't cure me. Because it was the *other* stuff—the problems that couldn't be seen in the MRI: the hormones, the fatigue, the elevated resting heart rate, the panic attacks, the bloodwork—that was the real problem. But overtraining wasn't publicly discussed and wouldn't be for several more years. So my back took the blame.

13

2016 OLYMPIC TRIALS

For the first time ever, when I came down from altitude, I didn't feel like superwoman. I still felt pain as I sprinted. I felt worse than I usually did without altitude training.

The Olympic pool looked exactly as it had in 2012, though this time, it held none of the magic. Four years ago, the water had been filled with potential and possibility. This time, the dim lights looked foreboding.

Warming up, it took all my energy to do hundreds at 800 pace. I tried to convince myself it would be fine. I'd had bigger miracles in my life—maybe I'd get another one.

I scratched out of the 400 IM, which was supposed to have been my first event and what I thought I'd be making the Olympic Team in just five months before. My IM training had fallen away in an attempt to save my freestyle.

The first night of Trials was torturous to watch. I would have been seeded second going into finals had I been where I was five months ago.

But you're not, I reminded myself. *You added eleven seconds in the last 400 IM you swam.*

I sat in the stands with my parents and sisters as the women competing in the 400 IM dived off the blocks.

Maya DiRado immediately opened a gap. But the rest of them . . .

They turned for the backstroke. My butterfly split would have been second. What were they doing?

Then the breaststroke. I held my breath. Would my time from Minnesota, the time I'd swum in the middle of hard training, have gotten me second? Have won me an Olympic spot?

This isn't happening, I told myself as I calculated what the second finisher's time was going to be. I would have been behind going into the freestyle, but there was no one I couldn't hunt down.

I watched Elizabeth Beisel surge into the wall second, securing her Olympic spot. I stared at the scoreboard as she touched—

4:36.81. Only .23 seconds—a single *breath*—faster than my best time.

I was a racer. I would have gotten that. I would have found a way to go .23 seconds faster.

What the fuck am I doing? Why didn't I swim that? What is wrong with me?

Everyone here knew me, and they were all watching. I couldn't react. I couldn't let my thundering heart leave my chest.

Thank God they couldn't see into my mind.

Would this have been my miracle?

I was back in Kazan, watching my dreams get snatched from beneath my fingertips yet again.

"The 800 is what counts," my mom whispered to me. I nodded numbly. It was déjà vu—Kazan faded, replaced with 2012. *The 800 is your event.*

My former teammate Chase won the Men's 400 IM. I watched Bob parade past my seat in the stands as Chase rose onto the stage, fire spouting into the air on either side of him.

I swallowed the knot in my throat. "Can we go home?"

The 400 freestyle, my first event that I hadn't scratched, got my meet off to a rocky start. I was fourteenth with a 4:11, over four seconds slower than my best time, which I'd swum a few days before the beginning of the end in Austin. It was slower than I'd gone at Olympic Trials four years before.

How was I supposed to salvage the 800? My body still wasn't responding.

I watched the 200 freestyle final. I was elated when Allison made her third Olympic Team.

So did another swimmer whom I'd trained with—and jealousy toward her overtook all my glee.

I should have been happy for her. She was a great athlete. She trained hard. But I was a *better* swimmer. I trained *harder*.

Why did she get to achieve her dreams, and I didn't? Why did she get the victory? Why did my body have to break down and betray me when I needed it most?

Stop thinking like this, I ordered myself. *You still have a chance in the 800.*

I stretched my arms and inspected them. They looked *normal.* Toned. Like my arms had looked six months before when I had been healthy.

Why aren't you working?! I mentally screamed. *Why can't you do what I trained you to do?! What is* wrong *with you?*

My arms didn't respond.

"Your training this year—it's been incredible. *Phenomenal,*" Erik said after warm-up. "That's all in there, okay? You can do it."

You can do it.

I gave a nod. "I know." I knew I *could*—my times had proved it themselves. *Res ipsa loquitur.* I just had to summon what I had once been—and still *might be*—capable of.

Last to the ready room. There was an empty seat beside Haley. I sat in amiable silence beside her.

I reflected on how much more comfortable the ready room felt than it had in 2012. I had beaten all these women before. Though somehow still the second-youngest, I was the fastest seed in my heat. I'd proven myself to be a formidable force.

Be that. But also be hungry. Like your fourteen-year-old self.

Lane 4. The fastest lane.

I shook out my muscles. *Just eight minutes. American Pie. That's it. You can hold yourself together that long.*

I gazed across the pool as I shed my parka and warm-ups. I'd seen the same view thousands of times over, but this fifty-meter stretch of water looked different. Longer. Unwelcoming.

I didn't want to jump in.

The long whistle sounded. I wrapped my toes around the edge of the blocks, doing a final sign of the cross. I turned off my brain, praying my body would take over. Praying it remembered how.

"Take your mark . . ."

BEEP!

I dived in.

Behind on the start. *Normal.*

Climbing my way back up to the others drained me. I felt like I was in Kazan, trying to fight my way back up to the pack after getting pummeled. And the race had just started.

I felt like a corpse after the first hundred. *Ignore it. Swim through it.*

I passed the outside lanes—the slowest swimmers. The competitors directly beside me were still ahead.

I passed a few more people until I was in fourth.

Fourth in this heat isn't going to get you into finals. There were still ten swimmers that had to race.

But I couldn't move any faster. My herniated back was the least of the pain in my body.

I got no pleasure out of the challenge. This race was pure survival. *Back half,* I told myself at the 400. *Do what you do best.* But I was hanging on for dear life, and no amount of encouragement from my mind could fuel my body.

When I touched the wall, the same thought from Kazan materialized. *Thank goodness it's over.*

I'd never felt so drained after an 800. I'd never known I *could* be. My body shook. I'd wrung every drop of strength my body possessed.

It took several long seconds to regain enough strength to look up at the scoreboard. Fourth. I'd fought tooth and nail . . . to go an 8:32.92. An eleven second add. Slower than I'd gone in 2012. My stomach plummeted.

I was muscularly, aerobically, and mentally depleted. It was a weariness that had spread from my muscles into my very soul.

I was on the verge of making finals. Based on the time and the placements, I assumed I'd be eighth or ninth.

In or out.

I dodged every familiar face as I hurried to the warm-down pool. I wound a rope tightly around a swirl of emotions, not allowing myself to feel them until I was in the safety of the warm-down pool.

The moment I was staring back at the black line, the silence thick around me as I swam as slowly as possible, I set my emotions free.

I expected anxiety. Fear.

But all I felt was hope. Hope that I *wouldn't make it.*

I couldn't imagine having to swim another 800 freestyle tomorrow. I wanted to go home. I wanted to spend the summer in the Chicago suburbs with my family. I wanted to go back into the forest behind my house and shoot my bow and arrow.

I wanted to pick up right where I'd left off five years earlier before I moved away to pursue . . . *this*. Whatever this was.

An unnerving sensation nestled into my body as I watched the final preliminary heat. I had no control over my destiny. Either four people in the final heat would beat me, and I'd have a shot at the Olympic Team, or five people would beat me, and my 2016 Olympic dreams would end here.

If I got a lane, would I really be able to go ten seconds faster? Would I be able to swim as fast as I'd been able to swim six months ago?

At the 400, it became clear that it was going to be close. I could barely breathe. The 500. The fifth swimmer and I would have been neck-and-neck had we been in the same heat.

700.

I didn't know whom I was rooting for. I didn't know what I wanted.

The swimmers darted into the wall.

She beat me. I was ninth. The first alternate.

I didn't make it.

Disappointment, quickly followed by relief.

"Dumb question! Are you scratching the 800?" I asked Ashley. Haley. Cierra Runge. Leah Smith. Every single woman who had beaten me.

"No," each of them replied.

Erik was aloof, his face stoic. It pissed me off.

"Well," I said, "I guess that's it. Cierra told me she's not scratching. Right?"

Cierra had already made the Olympics and had barely snuck into the final. Maybe Bob and Erik would pull her out so I could get in.

I was determined to triple-check my bases before I drove six hours back to Illinois.

"She's not."

"Okay."

"But . . . maybe someone will—"

"I've already asked everyone, Erik. No one's scratching."

I need to get out of here. The pool deck felt small. Claustrophobic. I avoided Bob. Jeremy. Michael. I needed to leave.

I was supposed to stick around in case something happened to one of the finalists, but I couldn't make myself. I couldn't bear the thought of having to swim one more lap or of being surrounded by my happy Olympic-bound friends.

When I found my family outside the CenturyLink Center, I said, "Let's go home."

My family escorted me to my hotel. As we hurried through the lobby, I spotted Allison.

I stood frozen in time as she hurried toward me. Wondering what had gone wrong. Wondering why I could never seem to put just the right amount of energy into swimming. The lead-up to Kazan had been too distracting, and the lead-up to Omaha too serious.

"Every year I've made the big meet," I blurted, "you haven't. And every year you have, I haven't."

"What?"

"Isn't that weird?"

"I mean, yeah, kinda."

My brain could never stop playing games. What were the signs pointing to?

Allison smiled like she wasn't sure whether she was supposed to be laughing.

"So this is *your* year to win," I said. "To represent us."

Allison searched my face. "What are you—?"

"I'm going home. Get some golds in Rio, okay? Promise me?"

"I will."

My mom drove me and my sisters back to the suburbs of Chicago that afternoon, my dad following in the car behind us.

We threw pretzels out of the sunroof at my dad's car. A song titled *Soy un Perdedor* came on the radio—*I'm a loser*. My family and I doubled over with laughter and replayed it on aux.

"This is your song, Becca!" they cheered.

"That's right!" My family made everything better. They never took anything seriously.

This was what I needed. Two months at home—the longest I'd been home since moving out at thirteen—before going off to college. Two months of no swimming. Two months of getting back on my feet.

The next morning, back in my childhood room, I got the text from Erik.

"Cierra is scratching the 800. Are you still here or did you leave?"

My heart stopped.

The last thing I wanted to do was go back to Omaha and swim another 800. The one yesterday had nearly killed me.

Why did I have to choose? Why couldn't I rest knowing I had given it my all, but it hadn't been enough?

I rushed to my mom and showed her my phone.

"You can fly back and get there in time."

"B—but I don't want to go back." The words felt dirty in my mouth, like I was confessing to a brutal crime. "I can't go any faster."

What if this *is your miracle?* Was this what I had been hoping and praying for? If there was a lane, there was a chance.

The universe was presenting an opportunity to get everything I'd ever wanted.

So why did the thought of getting it make me feel sick? What would happen if, by some miracle, I *did* make the Olympic Team? I would have to put off recovering. I didn't *want* to swim for another two months, even if it meant going to the Olympics.

My weary body begged me not to do it. It didn't want to get on a flight, warm up, and sprint 800 meters. It didn't want to have to face that pool again.

It just wanted to lie on the couch with Dock and not move for several weeks.

"Then don't," my mom said.

This was salt in the wound. It was my decision. I was the only person who could be blamed.

I texted Erik, *"Tell tenth place."*

Then, my fingers typing with a ferocity I didn't know I possessed: *"I'm burned out and don't even want to swim or go to Rio anymore."*

I stared at my phone screen. The bubbles appeared. I held my breath for what may have been eons. *"Ok. Will do. I just wanted to ask first."*

I waited for more, but nothing came.

Watching finals on TV was masochistic. A knife plunged into my heart with every stroke my competitors, peers, and friends took.

Leah Smith broke away from the rest of the field, claiming the second Olympic Team spot behind Katie with an 8:21.64, just .13 seconds faster than the 8:21.77 that I'd swum in Minnesota. *You're going to have to get through this,* I told myself. *Just make it out the other side.*

14

RECLAIMING MY YEAR

I needed the months at home.

Every day consisted of physical therapy and a long walk with my mom, with psychotherapy twice a week.

My regurgitation, still a problem since Clearwater, somehow got worse, despite not swimming. I got an endoscopy and was put on medication to avoid esophageal cancer caused by acidic scarring, which lined the entire tube.

It was a metaphor. I was scarred in places I couldn't see.

The mission was to get me into a better place before college. Every walk I took with my mom, we talked it out. I attempted to reconcile the past while looking forward to the future.

This was the first time in my life that I wasn't blazing forward. My entire career—regardless of whether I'd been winning or losing—I'd been in motion. I couldn't think of a single moment I'd been still.

There was nowhere to go and nothing to do.

Erik hadn't reached out since he'd scratched me. I didn't expect him to. I didn't trust him to.

Our partnership was over. I believed he had a fear of conflict, and I had a fear of being held back. So it felt right that we avoided each other.

When I felt I was treated poorly, I decided that whoever had made me feel that way wasn't worth it. Like Herbert.

And now Erik.

It didn't occur to me that Erik might also be upset or that the death of my dream could have been hard for him.

Instead, he died *with* my dream.

I had witnessed close friends struggle with post-Olympic depression, regardless of how they performed. It was the withdrawal—the comedown—after an addiction. I was terrified it would happen to me.

I was lucky that I had other interests. I'd gotten into cinema school. I was going to make a career of writing. But still—I had devoted my entire life to swimming. I knew nothing else.

Every night in my dreams, my subconscious tried to figure out what had gone wrong.

I was in Rio de Janeiro at the Olympics, but Rio looked like the OTC. I was in the back of a car, staring at the mountains, making the Olympic Team carpool karaoke music video. Michael drove, Allison rode shotgun. The wind swept through my hair as P!nk blared.

Everything was perfect. I was about to get a gold medal in the 10k. Or had I already won gold?

Except . . . I wasn't an Olympian, was I?

When I woke up, the dream tasted bitter in my mouth. Life outside of swimming felt fake until I flew out to Los Angeles for orientation.

School was new and shiny. There was so much to do. So much to see. Different people. Random clubs. Different people with diverse thoughts and ideas and opinions.

I finally *felt* excited for it. I allowed myself to think about what I wanted to do outside of swimming. For the first time in my life, I stopped thinking about it. I let myself be amused by the poetic nature of my failure.

I made a joke about it to my mom, to which she replied, "You can make 2020 if you want."

"You think I can just *make* it?"

"If you want to."

"Well, I *don't* want to."

My mom gave me a look like she knew she was about to get a lecture. I wasn't one to disappoint.

"I gave *everything* to that. I ate, I slept, I swam, and I recovered. That's literally *all* I've ever done. I can't do that for another four years. I can't do that in college. And I—I don't know if my body's even—ever . . ." I couldn't finish the sentence. *Going to be able to swim fast again.*

So maybe I wasn't as amused as I'd thought.

I was afraid I'd broken my body for good. My body wasn't just a temple—it had been a well-oiled machine. Now it was a broken, rusty pile of scraps smoking in a junkyard.

"It's going to," my mom assured me.

"Even if it does, I'm not doing another four years of that."

I couldn't imagine getting back in the pool, let alone going through it all over again. "I need to live a normal life. I have to try."

"Okay."

We walked in silence for a few moments. "It's just . . ." I paused, uncertain, then blurted, "What was it all for?"

"You had a lot of fun."

That was true. It was just hard to see it through my gray-colored glasses. "Yeah."

"And you're getting school paid for."

"Yeah."

I knew it was worth a lot. I knew that it wasn't for nothing.

I squared my shoulders. I had a blank page left in 2016 to write anything I wanted, so I would rise from the ashes, even if it was in a way that had nothing to do with swimming.

And that sounded like a challenge.

15

THE REAL-LIFE TEST DRIVE

After two months, the longest I'd been home in five years, I moved into my dorm at the University of Southern California.

I was excited for a new experience. A new look at life. I hadn't been to "real" school since I was eleven—a lifetime ago. The two months away from the pool had reinvigorated me.

This was my chance to test out the real world while still having swimming to lean on. This was my time to make 2016 *my* year.

I lived in a suite with five nonswimmers and one fellow USC swimmer named Gina.

Gina was a decent athlete—she'd gotten sixty-eighth at Olympic Trials in a sprint event.

"Becca and I are on the swim team," Gina told everyone we met. "We both have full rides."

"Oh, cool. Were you the best at your high school?"

"We were actually both homeschooled," replied Gina. "And I'm going for the 2020 Olympics."

I kept my mouth shut despite my building frustration.

Another suitemate turned to me, a knowing glint in her eye, and whispered, "You're better than her, aren't you?"

"What gave me away?"

"You're not talking as much, and your Facebook has a blue check."

I laughed, and with that, she became my first nonswimming friend.

It was still Welcome Week when Gina said, "You know, I would do literally anything just to be able to say I'm an Olympian."

I swallowed a laugh. "Really?"

"Well, wouldn't you?"

"No." Gina looked at me expectantly, so I continued, "I just love swimming. I wouldn't trade that for one swim meet or a label. Especially when I've lived my entire life like an Olympian."

Gina didn't know what I'd been through. Gina hadn't wrecked her body. Gina didn't feel pain in her herniated discs whenever she picked up something too heavy. Gina wasn't weaning herself off Prozac. Gina didn't feel weak and out of shape every time she jumped into the pool.

Gina didn't know that I wouldn't trade any of it for the journey because, now that my body and mind were healing, the fun of the challenge was what I thought about more than the failed goal.

But a part of me still wondered, *What is the next journey? What if you don't like anything as much as you like swimming?*

I wasn't even nineteen, but I'd already tasted what it was like to be the best in the nation. The sixth-best in the world. What if it was only down from here? What if the best years of my life were behind me?

There's something else out there, I assured myself. *You haven't tried anything yet. Get over yourself.*

I was going to chase the elation I'd felt in Baltimore. I was going to find joy in the small moments again. If I didn't put all my energy into swimming, I would have some left to put toward the search.

I was ready.

I started with something I already knew well: writing.

I was untrained and unknowledgeable about both the entertainment and book industries, but I trusted that the same principles I'd learned from swimming would get me where I wanted to go: hard work, discipline, and a willingness to learn.

I was nervous for the first day of class. The swimming world had been so familiar and comfortable that I hadn't felt nervous in *years*. But a first day of class? At a *college*? With kids my own age? Terrifying.

I walked into the classroom.

There they were. Eight of the writers in my cohort. Eighteen-year-olds had never looked so scary. I had a strong desire to flee. I had no reputation following me here. I wasn't special here. I had cemented my reputation in the swimming world when I was twelve. Even people who didn't know me knew that I worked hard, that I was loud, that I loved challenges, and that I danced to the beat of my own drum.

These students knew nothing. I had nothing to fall back on.

I can be anyone I want. That's cool. Be cool.

"Okay," the professor said. "Before we get started, you're all entering a career that's primarily relationship-based. If networking makes you uncomfortable, you need to be a novelist."

Networking. I only had four real friends outside of my family.

In swimming, I had been in control. My body had been a machine, my successes and failures had been my own to claim, and my ranking had granted me the luxury of being able to make demands that would likely be met.

Here, if something hurt, I wouldn't have five doctors waiting to fix me. I wouldn't be able to demand a regimen change from my professors if I thought something was wrong with the training. I couldn't just tell people that something needed to be fixed—I had to do the fixing myself.

None of us responded to the professor. I was determined to make it. And it might be fun to have more Allisons and Evas in life.

"And it's not for the weak of heart. It's going to take perseverance," the professor continued.

Maybe classes *would* be as fulfilling as swimming.

"That was intense," one of my peers said after class. "Why is he trying to scare us out of writing?"

"I think he just wants us to know that we have to work hard," I replied.

"It's the first day of school. Really is putting a damper on it."

I didn't know what to say. I liked them, but I felt like I was a different age—older in some ways, younger in others. My thirty-year-old friends hadn't told me anything about what teenagers on a more traditional path learned outside the classroom.

"Did you hear that one kid say he's here to win, not make friends?" another student piped up. "What's wrong with him?"

I swallowed a laugh. *I* had been that kid just two months ago.

I still was. But I was trying something new. I didn't want to immediately box myself in as my old self.

But if you're not going to be your old self, who are you going to be?

Remember, I reminded myself. *Be cool.*

Someone held out something that looked like a USB drive. "Want a hit?"

I looked at it. "A hit of . . . what?"

"Um . . . what?"

"Uh . . . no, thank you?"

She shrugged, put it up to her lips, and inhaled.

Before I could recover, a boy approached. "Becca, what do you think about *The Shining*?"

I knew of the movie, though I'd never seen a horror movie in my life—or even an R-rated one. I was too paranoid that horror would send my brain into a spiral.

"I actually haven't seen it."

"You *haven't*? Well, we gotta change that."

"I'm actually okay. But thanks!"

I asked him for his life story, from birth till now. He tilted his head, and this time, I couldn't stop myself from chuckling. *Okay, so maybe being "cool" isn't the best goal.*

I called my mom as I walked home. "I love it here!" I recapped my social interactions and my mom and I both cried from laughing so hard.

Over the next few days, I tried to find my social footing. I was insecure in my complete lack of cinematic knowledge. I applied for film school because I loved writing, and I wanted to write stories that spanned several seasons. I was a storyteller—not a cinephile.

I overcompensated. Had I seen whatever cool new movie was out? No, but "I've *definitely* heard of it and know the basics, but could you remind me again?"

Dating? I *definitely* wasn't afraid, and I *certainly* hadn't completely repressed my sexuality—it was just beneath me. I was too independent.

I'd wandered onto another planet. I was out of my league. But the more I interacted with the other students, the easier it became. I owned my awkwardness—and knew it was charming and hilarious.

Plus, I was determined to find my people, and it quickly became clear that I was not going to find them on the swim team.

For starters, they called nonathletes "NARPs." Nonathletic regular people.

"Why are they regular?" I asked after someone explained the acronym to me.

"Because they aren't *athletes*."

"That doesn't mean they're regular," I argued. "They've probably done other cool things. Like, maybe they're curing cancer."

"It's just a name."

"So we're special because we swim back and forth in a pool every day? That seems dumb."

"Yes. We worked hard to be here."

"They all probably did too."

"It's not the same."

I hated that. The swim team had decided they were campus celebrities because they knew how to swim. I couldn't do that. I was trying out the world without low-level fame.

I was going to try being a NARP.

One day, after a screenwriting class, I was invited to lunch with several new friends.

"I can't."

"You have something more fun planned?"

I hesitated. "I have to go to swim practice."

"What?"

We were several weeks into the first semester. I'd avoided telling my acquaintances about my swimming career—I had no desire to attempt to explain it.

"I'm on the swim team."

"The club team?"

"No, the college team."

"You're a student-athlete?"

"Yeah . . ."

"No way. That's so cool."

I did *not* want to talk about swimming. They were bringing up an ex that everyone assumed I was still dating.

"Yeah, thanks. See you next week."

No one mentioned swimming again, and I was okay with that.

As time passed and I washed the aftertaste out of my mouth, I realized that I *liked* not being defined by my swimming career. It was freeing. Being the girl who didn't make the Olympics didn't scare me anymore.

I didn't let people know that I had been addicted to endorphins, fame, training, competing, winning. Even to improving, to being better, to wanting *more*.

I leaned into my curiosity. I knew from training for open water that if I wanted something, I had to ask questions. And I wanted friends. *What was it like going to high school? Did you pursue writing your whole life? Were you in the school play? Have you ever dated anyone? What's your family like?*

It would take me a while to answer their reciprocated curiosity with anything more than a vague, "I swam a lot. Traveled a lot. It was really fun." My lack of backstory made it hard for others to connect with me, but my walls were coming down again. It helped that nonswimmers wanted nothing from me. They didn't care about the swimming world. I began to figure out how to protect my energy without being a complete enigma to those around me.

"I want to *make something*," Mary, a girl in my cohort, said. "I don't want to wait until I graduate."

Mary was one of the few freshmen I felt immediate kinship with. She was put together and didn't think of life as something that began after college.

"So do I." But the truth was, I knew *nothing* about how to "make something." I knew nothing about *anything* in this world except how to write.

And how to use what I'd learned from swimming to succeed.

I could learn from Mary, just like I'd done with Eva. And maybe I'd even get another life friend out of it.

"What do you want to make?"

16

THROUGH, NOT OVER

Even though I was doing well and enjoying life outside the pool, the scabs from swimming couldn't heal in peace. No. Instead, I picked at them every day when I was forced to go to practice.

During those three hours a day, I was miserable. And a miserable swimmer is a slow swimmer.

Practice, especially this early in the season, was painfully *easy*.

I still wasn't fully out of the hole from overtraining. But it was *boring* and, for a distance swimmer like me, a waste of time. The swimming I loved was challenging swimming. I loved pushing myself to my limits. I loved working so hard that painkilling endorphins rushed through my body and stilled my racing thoughts.

This was not that swimming. This swimming was designed for sprinters, just as Erik had warned. There was so much rest that I got cold, irritated, and antsy. I spent the practice staring at the clock, watching the seconds tick by until I could finally get out of the pool and do anything else.

I missed the high-stakes drama that was inherently borne of being one of the best in the world. I craved it, but my body was no longer able to perform at that level.

Madeline was my primary coach. We had our usual rapport. I made practice as fun as I could.

We did two beach workouts the whole season. That was it. There was no open water training.

I sucked it up. I needed to fully recover from what I'd put my body through six months before.

But I wasn't delivering the points that the team had paid for when they'd purchased me. My coaches' patience was running thin. *Is the racehorse going to run as fast as she did when we bought her? How long do we have to wait before we tell her she needs to step it up?*

I hadn't come with a warranty. They'd opened the box and seen that I was broken, but it was too late to return me.

Madeline never said this to my face. She acted like everything was fine, though I saw her frown as she watched me swim.

I was embarrassed by my inability to swim fast. Because it wasn't just the training. It was me as well.

I once again butted heads with the strength coaches. I should have come with a warning: *nine out of ten strength coaches do not recommend!* I had to show up two times a week anyway. I put my head down and hoped that no one would pay attention to me.

One Monday, the first day of a new regimen, I began a set of a new exercise and couldn't keep my balance.

"You're the least athletic swimmer I've ever seen," a teammate told me as she watched.

My family would eat this up. They would make endless fun, saying that meant I was at the bottom of our family's athleticism ladder.

I tried to harness the energy of proving them wrong. A year ago, I would have laughed. Because it *was* funny. I didn't care about dryland. Everyone knew I sucked at it.

But I was in a completely different headspace than a year before. I had been swimming so poorly that I felt guilty about it. Guilty about being on a full ride, about having been perhaps the best recruit in the nation, yet not even being one of the Top 5 highest scorers on the USC team. I couldn't manage a laugh. For the first time in my swimming life, I felt insecure. Past my prime.

"Well, thanks!" I said brightly. "That's very kind of you!"

The insecurity caused by this dumb comment woke me up. I needed to get out of this unhealthy headspace, regardless of how much I was thriving out of the water. The panic I'd been experiencing since getting overtrained had gotten better, but it hadn't faded completely—and the more I hated swimming, the more disturbing thoughts wormed their way into my brain.

I went back to therapy, sitting five feet away from a sports psychologist, though we were a million miles apart emotionally.

"Swimming isn't a reprieve. And then I'm worried my panic will be as bad as it was when I was thirteen. Or that . . . I don't know, what if I can't be good all the time? What if I mess up and don't make my ten-year-old self proud? What if I do something, and then I'm guilty forever, and I get stuck in an eternal panic attack?"

I couldn't look at her as anxiety overtook my body and mind. I hated talking about this—it made it more real. But it also made it sound ridiculous, which I suppose took some of the power away.

"Do you ever feel hopeless?"

"Only when I'm deep in a panic attack."

"I think you're depressed."

"I'm *not* depressed." I didn't know *what* I was, exactly, but it wasn't depressed. It was panic disorder—I was sure of it.

"Do you find pleasure in life?"

"*Yes*. I'm actually an exceptionally happy person."

"You can be a happy person and be depressed."

"But I'm *not* depressed! You don't understand."

I called my mom as I biked back to my dorm in tears. "I hate therapy. I want to quit."

Maybe you are *depressed*, whispered my brain. *Maybe you're so depressed that—*

"Tell them to find you someone else."

"I don't want someone else. I want to *quit*."

"You haven't even given it a try there. You just need to find the right therapist."

"I don't *want to*."

My mom was quiet on the phone, the spokes in my wheels and chatter of strolling students the only sounds I could hear.

"You need to suck it up and go back and tell your therapist you need a new one."

I rarely disagreed with my mother. I hated fighting with her because *what if something happened and she died, and we never got a chance to patch it up*?

Okay, so maybe I *did* need to go back.

I counted down the days before my next session, anxiety growing as the countdown neared zero.

"I don't think we're the right fit," the therapist said before I could tell her the same. "I'm transferring you to my colleague."

I love a mutual firing.

The next week, I went to my new therapist and repeated everything that I had told the previous therapist.

"What other things do you think?"

"Bad things."

"Like what?"

Things I would never even share with my mom—and certainly not with a woman I'd just met. So I changed the subject.

"But I'm *not* depressed. At least, I don't think I am. I think I have a panic disorder? But I don't know—I'm not a psychologist."

I waited, holding my breath, waiting to hear just how disturbed and unfixable I was.

"No. You have OCD."

I tilted my head. "But I don't have to, like, count before I do things. And I'm not a neat freak. Or organized. Well, I'm not *unorganized*, but I'm not, like, a spreadsheet girl."

I took a breath to continue, then closed my mouth, swallowing the urge to talk a mile a minute.

"That's not all OCD is. And you could have Pure O—pure obsessional."

"Well, I won't argue that I'm purely obsessional."

But I *did* have to count my strokes. And do the sign of the cross before every swim.

"You have disturbing thoughts and then your brain holds onto them rather than just letting them only be thoughts."

My intrusive, circular thoughts that I'd gotten when I moved to Florida suddenly made sense. The superstitions. The numbers. The constant movement so I didn't have to think too long.

"What if they're not only thoughts?"

My therapist gave me a pointed look, then continued, "In trying to get rid of them, you give them more power. The people who are distraught over the thoughts are actually the least likely to act upon them."

"But I do want to get rid of them."

"You get through them, not rid of them."

"No."

"No?"

"There's nothing I can't do if I put my mind to it," I insisted, staring at her with a powerful intensity that I was certain could make an army follow me onto a battlefield.

She was immune to my gaze. "That's not how this works. You're going to learn how to take away their power. To not let them have control over you."

"But they'll still be there?"

"Yes."

Having obsessive, intrusive thoughts—and having power over *them* rather than *them* having power over *me*—seemed more difficult than winning ten Olympic medals.

"No. I'm *here*, aren't I? I'll put in the work. I can get rid of them."

"Why is it so important for you to get rid of them? If they don't make you anxious anymore—if they have no effect on you—does it matter whether you think them?"

"*Yes!*"

Another look. She was challenging me, which, of course, I appreciated. "You will have to work. We're going to do exposure therapy."

"What's that?"

"It's about facing your thoughts and exposing yourself to them so they don't have power over you."

So, it's hell.

"The way through it is literal torture? I'm not doing that. I can't even, like, *think* the thoughts without having a panic attack. And you think I can just . . . expose myself to them? That's going to make me *worse*."

"You're not even able to talk about them. If you can see them as just thoughts, then they won't have power over you when you do think them."

"That sounds—" *Like it honestly might work?* "Like there's an easier way to do it."

"We'll start small."

I was petrified. This felt like how it would get as bad as it was when I was thirteen. I couldn't go back to that. Just thinking about it made me nauseous.

But maybe the technique could help with something else.

I went back to my dorm room and finally allowed myself to *really* reflect on my swimming career.

I'd never celebrated my accomplishments or even stopped to be proud. I'd just moved on to the next goal. But in that moment, I celebrated who I'd become thanks to the journey toward those accomplishments.

I reflected on the 2012 Olympic Trials. Instead of feeling the pain of not making the team, I remembered that I'd learned how to compete at the highest stage. I belonged with the best. In swimming, in writing, in *anything* I chose to do.

I thought about winning both Open Water National Championships. What it had felt like to be the best person at something in the *entire* nation. How it had felt to win by a landslide the first time and how hard I'd managed to fight for the second victory. I hadn't given up. I could still feel the joy.

But I didn't think I'd learned anything from that race. Had failure taught me more than success? In this instance—maybe. After that race, I'd gone back to my hotel, and Julia had badgered me into going to the beach with her. Despite being *the best*, I'd returned to normal life.

Kazan. That had made me strong. I knew how to keep moving forward amid heartbreak. I was resilient. I would *always* be resilient.

The 2016 Trials. I paused, unable to write anything down. It was still too fresh.

Why did you swim? I asked myself. *Why did you work so hard? Was it just because you wanted to be the best? Whether it was the best version of yourself or the best out of everyone?*

No. It was because I *loved* it. More than anything.

I loved swimming. I loved the adrenaline, the endorphins, the feel of the water. I loved the pain of pushing my body as hard as it could go and the satisfaction that followed. I loved trying to be better than I was the day before. I loved how it made me feel about myself—joyful, strong, proud.

I loved swimming as much as was humanly possible, so I thought that meant I deserved to be the best. But that didn't matter. I was *my* best. Swimming had made me my best self. And now my best self could go do other amazing things. And, because my OCD had to ask—*what if your best self is stuck in swimming? What if that means you're only going to be a worse person from here on out?*

I had made no major mistakes in life. *And I'm going to,* I realized. *I'm nineteen.*

Then I'll learn and move on. Because if I wanted to live—*really live*—I was going to have to test the strict rules I'd made for myself. It seemed a lot of the things I did and didn't do were because my OCD had instilled a deep-rooted fear in me.

It was constricting to live by rules constructed from fear. That wasn't the person I wanted to be. *And that's dumb. You're not dumb.*

I'd been acting like an adult since I'd moved out when I was thirteen. Maybe I needed to be a teenager this year.

Maybe I'd drink when I was twenty-one. Maybe I'd acknowledge my sexuality, and that I was probably queer. Maybe I would start wondering what *I* thought instead of just believing what my family believed. Maybe I'd challenge them when I didn't. Maybe I didn't need to be perfect all the time. Maybe I'd swear occasionally, in an appropriate situation, if it was a better way of communicating. Maybe I'd stay up past 10:30 p.m. Maybe I'd challenge some of the rules of Catholicism that I thought were stupid.

Because for someone who loved adventure so much, I'd sure been determined to live in my comfort zone.

I took a deep breath, enamored with the idea of liberation.

I can do this on my own, I decided. *I don't need a therapist. Or exposure therapy.*

But would I really be liberated if I was a slave to my intrusive thoughts? I was strong and capable . . .

And really good at making excuses, apparently.

I chuckled. I needed to suck it up. I needed to change things if *I* wanted to change. I was never going to move on or be at peace if I didn't.

I didn't know this woman, though. How was I supposed to trust her to—?

Excuses, excuses, excuses.

Trusting people had never—

You know this is different.

I sighed.

You have to. The stakes are too high.

But I'd lost my courage by the time I showed up the next week.

When I visited my therapist, I said, "So I don't want to be all the way fixed."

I had a feeling she was trying not to roll her eyes. "Fixed? Can you elaborate?"

"I think my OCD is part of the reason I was so good at swimming. I was *always* obsessing about ways to improve. If I lose that, I'm not going to be excellent at whatever I do next. So, is there a way to, like, keep the good and get rid of the bad?"

I didn't notice that I'd used *was* instead of *am* until after I'd spoken.

"You can be excellent without being obsessive."

"How?"

"Because thoughts aren't actions."

I mulled that over. Maybe she was right. If I hadn't been obsessive, would I have gotten overtrained? Probably not. Maybe I would have made the Olympics.

But if I hadn't been obsessive, would I have been anywhere near as good as I was? Maybe . . . maybe not.

Maybe I could have just worked hard, worked smart, and *not* devoted every waking second to *thinking* about swimming. Maybe I could have had fun outside the pool *before* I was seventeen years old.

But I was failing at swimming while dividing my energy between it and school. Wasn't that proof that I couldn't nurture multiple passions at once?

Or maybe you're just in an environment that doesn't work for your swimming, a voice in my head told me.

"Your intrusive thoughts aren't what make you great at what you do."
You need to be brave. You like challenges.

"So how does this exposure therapy start?" I asked before my courage could abandon me. I wasn't going to enjoy this challenge. Not at all. But I had to do it. So, rather than swallowing my fear, I let myself feel it.

About six months into the college season—eight months since Olympic

Trials—I was sat down for "the talk" with my coaches.

"You need to think about what you're doing outside the pool. You need to start showing up for this team. You need to lose weight. You're not even qualified for NCAAs. You need—"

"I need harder practices," I interrupted. I was a year removed from the beginning of overtraining, and my body had finally begun to feel like itself. An out-of-shape version of itself.

Res ipsa loquitur had never been truer. My poor training was reflected in my performance.

But I hadn't felt a hint of fatigue from overtraining in a month. It was time to see if I could get it back.

I looked at Madeline to back me up. She didn't meet my gaze as she replied, "Our practices have worked for other open water swimmers—"

"I'm not other open water swimmers." Haley and I were as opposite as it got when it came to training.

I stared at Madeline, willing her to be the person I'd thought she was. I needed practices like the ones she'd written on our Open Water National Team trips.

She said nothing. She wouldn't save me? Fine. I'd save myself.

We had a dual meet in two weeks. I wondered if I would be able to put up a decent time if I worked really hard until then.

"How about you give me two weeks of distance practices? *Hard* ones: 7 to 8k per workout until our UCLA meet. I'll qualify for NCAAs."

They reluctantly agreed.

I did my first challenging practice in a year. Conor Dwyer, who had also moved to LA, did it with me.

For a moment, I was back in Baltimore. I was my old self, swimming through the pain until endorphins coursed through my body, and I was in the high of a hard set.

Even though I was nowhere near my old practice times, it was the first time I'd done something physically difficult without my body giving out on me in eight months.

"That was a tough practice, Hype Beast," Conor said.

No one had called me that in a long time. I grinned.

Erik's words when I told him I was going to USC echoed through my memory. "*You're not going to get what you need there.*" He was wrong. I would make sure I got what I needed—I just needed to stay in the driver's seat.

The meet came. My mom flew in to visit me. Her presence gave me a boost, as it always did—there was someone rooting for me. Someone who didn't just see me as a robot. Who saw my swimming career as more than points at a college swim meet.

I felt like my old self. *Truly* like it.

"Swim for your teammates," a coach told us in the team room.

I did—for the team of myself and my mom.

Sure enough, I put up a decent time. A time that not only qualified me for NCAAs but would put me in the fastest heat. I almost beat Haley's team record.

Huh. That hadn't taken much.

Was I actually *back*? Could it be that easy? Was my swimming career not as over as I'd thought it was?

I called a meeting with the coaches. "I need more of that."

But it was taper time.

"I don't need a taper," I insisted. But I got one anyway because I had to do the same workouts as the others.

My strength went as rapidly as it had come. I'd only felt it—and been able to enjoy it—for about four days. The power of my pull, the feeling of the water, slipped. I grasped at it for dear life, but it trickled through my fingers like the water. Slipping, slipping, slipping . . . until it was gone.

It was too much rest again.

"Can I please get some hard workouts again?" I asked Madeline every time I stepped onto the pool deck.

"You're back. Just trust the process."

I had nothing to taper off. I'd been tapering for a year.

I tried to focus on other things to distract myself from my disappointment in my coaches. I hung out with my friends. I wrote. I helped Mary out with the web series she was creating.

At NCAAs, I put up a somewhat decent 500 freestyle, but I had no endurance for my mile. I was seeded *last* in the 400 IM. Something had happened to my breaststroke technique when I'd gotten overtrained that I hadn't been able to fix.

When I saw the seeding, I roared with laughter and told my roommate, "I'm seeded *last* in the 400 IM."

She stared at me, uncertain how to respond.

"How the mighty have fallen!" I exclaimed.

Thankfully, I managed to beat one or two people in the actual race, so I didn't get *dead* last. I let myself bask in that small victory.

I didn't let myself watch the race in finals. I didn't let myself ruminate on the phone call I'd had with Madeline a year before, on the day my overtraining culminated into a panic attack, when I told her that I planned on being the fastest 400 IMer in the world at this meet.

It was okay. I had expanded my world. I had seen more than swimming. I had one foot in the future—in what came after. I didn't think I'd made 2016 *my year*, but I'd done a damn good job salvaging it.

I looked at the bright side. College season was over, which meant I could focus on what I loved for the first time in what felt like a millennium.

Open water.

17

THE 25K IS EASY

After the collegiate season was over, I convinced the coaches to give me some harder workouts again. Madeline delivered. The harder the practices, the more my love of swimming returned. The strength returned.

I felt like a superhero who had lost her powers and had finally unlocked them once more.

Even my bond with Madeline, which had gotten a bit shaky, reformed.

I was third at the Open Water Nationals, behind Ashley and Haley, and managed to qualify for the 25k at the World Championships.

I was *back*. Somewhat, at least. Enough to compete on the highest stage again.

But not enough for the swimming world to care about me again.

People only love a comeback story if it's a record-breaking comeback. It didn't matter to me. *I* was happy.

I'd wanted to swim the 25k for years. The only reason I'd turned it down in 2015 was because I had pool events to swim in Kazan after the open water competition was over.

I was thrilled. Plus, Eva had been waiting for me to swim the 25k so I could eat the words I'd told her back in 2013: *"The 25k is easy."*

After qualifying, I texted Eva, who was a 25k World Championship bronze medalist. *"So, you got any tips for the easiest event at Worlds? Not that the 25k's hard or anything."*

Within seconds, Eva and I were FaceTiming. "The 25k," Eva said, "is all about not giving up when you want to."

"Easy."

"There are going to be *less easy* parts. Just get through them. It'll get easier at some point."

"Maybe your *less* easy is my *very* easy."

Eva laughed. "When the boys lap you, hang on as long as you can. The woman who hangs on the longest is the one who wins."

This was going to be a test of true endurance. The men started ten minutes before the women on a 2.5k course—which takes approximately thirty minutes to swim. The women went slow enough at the beginning so the men would lap us around twenty kilometers into the race.

The women who would medal would draft off the men until the last loop.

"Be prepared to go from easy to *super fast* in a literal second."

"Or super easy to somewhat easy."

"Exactly."

Whoever didn't get dropped won. Simple as that.

I wasn't worried about five-plus hours of swimming. I was built for races like this.

I did some four-hour practice swims: one in the Long Beach canals and one in Manhattan Beach. I joined the other Team USA 25k swimmers in a 15k workout. Alex Meyer came out to LA to share more of his secrets.

I was excited, though nonchalant. Haley would be feeding me. I told her to have chocolate and a banana with Nutella out at the 20k.

"You're not going to be able to eat that," Haley said, deadpan. She'd swum the 25k back in 2009.

"If I can't, I won't. May as well have the option."

Before I knew it, I was back in Lake Bled, Slovenia, for a training trip. It was as magical as it'd been in 2015.

For the first time ever, I wasn't the youngest. Seventeen-year-old Cat Salladin would be taking on the 25k with me. At some point, I'd become a veteran.

After training camp, Team USA flew to Hungary.

The day before the race, I asked to lead the nightly cheer in the team room. Usually, it was a quick, "USA on three. One, two, three, *USA!*"

Instead, after everyone put their hands in the middle of the circle, I said, "250 percent the distance, 250 percent the fun on three. One, two, three, *250 percent the distance, 250 percent the fun!*"

Only a few people managed to get it right. I grinned. It was an ode to Fran Crippen, a USA swimmer who had died in an open water race back in 2010. Eva told me that he always used to say, "Half the distance, double the fun," regarding the 5k. Based on everything I knew about him, I figured he would have appreciated the 25k cheer.

Jordan Wilimovsky held out his phone as I headed to the ready room. "Do you want me to live tweet the race from your account?"

"Sure," I said, signing him in, not thinking anything of it.

"Good luck. Not that you need it. The 25k is easy for Hype Beasts."

"And don't you forget it."

On Twitter, "I" posted, "*I, Becca Wilke Hypebeast Mann, am about to swim the 25k. Follow along as I swim and simultaneously live tweet my own race. #FINABudapest2017*"

When we walked onto the start pontoon, everyone sat on the edge to pee. Cat approached and sat beside me.

"Are you peeing?" I asked her. We were roommates, and this was her first Worlds.

She was a bundle of nerves. Later, she told me that she was much too anxious to even *consider* emptying her bladder. "No."

"Oh." In an attempt to lighten her mood, I added, "Well, I am."

My Twitter read, "*Just walked out of race briefing. Officials said no phones, but I was like nahhhhh. Gunna tweet updates every time I stop for a feed.*"

I don't think I would have been anxious if my suit had ripped as the gun sounded. This was a test of endurance. I was back at Worlds. I was here to have fun, nothing else. Yes, I wanted to win, but if I didn't—I was here. And I was proud to be here.

When the gun went off, only a few girls, including me, dived off. Most of them finished stretching for a few seconds before jumping in, feet first. Some didn't even have their goggles on.

We started off at a very leisurely pace.

Easy, easy, easy.

No one wanted to lead. Everyone wanted to draft.

The boys are going to pass us at the 7k, I thought. This sluggish pace was just going to make the race *so much* harder. Didn't the others get that?

My Twitter read, "*@SwimHaley with my feeds is like the Gandalf to my Bilbo Baggins, the Samwise Gamgee to Frodo Baggins . . . But out* *of all the Lord of the Rings references I could make . . . I am Gollum, and you're my precious."*

I didn't want to drink at the feeding station. I wasn't exerting myself enough to. I forced Gatorade down my throat anyway. That was another rule I'd been given by Eva: "Even if you don't want to feed, feed. Drink it all. I don't care if it makes you want to throw up."

On the third of ten laps, something interesting happened.

I'd managed to fall back into the middle of the pack, so I didn't accidentally end up leading when I sighted and saw that four women had broken away and were over twenty-five meters ahead of the rest of us.

What the hell?!

I was naive enough to think that this was what was deciding the race. I had to catch them, and the five of us would be the Top 5.

I raced up the side of the pack.

For a moment, the sprinting felt great. It was a release of the energy that I'd been conserving.

It was going to take me a while to make up twenty-five meters.

Thankfully, I was rested and ready.

It was a logical approach and one that wouldn't waste unnecessary energy. It was something I'd been applying to my life and my OCD— when things weren't going well, I couldn't judge or wonder how I'd gotten there. Instead, I made a plan to get where I wanted to go.

The mindset set me free, allowing me to catch the leaders with a kilometer of intense focus.

When I did, I saw there was an even larger gap between us and the others—fifty meters. We'd broken away.

I had only joined the pack for about a minute when the leader stopped swimming.

She just floated there. I expected someone else to take the lead. For the second person to take a turn. If we all worked together, we could get even farther ahead—

Nope.

The second person stopped. The third stopped. The fourth.

We all just floated there, treading water.

Two of the girls were *chatting*. One of them took off her goggles and fixed them.

I was furious for about two seconds. Just like that, all the work I'd done was gone.

Accept and assess. Should I take over the race?

It was tempting. I almost did.

But then I realized I didn't have the energy to lead after that sprint—especially not this early in the race.

I floated with the others, slightly annoyed.

Thirty seconds later, the rest of the pack caught us.

I couldn't quite bring myself to appreciate the unpredictability of the sport.

I brushed it off. I'd made what I thought had been the right call. So, it hadn't been. Whatever. Sometimes I made bad decisions. That was life.

We went back to the sluggish pace. For the next hour and a half.

We circled around the halfway point.

"Just finished half the race . . . so easy!"

If I'd looked at the giant screen that they'd set on a platform in the middle of the lake, I would have seen my tweet broadcast to all the coaches and spectators.

At fifteen kilometers, the peace shattered as a vacuum pulled me backward.

Before I could figure out what was happening, three men thundered past like a tsunami.

One moment, we were swimming steadily; the next, women were getting run over and sprinting.

Sometimes, life just speeds up like that. Five kilometers earlier than I'd expected, though I wasn't surprised given our speed up to this point.

"Just swam by and saw my tweet up on the board. Shoutout to the iPhone 7 for being waterproof!"

I settled into the men's pack. The new pace was difficult, but I was determined to stay in there as long as I could. It wasn't a violent race—it's hard enough to swim a 25k without elbowing, punching, and kicking.

"@SwimHaley on my next feed, I'd like some pulled chicken, no salt, no seasoning, please and thank you."

20k.

My banana and Nutella came out on my feeding stick.

Just looking at it made me want to vomit. Haley smirked from the dock. I would have rolled my eyes if I'd had the energy.

Five kilometers was nothing. But my speed was failing, the milky water spinning beneath my fingers.

I was exhausted.

The feet of the man in front of me got farther and farther away until—about one kilometer later—I was on my own in Lake Balaton.

"@Eva, how fun are 25ks!?!?!"

I threw in a few meters of backstroke, then promptly couldn't tell which way I was going when I turned back onto my stomach. I couldn't get my bearings.

This is fun, I reminded myself. *Challenging myself is fun.*

My Twitter agreed: "250% the distance, 250% the fun!"

I wanted to be done. My body was at its limit.

But the 25k is easy. Remember that. This is easy. I snorted into the water.

During the final hour, I was unsure about how fast I was going or where I was in the rankings. I didn't know how many women had been able to hang with the men longer. My muscles were failing, every movement depleting.

"*About to come home around the final buoy. @USCswim if you wanna see why I should be on the 4x100 free relay, tune in now.*"

I finished seventh, a few minutes behind the leader. My highest ranking at the World Championships.

When I stumbled out of the water, Jordan asked, "How was it?"

I grinned, "Easiest thing I've ever done."

I broke into a fit of laughter, and didn't tell anyone otherwise.

18

DON'T GET STUCK

I traveled internationally for three months that summer, training in Hungary, Italy, Thailand, and Taiwan.

I went into my sophomore year of college excited about swimming, excited about school, and excited about life.

The college team had other plans in store for me. After our first dual meet, in the basement of some sketchy hotel, the torture began.

"Put your phones in the bin," a woman I'd never seen before said. The first sign we were about to be treated like children.

My immediate dislike increased when she met my eyes, squealed, and wrapped me in a hug.

Annoying sibling-like bear hugs from Allison and Michael were one thing. A hug from a stranger pretending to be my best friend? Not ideal.

"Becca! It's so great to see you!"

I had no idea who this woman was.

Maybe we'd met before at a swim meet when I was younger? But I felt like such an eccentric presence would have been difficult to forget. I went with a polite, "Yeah, you too."

We each took our assigned seats in a big circle.

"Who is this woman?" I whispered to one of my friends.

"You don't know her?" she asked, having just witnessed the greeting.

"Nope."

"I think she knows you."

"It certainly seems that way."

I hoped whatever this was would be short. I had things to do. Ideas to ponder. Words to write. Songs to sing. Homework to do. Sleep to get.

Once we were seated, the woman said, "For those of you who don't know me, my name is Agnes, and I'm here to heal your team culture."

She instructed us all to fill out packets with random questions, starting with "What is your name?" and going from "What are my weaknesses?" to "What is my greatest disappointment?"

After Agnes handed out the packets, she said, "I'm going to ask all of you to be vulnerable with me."

Alarms went off in my mind. *PROTECT! PROTECT! PROTECT!*

Yes, I had made progress, but I was still nowhere near working through my trust issues. Not that I would have shared even if I had, because I immediately could feel that this place was not—

"This is a safe space," Agnes said.

I bit back a laugh. I was never well-behaved when I was on the defensive.

Madeline glanced at me out of her periphery. She knew I had specifically chosen not to visit Cal Berkeley because I knew they did lots of team-feeling-sharing stuff.

I later learned that Agnes had been Berkeley's leadership coach before being hired by USC.

"Fill out the packet, then we're all going to share something from it."

I skipped some questions. I made some stuff up. I scribbled down follow-up questions in response to the questions. I doodled.

"Time's up," Agnes said after fifteen minutes. "Now I want you all to share something from your packet. Any answer."

When my turn came, I read, "My favorite quote is '*Res ipsa loquitur.*'"

Everyone stared.

"It's Latin."

Agnes said, "Could you pretend that maybe we all don't know Latin?"

"It means, 'The thing speaks for itself.' And the thing can be whatever you want it to be. It's a common phrase in law."

I got more stares and a few eye rolls from the people I didn't get along with. My muscles tensed, my fight-or-flight response ready to kick in if needed.

"Ohhhhhkay. Next up."

After this *exercise*—though the only thing it was an exercise in was patience—Agnes said, "I noticed that none of you shared your more vulnerable answers."

Because we're not idiots.

"Now, the secret to trust—and you're a team, so you all have to trust each other to work together—is vulnerability."

I disagreed. All we had to do was individually swim fast across a pool. We weren't Navy SEALs.

I could name five people in the room who actively disliked me. I could name twenty who didn't know more about me than my name, what events I swam, and that I liked *Wicked the Musical*.

I could only name two who actually cared about me as a person.

"Everyone stand. I'm going to read a statement, and if it applies to you, I want you to step inside the circle."

"I have siblings."

I stepped into the circle. Whatever.

"I grew up in a city."

Sure. I stepped inside.

"I grew up religious."

Hail Mary took a step forward.

"My parents are divorced."

Some people stepped in. I began wringing my hands behind my back.

"I have an eating disorder."

I tilted my head, not liking where this was going. Again, people stepped in. I forced my hands to still, but I found myself filing beneath my nails the moment my attention slipped.

I didn't like this game. I was done playing.

"I've been lonely before."

I was one of two people not to step in.

"I've been diagnosed with a mental illness."

I had no desire to talk about my OCD, especially what I'd experienced when I'd moved away, with any of these people. I didn't want to answer follow-up questions. And I sure as hell wasn't going to step into this circle just because some lady told me to.

"I've been sexually assaulted."

What. The. Actual. Fuck.

My mouth fell open. I couldn't believe that Agnes had the audacity to ask young women she'd *never met before* to step into a circle and admit this, not bothering to ask if they were comfortable. In front of all our coaches and their peers.

Should I leave?

I glanced at Madeline again. She gave me an almost apologetic smile. *Stay and don't participate.*

After what felt like five years, we got a bathroom break. "You're not allowed to talk in the bathroom," Agnes said. "Reflect and process what you just learned."

All I could process was that whatever had just happened felt violating.

We went to the bathroom. I made eye contact with a few people. Finally, I said, "Are we all just going to—?"

"Be quiet, Becca," a girl who'd rolled her eyes at me snapped.

I didn't trust that they wouldn't use any information I gave against me.

I put my hands up in surrender.

I approached Madeline after the session. "I *hated* that."

"I know."

"Are there going to be more of them?"

"I don't know."

"Can I be exempt?"

"I think you'd have to talk to Dave."

The answer was no.

Some of the swimmers claimed Madeline loved Agnes, and others claimed she hated her. My trust in her wavered. Rachel's words from four years ago came back to me.

"Don't trust that woman."

She's only telling me what I want to hear. I felt as if I could finally see Madeline clearly. I ran through our previous interactions, such as when she had given me an inexperienced feeder at Pan Pacs. When she'd said I could regularly practice open water here. When she'd tapered me despite me insisting I didn't need it.

As I'd suspected, after the meeting, the team used everything that was discussed as ammunition.

The Agnes meetings became a regular part of the schedule, and I began to dread even approaching the pool. I felt myself drifting from my healthy relationship with swimming. I was slipping back to where I'd been in freshman year, hating practices and the culture. I couldn't find any silver lining.

I can't do this for three more years.

"I can't make this meeting," I began to lie whenever we had an Agnes session. "I have a group project."

Every time I couldn't make up an excuse—such as when the meetings took place during practice time—Agnes would ask me, and *only* me, if I had something to share. Like she was trying to get me to spill some secret.

Does she want me to confess that I've been making up the group projects?

Does she want me to admit that I actually have been lonely before?

Does she want me to tell them I'm queer?

Does she want me to talk about how these meetings are making me hate swimming?

It didn't matter. Whatever she wanted from me, she wasn't going to get. I never had anything to share.

Why am I still on this swim team?

Because it was paying for college. That was why. I was stuck between a rock and a hard place—making myself miserable so I could stay at the school I loved.

Writing was an escape again, just as it had been when I'd moved away from home and needed an escape from my OCD. I was able to live vicariously through my characters, recreating the excitement swimming no longer gave me.

I was angry with myself—my positivity was nowhere to be found in the pool. I'd lost all passion for it. What had changed?

I hate swimming here. That was what had changed. I got slower at every practice and didn't even ask for harder ones. I just wanted to get in and out. Make the smallest splash, the least amount of noise. I didn't want to be noticed.

But I was. My lack of speed made more noise than any scream.

Every day, Agnes waited on deck with a cheesy inspirational quote that sounded vaguely like a threat. I felt like Madeline was making empty promises just to placate me. I was bored and antsy in the pool.

I bought underwater headphones so I could focus on something besides the fact that my body couldn't seem to remember how to swim fast and that my mind was never at ease around Agnes and Madeline.

A few months into the season, I swam a 400 IM that was thirty seconds slower than my best time—I would have *lapped* myself two years ago.

I couldn't look at anyone as I climbed out of the pool. I felt nauseated—not from the race, but from the embarrassment. It had only been a few months. How could I have fallen so far from my summer form? Had the summer just been a fluke?

Madeline beckoned me over. I sensed what was coming. I'd been "in trouble" enough times to recognize the stern frown on Madeline's face. I swallowed my guilt, my shame, my trepidation and slipped a stoic mask onto my face.

"This is getting out of hand," Madeline said the moment I was within earshot.

"I know."

"You don't even look like an athlete anymore. You aren't doing the work outside of the pool."

I'm not doing the work in *the pool either!*

"I need—"

"You need to be *accountable*," Madeline interrupted.

I need to quit.

I stared at her. She was right. I had to make do with what I could. I was the only one responsible for my swimming career.

But I still wanted to ask, *Where's my open water? Where are the hard practices? Where's the fun? Where's your accountability? Where is what you promised me when I was fifteen?*

But I was responsible for what came next. I needed to grow up and stop whining about what I'd been promised, even if I didn't have a plan forward. "Okay. I will be."

Following that meeting, the tension between me and Madeline was palpable.

I need to stick it out. This is the sacrifice for school.

I wished I could just stop caring about swimming. But it was impossible. Not when it had been my entire life. But I couldn't live in this in-between.

Soon after, Agnes called a meeting. I was feeling ill and told her that I didn't think I could attend.

I'd cried "wolf" too many times. She didn't care that I was sick. *I wasn't even sure whether I was actually sick or just physically feeling the negative ramifications of hating swimming.*

I showed up in three pairs of mismatched pajamas and my clown UGGs.

"I love the outfit," my one friend said genuinely.

I shivered as Agnes began lecturing, not bothering to pay attention.

I'm going to pretend I'm in an acting class. I'd pick a character and react the way *they* would.

But all I could think about was *how hot* I was. I began stripping off layers of pajamas.

"Becca," Agnes said just as a violent tremor went through my body. "I see you jumping. Don't worry; you don't have to be nervous."

"I'm not. I'm *cold*." I pulled the pajamas back on.

"We need to talk about how you behave in practice."

"I'd love to have an intimate discussion about my behavior with you and my twelve closest friends."

Agnes gave me a pitiful smile. "And how you use humor to deflect."

I laughed so hard that tears sprang into my eyes. "I'm flattered that you think I'm funny. I can also burst into song to deflect if you'd prefer."

Agnes tilted her head as if I'd just proved her point. Another shiver went through my body. I was acting like a child. I supposed that when my immune system went down, my filter fell with it.

"You're never satisfied after practice."

"Yes."

"It makes your teammates uncomfortable."

"That sounds like their problem."

I pictured an outsider walking in on this meeting—a shivering, sweaty twenty-year-old in pajamas facing off against a middle-aged woman while a dozen athletes watched. It was ridiculous.

"And when people tell you 'good job' after practice, you tell them that you *didn't* do a good job."

I held back another laugh. When I didn't want to be at the pool, I smiled anyway because I wasn't going to taint the water with bad energy. But—yes, when my teammates gave me a high five and told me, "Great practice," I shook my head and replied, "Not for me, but you had a good one!"

I couldn't accept the empty praise.

"I don't see what the problem with that is," I said, bundling my pizza flannels around me.

"Do you understand what I'm saying?"

"*Yes*, but I don't agree."

"Can you at least *try* to put more effort into seeming satisfied after practice? For Madeline and your teammates?"

Fury exploded out of my chest, poisoning every cell. My face heated—whether from the anger or the fever, I wasn't sure.

"But I'm *not* satisfied." And I sure as hell wasn't going to do *anything* for Madeline. "I'm not going to be until I'm faster than I was two years ago."

It was a statement in direct opposition to my attempt to forget swimming. To be better than my previous self.

It's a convoluted mess that I don't need to explain the intricacies of.

"But do you understand what I'm saying?" Agnes repeated.

"Yes, *I understand*." My voice was lethally calm. "And I *still* don't agree." And, for good measure, since I'm a dramatic musical nerd, I added, "I've never been satisfied, and I *will* never be satisfied."

I will not settle because you want me to.

I waited for the repercussions of the meeting, but they never came because I was gifted with the flu and didn't have to go to practice.

I was bedridden for two weeks, recovering three days before our next dual meet against UCLA.

"I don't think I should swim," I told Madeline.

"We need you to get the points."

I was still weak. It was going to be *ugly*.

But two days before the meet, I was blessed with yet another sickness.

Pink eye.

I sent a picture of my disgusting gunk-filled eye to Madeline, to which she replied, "Wow, that's so bad that it doesn't even look like your eye!"

Did she seriously think I was *faking* it?!

I went to the doctor. "Take this antibiotic. You'll be able to swim by Friday."

"No."

The doctor gave me a confused look.

"I don't want to give my whole team pink eye. I just gave them all the flu."

"You won't be contagious on Friday—"

"*Please*," I begged. "I shouldn't swim until Saturday."

He must've seen the desperation in my good eye. "Another day can't hurt."

I told Madeline that the doctor said I couldn't swim the meet. She didn't think it was real? Fine. It wouldn't be real. For the first time in my life, I had a fake injury.

I watched the meet in dark sunglasses so no one could see that my eye was no longer discolored.

I was the lap counter for a fellow USC swimmer. My discontentment grew with every number I turned. I *should* have been swimming. I should have been able to throw down a decent 1000, even after the flu.

How could USC Swimming have done this to me? How could I have let this happen?

I'm done. There had to be a way to quit and keep my scholarship.

The athletic compliance office overlooked USC's campus. I watched students rush to and from class, wondering if they just worked out for fun.

I wondered if I'*d* ever be able to.

"I want to quit the swim team," I told the compliance officer the moment I was escorted into the office, taking my sunglasses off. "But I want to keep my scholarship."

"Do you have an injury?"

"I'm having. . . mental anguish."

The compliance officer looked me over. "You might be able to medically retire. If you can prove your . . . mental anguish." That was a worst-case scenario, but one I was willing to accept before continuing like this for two more years. "I don't want to quit swimming altogether. Is there anything else I can do?"

"Transfer."

"No." I loved USC too much. I wasn't going to leave my program.

"I'll look into other options, but . . . I don't know if there are any."

My heart sank.

Was there no exit strategy? Was I condemned to suffer on the USC swim team for two more years unless I stopped swimming altogether?

I *hated* not knowing what to do. If there was a plan, there was hope. Without a plan, I was stuck.

I continued to feel like I was drowning every time I jumped into the pool; my body's connection with the water was nowhere to be found. But I couldn't quite stop caring about swimming. It wasn't in my nature, so I still tried my best to salvage whatever I could from the practices.

I continued pouring myself into other areas of life—and loving it. I took a pregnant cat into my studio apartment. I found lifelong friends.

The Stanford dual meet came. I was once again next to Katie. For the first time in my life, I wasn't looking forward to swimming beside her.

Every stroke was torture. Katie lapped me, and I swam slower than I had since I was twelve.

I held it together for a few seconds and exchanged a few normal words with Katie as if I hadn't just humiliated myself with the slowest swim of my entire life.

I hopped out of the pool, grabbed my parka, and rushed into the locker room, locking myself in a bathroom stall. I pulled out my phone and texted my mom.

"I can't do this anymore. I hate swimming. I want to quit."

I *felt* like a quitter. How could I have come to despise my favorite thing so strongly, so quickly?

"Where are you?"

"Hiding in the locker room." Tears were pooling in my eyes. I sniffed the snot up my nose, then added, *"Lol."*

I was ashamed that I couldn't pull through for the coaches who had purchased my swimming career. Ashamed that I didn't enjoy swimming. Ashamed of my attitude.

"You can quit, but don't be one of those kids who cries in the locker room."

She was right. I still had two more races.

But I couldn't quit. I wasn't going to make my parents pay for the last two years of college when they'd already invested so much into my wretched swimming career.

I should have gone pro when I was fourteen.

I pulled myself together and stepped out of the locker room.

Maybe you've been playing the victim. You aren't a victim, I told myself. *Maybe a medical retirement is what you have to do.*

Madeline was the only coach who didn't ignore me. "I'm going to get ready for the 500," I told her before she could speak. "Forget about this race."

She just shrugged as if she were done caring about me. *Good.*

The next races were just as bad, but I managed to hold my head high. To mask just how painful it was to swim so slowly.

Swimming, which had once given me purpose and energy, was draining me.

I'd found my footing outside of the pool. But at the cost of what brought me the most joy. Was it not possible to live a life that wasn't singularly focused on one passion? Did I have to sacrifice swimming to thrive outside of it? *What if I can only—*

What if these are just thoughts? I interrupted the irrationality. I let them be. I didn't fight them, as I'd been learning. I just knew that I couldn't end my career on this note. I couldn't end *hating it.*

I walked back to the compliance office. "Have you looked into more rules?"

"I was just about to email you . . . there is this one rule . . . If you withdraw from the university with the intent to professionalize and make significantly over $700, the former athletic department will match your scholarship."

I would have to leave, go pro, then reenter college.

I was both elated and torn—I didn't want to be in a new screenwriting cohort. Returning to a life of only swimming, especially in the shape I was in, felt like a giant step in the wrong direction. It was dramatic and extreme—I would be going back into a world with no balance but without the times to back it up.

But it would only be for a year. The end of my gap year would be summer 2019—Olympic Trials for Open Water.

Maybe this was my chance to give it one more shot. Regardless of what happened, I could finish swimming the way *I* wanted to in an environment I enjoyed.

I liked being extreme. I could be extreme one more time.

That was the plan. I'd drop out of college for a year—two if I somehow revived my career and made the open water Olympic Team—and tell Madeline and Dave I was quitting after NCAAs.

I was ignored by most of the coaches at practice the next day. They were really trying everything. Except for giving me hard practices, of course, because that was far too radical an idea.

I turned on my underwater headphones and dove into the pool. Madeline's expression suggested she wasn't happy with me.

How things had changed since Barcelona. We'd had so much fun when all she'd had to do was say *yes* to everything I'd wanted. When all she had to do to win me was laugh about which sub she wanted out of a swim bag.

We'd really never stood a chance, had we?

My pregnant cat was extremely stressed—and about to pop—when I got on the flight for the NCAAs in Indianapolis. My last collegiate swim meet, thank God.

I couldn't bear the thought of missing the birth, but I couldn't get kicked off the team before I quit. The next two years of college depended on it.

On the first day of the meet, a day I wasn't swimming, my friend FaceTimed me for the birth. I watched eight kittens enter the world in the closet of my studio apartment.

I paraded around the pool deck in my UGGs, showing every person I knew—and people I didn't—my cats.

I found Katie, not caring that she was getting ready to swim. "I'm a mother. Want to see my eight kittens?"

"Yes."

I saw Erik on the other side of the deck. He had gotten a new job as a collegiate coach. I didn't approach.

I found Bob instead. "Look at my nine cats," I said, shoving the phone into his hands.

"You're a crazy cat lady already?" Bob asked, his voice dripping with sarcasm.

"I've always been a crazy cat lady."

The amused glint appeared in his eyes. I looked around, lowering my voice. "Can I come train with you this summer? I need to get out of USC."

I had done my best under Bob's coaching, and Allison was getting back in the pool after a few years off.

I wasn't sure whether I *trusted* Bob, but I trusted his training. I trusted Allison. I trusted that my time in Baltimore, with Bob at the helm, had been the best training of my life.

Maybe that was enough.

"You're always welcome to train with me. Are you bringing your cats?"

I grinned, practically sagging with relief. "I'll be an empty-nester by then. They grow up fast."

I turned back to my team. Madeline stared, just out of earshot. I wondered if she thought I was transferring to ASU.

I was making USC look *good* by not transferring. People would think that I'd negotiated these terms before I'd committed to USC. The swim team would get their scholarship back, which they could use to buy a sprinter who could actually score them points.

Once again, I swam poorly at the meet.

After my 400 IM, I noticed Erik *not looking* at me. I stared, willing him to meet my gaze.

He didn't.

I jumped into the warm-down, occasionally seeing him on the side of the deck when I breathed. *Are you glad you're right? Do you wish you could say that you told me so?*

I knew Erik wasn't like that, but my frustration was easier to manage with a target in mind. The only thing he was guilty of at that meet was not seeking me out.

The 500 came. I didn't even make the B final. My best time would have put me second behind Katie.

Stop, I ordered myself. *It's about where you are now.*

I watched the 400 IM American record get broken. The very same record I had promised Madeline I'd get before I started school.

I was pissed. Pitiful. Envious.

It's about getting back to the lead pack. Not feeling bad that you're not winning.

Maybe it was good that I still felt something. It meant that I still cared. It meant that it was the right decision to keep going. *You'll be better when you get out of here,* I told myself.

When I went back to my hotel room, I sang show tunes with my roommate, knowing I would be in greener pastures soon.

The day I got back to USC, I called a meeting with Madeline and Dave.

I was giddy as I perched on the edge of the couch in their office. "I'm going pro," I announced.

I wasn't sure what type of reaction I was expecting. Joy, since they would get a scholarship back? Relief that they didn't have to deal with me anymore? Anxiety because they were low on distance swimmers? Anger since this meant I thought they weren't good enough?

"We wish you the best," Dave said, as if he were reading off a script.

The weight of the USC swim team lifted from my shoulders. I didn't have to worry about *points* or *my teammates* or how much money the swim team had spent on me.

I could return to swimming for myself. I no longer owed anyone anything.

"I'm *so* happy for you!" Agnes squealed when she saw me.

"Thanks for helping me with my decision!" I said brightly, not bothering to stop.

While finishing up the semester at USC, I swam by myself. Training with Dave and Madeline would have been too much drama. I also had some losses in my personal life.

I needed the water to be my comfort. I became grateful for it again. I told myself I would never again have a victim mindset.

But I was still swimming in the same pool at the same time as the USC swimmers. I was still mentally recovering. As I got ready for Nationals, I sent my cats to their new homes, counting down the days until I could leave.

At 2018 Open Water Nationals, I placed seventh and missed the National Team. My worst Nationals since I was thirteen. Since before I'd learned *anything* about the sport.

Madeline gave me a small smile when our gazes met. Maybe she was gloating, or maybe she simply wished that things had been different like I did.

I needed more than the water for support. I wanted to tell someone about what my life had been like since Kazan. Someone who would understand.

My eyes landed on Ashley Twichell, who had just won her third consecutive National title. People congratulated her. She took time to speak with every one of them.

We'd always gotten along on National Team trips, but I'd been so enveloped in my USC bubble that I had never gone out of my way to really *know* her.

She was always kind. To *everyone*. Her competitors, her teammates, her coaches. And they didn't drain her energy. It was just how she moved about the world.

I thought about the text she'd sent me in Kazan. How I hadn't taken her up on her offer. I wondered if it still stood.

I asked her and her husband to coffee. I told her everything. How I hated swimming, but I knew I could love it—could be good at it—again. Ashley listened—actually listened—and even though we didn't know each other well, she *cared*. She was the type of person who saw her competitors as *people*, and everyone she surrounded herself with was better off after being in her presence.

"Unless I get Top 2 at Nationals next year and make the Olympics," I told her, "I'm done after this year. Onto the next adventure."

"You can come train with me in North Carolina," Ashley offered.

But I was fixed on Arizona. I knew it would be fun, and, unlike in 2015, that was what was most important to me.

"I can't, but let's do some training trips at the OTC."

Ashley's friendship was one of the final gifts the sport gave me.

I had gotten trapped at USC. Madeline had been right when she had told me to "be accountable." I was accountable for getting myself out. USC didn't owe me hard practices, a supportive swim team, or *anything*.

As I packed up my apartment, the only regret I had was that I hadn't *tried* to make it more fun. I'd been imprisoned, but that hadn't meant I had to be unhappy. I should have pulled pranks. I should have tried to connect with the others more.

I was going to do things differently this time. I could give swimming the ending it deserved. One final try, but for the fun and the love of it. It would be a celebration of my swimming career and a final chance to push myself and see what I could really do. This was my victory lap.

11

GRATITUDE

It was like not a day had passed between Allison and me. I knew that, regardless of whether I was in Baltimore, Los Angeles, or Arizona, we would always be close friends. Carving our initials into the concrete in Baltimore really *had* cemented our friendship.

My summer of training in Arizona was fantastic. I healed. I got to do the ladder set again.

At 2018 Pool Nationals, I was treated like a *regular* swimmer by my fellow athletes. Average. Mediocre. But mediocrity didn't terrify me anymore. Not when I was improving.

It was odd to see how I was treated in Allison's presence versus on my own. When Allison was by my side, people who had ignored me since I'd been overtrained acted like they'd never stopped speaking with me. People pretended to care about what I'd been up to since disappearing off the map of elite swimming, though they hadn't bothered to ask without Allison around.

This secondhand acknowledgment was a taste of the fame I'd had before. But now I could taste the arsenic beneath the honey.

I told Allison as much. "Yeah, the same happened to me in 2013 and 2014."

"That's screwed up," I said. "And stupid."

No one cared how good I had been before. Maybe I shouldn't, either.

But the dopamine of being known was still addictive. Like getting likes on Instagram. Like fitting in with the popular kids.

I enjoyed it. Being talked about. Having people know who I was. I felt the craving again. I'd been two years sober from fame, but I could smell it in the air.

I had to have the strength to ignore it. I couldn't associate with people who only cared about me if I was shiny and successful. I could still *be* successful, but not for the accolades.

I'd thought that, once I got the title of *Olympian*, my improvement would be complete. But there was always room for improvement, and skills didn't always equate to recognition.

I was on my way to feeling satisfied with the work I'd done, even though the recognition had not come.

My training partners in Arizona inspired me rather than bogged me down as they had at USC. I traveled. I raced internationally again.

I improved. I tried to return to my pre-overtraining times but fell just short. I suspected that I never *would* be able to achieve that again.

For the first time ever, I was okay with it.

A few months before Open Water Nationals, I received a text from Ashley.

"Want to come train at the OTC with me and Coach Rose before Nationals?"

I was getting a final chance to train with Coach Rose. I wondered if the universe had been trying to make it happen for years.

This time, I didn't ask anyone's opinion. *"Yes PLEASE!"*

Ashley was exactly the training partner I needed to end my career with.

It was the best time I'd ever had at the OTC. Ashley and I were perfect companions. Both of us loved being at the pool, we both loved Coach Rose's jokes and workouts, and we motivated each other. Training with her made me realize that I'd been missing out my entire career—I had never trained with anyone who swam the same events as me and genuinely *wanted* me to succeed. Who wanted me to be my best, not caring that maybe that would mean *she* wouldn't be the best.

I reciprocated the feeling.

My last Open Water National Championships was one of the most fun weekends of my life.

I showed up with Coach Rose and Ashley. When I ran into Madeline, I just nodded from afar. She had no power over me. I had found my people. I had rediscovered my passion.

Nothing would bother me. Nothing could.

Bob wasn't there, but I didn't mind. Open Water Nationals was always mine. Herbert had never accompanied me—it was just me and my family. Ashley's North Carolina coach fed me.

Ashley and I did a warm-up loop around the course, enjoying ourselves. Knowing all the work was done.

It was the same selection criteria as it had been in 2015: Top 2 at this race swam the 10k at Worlds, and Top 10 at Worlds made the Olympics.

It didn't matter what happened because I was going to love it no matter what.

I was grateful. I'd achieved my goal of falling back in love with swimming. I was already a winner.

The joy continued during the race.

I applied a technique I called "chunking." It was what got me through long and hard swim practices, and it wouldn't let me down now. There were six loops, and each one I mentally dedicated to someone I was grateful for. When it got hard, I would think of the people who had gotten me here—back to this love of swimming.

The first loop was dedicated to Coach Rose, who had always offered me a home with him, even when I was on my way out, and to Allison, who had shown me what friendship was.

Then to Eva, who had taught me how to swim open water and had shared my pure joy for the adventure that can only be found in the open waves.

Loop three was for Rachel, Julia, and my dad, who had all loved and supported me and kept me as humble as they could.

The fourth was for Ashley, whom I aspired to be as kind as. Whom I wanted to make the Olympic Team almost as much as I wanted myself to. Whom I swam beside as we raced.

The penultimate loop was for my mom. I'd shown her my dream, and she'd seen it just as clearly as I had. She was the reason I was here, doing my favorite thing. She was the person who believed in me even when I didn't. I didn't know who I would've been without her, just that I wouldn't have been as good—or as great, happy, or strong—as I was now.

The last was for me. For the Hype Beast. For the work I put in. For my unmatched back-half speed. For the hours I'd spent staring at the black line. For everything I'd sacrificed for my vision. For my mindset. For my resilience. For seeing my vision through. For heeding the call. For my love of swimming.

I fought into the finish structure, just getting touched out. Fifth place.

The Top 4 made the World Championships, with the third and fourth athletes swimming the 25k. I had just missed it.

As I caught my breath beyond the finish structure, I turned to Ashley. "Did you do it?"

"Yes."

I threw my arms around her. I was happy—despite just missing my goal—because I'd done what I'd set out to do. I'd improved from the year prior. And I'd had a pretty great time doing it.

I was satisfied.

I waded back into the bay after my race to warm down, the sand mushy beneath my toes. I plopped into the water, watching my forearms disappear into the murky waves.

I stopped, treading water as I took in the skyline of Miami.

This was the same bay in which I'd swum my first ever 10k when I was just an eight-year-old drafting off Rachel. I'd gone half the speed I'd just swum at. I could almost see that version of me doing her best to stick with Rachel, a determined and ambitious dreamer.

She did it. I did it.

Tears sprang into my eyes, catching me off guard. *I'm going to miss this. I'm going to miss this so much.*

I had been to every Open Water Nationals since 2010, besides 2016. It was my *favorite* athletic event.

It was hard to explain exactly what Open Water Nationals meant to me. What could I possibly label the event that had been my goal, my inspiration, my teacher, my love, my pain, my breakthrough, and my call to adventure?

I didn't want it to be over. Hundreds more wouldn't have been enough.

Thank you, I said to the bay. *Thank you, open water. Thank you for taking care of me. Thank you for making me who I am. Thank you for always calling me back.*

What a gift I had been given: to be able to pursue my passion from childhood into adulthood. To be able to compete in an annual event that brought me infinite meaning and joy.

I caressed the water before I swam back to shore, shedding tears of joy, sorrow, and everything in between. *Res ipsa loquitur.*

My race had re-qualified me for the National Team and the Pan American Games.

I may not have risen from the ashes a better swimmer than I had been before, but I rose a better person. And that was what mattered.

The end of my swimming career was falling into place. I went back to the OTC to train for Pan Ams with the National Team.

It was on that trip that I happened to make peace and get catharsis with several ghosts from my past.

The first was with Jeremy.

Ashley and I were going to walk over from the recovery center to the USA Swimming building for a meeting. But when I arrived at the rendezvous, Ashley was nowhere to be seen.

Jeremy was.

"Have you seen Ashley?"

"No."

"I have no idea where this meeting is."

"I'll walk you over there."

I thought about protesting, but I was late.

Jeremy started talking about swimming. *Men's swimming,* listing one hundred breaststroke times. *So-and-so did this time in the one hundred breast.*

"All of this is going over my head," I murmured. "I don't really follow men's swimming."

"Well, you've only ever cared about yourself, haven't you, Hype Beast?"

I took him in, my eyes narrowed and face impassive as my heart pounded in my chest.

I wasn't the sixteen-year-old girl who couldn't catch a medicine ball anymore. Now I was a twenty-one-year-old woman who still couldn't catch a medicine ball but had seen the world beyond the dojo.

I had a tendency to put myself first. I owed that to myself. I would be the first to admit I wasn't perfect.

But I thought about helping Allison. I thought about standing up for Eva. I thought about how excited I was to watch Ashley make the Olympic Team.

I thought about how seeing life outside of swimming made me realize just how important it was to have loyal, good people in my life.

"That's right, Jeremy," I drawled. "And I can get to the USA Swimming building myself."

That was the last time I spoke with him. Jeremy's power was gone, unlike the other ghost's.

Erik.

He was one of the four coaches overseeing the training trip. Whenever he coached my practice, I ignored his presence, and he didn't speak to me.

"He's being a baby," I complained to Allison.

"So are you."

"Well, he's *older*," I argued, but even I knew that the words proved her point. I was being immature. "And *the coach*," I added, though my voice carried significantly less self-righteousness than it had a moment before.

Yes, I was eighteen when we'd had our "not-fight." But I'd grown up. Maybe it was time to start acting like it.

The next day, Allison and I were walking from the dining hall to the pool when we happened to fall in step with Erik.

"Hi, Erik," Allison said.

He averted his gaze when he saw that she was with me. "Hi," he said, his voice basked with trepidation. The greeting was very much directed at Allison—not at me.

Unless I wanted it to be?

Just two words. That was all I needed to say. I took a deep breath. "Hi, Erik."

He glanced at me, surprised. A flash of hesitation—and maybe relief—crossed his face before he said, "Hi. How are you?"

"Good."

"I'm really, really glad to hear that."

"Have you been liking coaching at Penn?"

The ice was broken. From that moment forward, greetings were exchanged, and times were read. There was no bad blood with anyone or anything. Maybe there was even warmth.

I was at peace—or as close to peace as I would ever be—with not making the Olympics.

But it didn't feel right to end my career on an *almost.*

A familiar itch was spreading through my soul. A call to adventure.

The Pan American Games was a big competition, but it wasn't the competition I wanted to end on.

I was practicing with Ashley and Haley, the two swimmers who were likely going to secure the 2020 Olympic spots in a month, when I had an epiphany.

I was having an exceptionally good practice. I cut through the water like a knife, my strokes propelling me ahead of both Ashley and Haley. *I* was the best swimmer in the pool—which also meant I was likely the best swimmer in the country—that day.

But it doesn't matter, I thought bitterly as I glided into the wall.

They were going to get the Olympic spots. And I wanted them to. Ashley deserved it. I was more than happy for her—I was proud of her.

But I was infuriated on behalf of myself. It *could* have been me. I had come *so close!* Why did *they* get what I had so desperately wanted my whole life?

Not allowed, I told myself, pushing off the wall again. I stared down at the black line, watching myself fly over it.

I despise self-pity.

You need to do something else.

A pivot.

I reflected, the silence of the water thick in my ears. My goals. My dreams. Everything I had wanted to do.

I couldn't just swim at Pan Ams and then disappear from the swimming world. I had worked hard—so hard that only a few people could even conceptualize it. I knew that it hadn't been for nothing. I had gotten to see the world, compete at the highest level, and train with the greatest athletes of all time. I had learned how to behave as a role model to people I didn't know but who knew me.

I needed to take everything, all my skills—my resilience, my endurance, my love for swimming—put them together and do something that *no one* had ever done before.

Something only *I* could do.

My swim across the Au'au Channel at ten years old had been one of the most rewarding experiences of my life. And I'd only been competing against myself.

I flipped at the wall. Ashley gained on me. A smile tugged at my lips. After a decade of elite swimming, I *still* had the worst turns in the pool.

No more turns.

I wanted to do another channel swim. While I was still close to the best shape I'd ever be in my entire life.

I went back to my barrack and emailed Steve Munatones, the founder of the World Open Water Swimming Association. *"Do you know of any channels that haven't been done before or that I would be able to get a record in? I need something big."*

I wasn't going to disappear into the darkness, never to be heard from again.

I was going to go out in a blaze of glory.

An hour later, Steve sent me an answer: the Maui Nui Triple Channel Crossing. Maui to Molokai to Lanai and back to Maui. Three channels in one, spanning approximately forty miles. It had been attempted twice before by a channel swimming legend named Harry Huffaker in the eighties, but it had never been completed.

It was especially difficult due to the triangular nature of the course. One of the channels would *always* have a strong current, so both speed and endurance would be required to make progress at all.

I was electrified.

"Sign me up. What are the next steps? Is August too soon?"

It was May. Steve put me in contact with a boat crew. It was actually happening.

When I went to afternoon practice, there was a bounce in my step. I approached Haley as she stretched. "Look at the channel I'm doing."

"What?"

I showed her the map, beaming. "I'm going to swim this. Forty miles."

"When?"

"August."

"Ohhhhkay." Haley went back to her rolling, clearly not believing me. Why would she?

She wasn't alone. *No one* really could fathom that between morning and afternoon practice, I'd decided I was going to swim forty miles across the ocean—through the night, at that—and that I had already set things into motion.

Except Ashley. She took in the map. "You're really doing it, aren't you?" She saw the glint in my eye and knew I was going to swim across that ocean or die trying.

"Yes. I am." It was a promise. Yes, in some ways this had been a spur-of-the-moment, impulsive decision. But I also felt as if the idea had been marinating in the back of my head since I had crossed the Au'au over a decade before. I didn't wonder. I didn't think about everything that could go wrong. I just heeded the call.

I contacted Harry Huffaker and asked him about his two Maui Nui attempts.

He gave me a hundred-page dossier on his experience. I started reading.

The first words I read were, *If the doctor tells you that you have only one year to live, you better take up long-distance swimming. It will seem like ten years.*

I chuckled.

"What on earth makes you do it?" Sometimes, the query is conversational stonewalling while the questioner looks for someone more normal to talk to. In this case, it is permissible to score first by telling him it is done to get away from tedious people for a couple of hours every day. At other times, the inquiry may come from someone genuinely interested. An appropriate reply in this instance would be, "To be acknowledged as an expert and do something better than most other people."

That wasn't why I was doing it. I was doing it to do something better than failing to make the Olympic Team three times in a row.

Harry had struggled during his attempts, but rather than make me fearful, it excited me.

When sharks had appeared during Harry's attempt, he'd decided, *If I stop looking for sharks, I probably won't see any.*

It would be *all* about my mindset. I would only see the sharks—metaphorical and literal—if I looked for them.

"What are you going to do to train for it?" everyone started asking.

"Just what I've been doing. I've been training my whole life for this."

I could physically do it. It was going to be about the mental battle. I was looking forward to seeing how I would mentally hold up after fifteen hours of swimming.

The Olympics were a big deal, but they were only "more important" than the many other competitions I'd done because they showed *other people* how great an athlete I was.

This swim was for me, not for them.

Ashley went to World Championships in South Korea. I watched from the OTC. When she touched in the Top 10, finally becoming an Olympian, I cried for her. There was no one more worthy.

I continued training for the Pan American Games, but the tri-channel swim was all I wanted to talk about. All my National Team teammates thought I was insane.

My coaches did as well. "What about sharks?" Bob asked.

"If I don't look for them, I won't see them," I replied, quoting Harry.

I wasn't worried about the wildlife. I wasn't really worried about anything. It seemed so far away. Too far away to be anxious.

I flew to Peru, as ready for the 10k as I could be. I would go straight to Hawaii from there, a few days before a week-long window of potential swim days, dependent on currents and weather.

But a day before the 10k, I got a call from USA Swimming.

Haley, who had been selected to swim the 400, 800, and 1500 freestyles at the Pan American Games, was instead going to the Open Water Olympic test event. Now they only had one of two swimmers for Team USA in Haley's events and wanted to know if I'd stay in Peru for another week and take her spot.

This was a no-brainer. I had assumed my pool career was over, ending anticlimactically at a random meet in Texas. This was kismet. I would get one last chance to represent Team USA in the pool, something I hadn't done internationally since Kazan.

It would mean another week of racing in Lima and fewer days of prep for the Maui Nui Triple Channel. But that was fine with me. I wouldn't turn down an international competition *now*, so close to the end of my career. My mom's words from years before echoed through my mind, *"Never turn down an opportunity to see the world."*

Yes, there would be fewer days of adjusting in Hawaii, but I was prepared. And failing to make the Olympic Team had taught me how to adapt.

My 10k didn't go well, but I didn't dwell. I pivoted my mind to the pool competition.

The 400 and the 800 went decently for being just a few days after the 10k, with me just missing the podium in the 800. But I knew the *real* race, the one that I could medal in—and perhaps even win—was the 1500. The event that had *finally* been named an Olympic event for women.

My best pool event would be my *last* pool event.

They were timed finals. No preliminary heat. My final day in Lima before I'd fly to Hawaii.

Get a medal, Becca. This is your moment.

I soaked up every moment in the ready room, knowing it was likely the last time I'd ever sit in one. I sat in my assigned chair and watched my competitors go about their routines. They had years of swimming ahead of them. I wondered if they thought that I did too.

They're definitely not thinking about that. I grinned.

We paraded out onto the deck. I thought about 2012 Olympic Trials and how the march to the blocks had felt like my debut into the swimming world. Now it felt as familiar as diving into the pool for swim practice. I made myself look into the bleachers to take in the spectators. I couldn't let this be regular. Not today. This was a race I needed to take in.

To enjoy. To remember.

Dozens of countries' flags waved in the arena. As the announcer announced my name, Team USA's section roared. I broke my routine—ignoring them and staring into the water—and waved, a grin on my face.

The starter blew the long whistle. I stepped onto the block and did the sign of the cross.

One last time. Make it good.

Make it fun.

"Take your mark . . ."

The BEEP sounded. I dove in.

I felt powerful. In control. I was floating over the water rather than swimming *in* it.

A woman broke away early, another competitor and I doing our best to hang with her, breaking away from the rest of the heat in the process.

I enjoyed every stroke. I relished holding off the girl in fourth. I basked in the endorphins.

I touched third, beating the woman who had won the 10k the week before by over ten seconds.

I won a bronze medal for Team USA in my last pool race. It was nowhere near a best time, but I didn't care. I'd gotten the medal. I'd gotten the thrill of an international competition again. The time didn't matter—the fact that I had been able to medal in an event I hadn't even been signed up for *did*.

Everything was perfect.

The team manager escorted me to the award ceremony.

The pool deck was dark as we marched to the podium. I beamed as my name was announced.

As I took in the stadium, I was nearly brought to tears. Standing there, I was grateful. Grateful for swimming, grateful for what it had taught me, grateful for the lessons I had learned, grateful that my pool career had received a proper closure, and grateful for who I had become.

My swimming career spoke for itself.

No, it wasn't *my* national anthem playing, but I was there—on the podium—again. I hadn't been on an international one since 2013. Call it fate, divine intervention, luck—but for me, in that moment, it was exactly what my swimming career had been: not quite what I had wanted it to be, but magical nonetheless. I was in a beautiful foreign land and had gotten to compete and medal in a coveted competition that I hadn't even qualified for.

I celebrated who swimming had made me rather than what I had or hadn't achieved. Rather than what *other* people defined as success. I had gotten to embark on an incredible journey of ups and downs that had forged me into someone who would never again be affected by the concept of falling short.

But my journey wasn't over yet. I still had one more swim.

20

THE MAUI NUI

I flew to Hawaii after a twenty-two-hour travel day, meeting up with my parents in an Airbnb on Maui.

My crew got in touch with me and told me it was looking like the weather would be best on August 18, meaning I had five days to prepare. The perfect amount of time.

I swam in the ocean for two hours the morning after arrival—in one of my favorite bays. I shook the travel and the week of racing out of my muscles, keeping it easy and enjoying the wildlife on the reef below.

This swim will be fun.

It was perfect. Until about an hour and a half in, when my understimulated brain got pulled into a spiral.

This has only been ninety minutes, and I'm already kind of tired.

Anxiety ate at me.

I'm going to be trapped in my mind. There's going to be nothing to distract me from my thoughts.

Then, *there's nothing to distract me from my thoughts* right now.

I swam back to shore. I needed to keep my brain as calm as I could manage this week.

That just made the anxiety *worse.*

This was my first time ever being fully *nervous* about a swim.

It didn't help that I was fighting off a cold and that my only job was to rest and conserve energy.

On day two in Hawaii, I only swam for forty-five minutes. My stomach churned in the water.

Am I getting seasick? What if I get seasick, and that leads to anxiety, and the anxiety spirals into fear?

"Are you excited?" my mom asked as we sat outside that night, looking across at Molokai, the first channel I'd be crossing.

I hesitated. "Yeah."

"What's wrong?"

"Looks . . . far."

"I know," my mom agreed.

"But that's good," I said.

"You'll be fine."

"I know."

My parents and I shopped for Gatorade, bread, oatmeal, juice, high-calorie protein drinks, energy gels, bars, ropes for my feeds, Vaseline, and lanolin. I walked through the baby aisle and decided I might want baby food.

It was hard to anticipate what I'd be craving eight or fourteen hours into the swim, so we bought a little bit of everything.

On the third day of prep, we went to breakfast with my captain, Mike, and one of my three kayakers, Shelley, who had competed in the Olympics.

They were an eccentric couple. They seemed a little full of themselves, but they'd escorted multiple swimmers on other Hawaiian channel crossings, so I supposed they knew more than I did when it came to navigation and logistics.

"Get red lights for your goggle straps," Shelley told me. "Other colored lights will attract the big fish."

"Sharks?" my dad asked. He had a probably normal fear of the creatures, one that I didn't share.

"If you can't find red, find green," Mike added. "They're not as good as the red, but they'll do."

After breakfast, my dad went on a wild goose chase around the island of Maui, scavenging through every sporting goods store.

"I'm *fine* with a green light," I told him when he came back empty-handed that night.

"It's not worth it," my dad said.

"What? Getting eaten?" I was grinning.

"That's not funny."

"It's kinda funny."

"I'm gonna call some other stores."

"If we don't find one, I don't care."

"*I care.*" His forehead was wrinkled with concern. Sympathy wiped my smile away. My dad was a cautious man, one who measured every possibility before making a decision.

His daughter was a girl who had decided to move across the country on a whim, chasing an impossible dream, expecting everything to work out.

I was about to brave uncharted waters, and he wasn't even going to be on the boat.

"I know. Thank you for that."

Despite my lack of fear of sharks, I was not fearless.

The moments in which I was most afraid were the moments alone on the beach, staring at the whitecaps across the Pailolo Channel—the body of water between Maui and Molokai—which was the first channel I'd cross.

I studied a couple sitting on the beach several meters away as they gazed into the pristine ocean. They were lost in the beauty of the landscape.

Not me. The channel looked long and wild. More untamed than even I was.

Clouds cloaked Lanai. If I didn't know better, I wouldn't think there was land there at all.

You're in over your head, the voice in my head sang. *You've never swum for longer than six hours, forty-six minutes, and forty-six seconds. You were hanging on for dear life at the end of that 25k, and this is going to be three times that.*

The unwelcoming ocean raged. There was really no way of knowing whether I'd be able to cross it. I had never done anything like this before. And I *hadn't* been training for it. Not really.

Goosebumps rose on my skin.

What were you thinking?

I'd raised $5,400 to help pay for the boat. If I couldn't make it, I would be letting people down. It wasn't just my legacy on the line—it was dozens of people's generosity.

I took a deep breath, tasting salt on my tongue. I was capable. This was just my anxiety casting doubt in my mind. I wasn't afraid of the ocean. I wasn't afraid of the unseen depths beneath the water or what lurked below.

I was afraid of being trapped in my own mind.

I'd sacrificed my family. My trust. My mental health. All for a goal I hadn't achieved.

I would be stuck in the water with nothing but my brain to distract me. I'd had panic attacks caused by the knowledge that a panic attack would "ruin" everything. If that happened during the swim, it would tire me out. Drain all my energy so I couldn't finish the swim. Or my OCD could spiral with no distractions to pull me out of it.

If I didn't make this—

I would still have gained more than I'd sacrificed. I would still have everything that swimming had taught me.

I could have doubts, but that didn't mean I was going to fail. I wouldn't let it.

You will weather it, I promised myself. I had to. This swim was a celebration of my career. Of my athletic life. Obstacles would just make it more impressive. If my mental state was bad, and I got through it despite that, more power to me.

Even if I were in an eternal panic attack the whole race, I would not let myself touch the boat.

What if that's a promise you can't keep? my OCD asked. *What if you just made yourself an impossible promise that will lead to your never being able to trust yourself ever—?*

I stood up and walked away from the water, dusting the sand off my butt and focusing on the wind prickling my skin.

If a storm came, I was strong enough to plow through it.

"How are you feeling?" my mom asked when I got home.

I sat down, sighing. "It looks long today. *Really* long. What I could see, anyway."

My mom took me in.

Before she could say anything, I blurted, "Am I insane for thinking I can do this?"

I waited for some humorous tough love about how it was too late now—may as well get in and just force myself to keep swimming until I reached land.

Instead, my mom said, "If you were positive you could do it, you wouldn't have wanted to. That's just who you are."

It was true. "Yeah, I know."

"Just get to two islands," my mom continued. "That will be easy. And then you'll only have one left."

I let my thoughts be.

The next obstacle that arose was the course.

The first channel swimmer to reach out to me was Mike Spalding, who had been bitten by a cookie-cutter shark in these very waters during a night swim.

I was walking on some rocks by the ocean when I got the call.

"Hello?"

"Becca," he told me, jumping right to the chase. "You need to start at dawn."

I was planning on an afternoon start. "I think we're—"

"The sharks come out at night. You need minimum night swimming."

I still wasn't worried about sharks, despite knowing that Spalding had a crater in his calf from the cookie cutter.

"And why are you starting on Maui? Going into Club Lanai instead of Shipwreck is going to add six miles to the swim."

I bit my bottom lip, trying to ignore the gnawing worry in the pit of my stomach. "The reefs on Shipwreck were the reason that Harry didn't make it," I said. My voice was uncertain. I was trying to convince more than just Spalding.

"Start at dawn, time Shipwreck Beach with high tide in the daylight, and you won't have the same problem. You're making this swim a lot harder than it has to be."

I paced the rocks, looking at Lanai across the water. Six miles was *a lot* of extra distance. Navigating the landing on Shipwreck Beach shouldn't be *that* hard, should it? Harry's crew had tried, and the only reason they hadn't been able to was that he'd ended up getting there later than anticipated when it was too dark to navigate safely. If we timed my swim right, that wouldn't be a problem.

"I think you're right," I said to Spalding. I disregarded the suggested early morning start time—I *wanted* to experience swimming through the night, and for some reason, still unbeknownst to me, I couldn't manage to concern myself with the sharks. Even the man with a chunk missing from his leg couldn't convince me.

I sat on a rock and called Captain Mike, relaying all the information Spalding had just shared.

"Don't fret," Captain Mike said. "Spalding's just traumatized. I've planned this whole course out. I know these waters."

But Spalding knew the waters too. "I don't—"

"Becca. Landing on Shipwreck is impossible. I've already carefully routed the course. Maui to Molokai to Lanai to Maui is the best way."

His tone felt patronizing to me. *"I know more about this than you do."* While true, I still wasn't convinced, and frustration was building in my chest.

"But what about—"

"I have to run. We'll talk tomorrow in person, okay?"

I couldn't swallow the nagging feeling that this course had been plotted incorrectly. Anger prickled beneath my skin. I wished I knew more. I wished there was enough time for me to study the tides and the currents.

How was I supposed to trust people I didn't even know? It was the same issue I'd had my entire swimming career—only this time, I wasn't an expert. I was out of my league, so I couldn't rely on my own experience and knowledge. I didn't have any.

I thought about how I'd mirrored Eva when I knew nothing.

Steve Munatones knew more than I did, and I trusted his judgment.

I returned to pacing as I dialed his number. "Steve, I need help."

Steve was quiet for a long moment after I divulged my concerns, playing with the strings of my hoodie.

"Becca. None of this matters."

"What?"

"You're going to complete the swim regardless of the course or what time you start. Trust your captain and do the course you originally plotted. You're capable of doing it even if it's longer."

Steve was right. It didn't matter. This was all distraction. I would trust my crew.

If I had to swim an extra six miles, so be it.

The next day—the day before the swim—my parents and I met again with Mike and Shelley on the support boat to drop off some of my feeds.

It was decently sized, with a small cabin, a spacious deck, and two wheels.

Shelley held two long rope-like devices, practically giddy, as she displayed them to me.

"These are the shark shockers. They'll hang off the kayak, creating a force field that will keep the sharks away."

Everyone sure loved talking about the sharks.

"Okay."

"There's almost *always* a shark sighting during these swims, but these shockers are the best," Captain Mike added.

"On one of our recent escorts, two giant mahis followed right behind the kayak as a shark circled our swimmer. The mahis recognized that the kayak had a force field surrounding it," Shelley continued.

"Shelley used to have to hit the sharks with her paddle before we upgraded to the shockers."

I laughed, but my parents exchanged a glance. This was *not* the pep talk they needed.

"The weather and the currents are looking good, so we'll plan on a 1 p.m. start tomorrow," Mike said.

"Sounds great."

I went home and made some overnight oats for the swim, then packed up a dozen bags of feeds and backup equipment.

I decided to do an hour-long feeding cycle with a different feed every twenty minutes. It would begin with Cytomax, a sports drink that USA Swimming had given me a big container of after Pan Ams. Twenty minutes later would be a Gatorade with an energy gel dissolved in it. At the top of the hour was a high-calorie weight-gain protein drink paired with either a Gatorade or a Cytomax. Rinse and repeat.

My dad's nervousness made me anxious, so I kept to myself that night.

I slept for nine hours, woke up, ate breakfast, then took an hour-long nap.

"How are you feeling?" my mom asked when I awoke. She was leaving for the boat two hours before I'd go down to the beach for takeoff. Our Airbnb was in Kapalua, and my starting point, Kapalua Bay Beach, was a mere five-minute walk away. I would meet the boat there for a 1 p.m. start.

"Good. Normal."

"I can't believe you're doing this."

"Me too."

My mom would watch every stroke of the journey and feed me every twenty minutes. I needed her there, just like I'd needed her at every swim meet. Just like I'd needed her for the Au'au Crossing.

"I put everything into the feed bags," my dad said. He was leaving for the airport at 12:30 to pack Julia up for college and would be on a plane for the first half of my swim.

After my mom left for the boat, my dad helped apply ten layers of zinc oxide and a bottle of lanolin to my skin.

Then it was time for him to go.

"Be careful, okay?" he said.

I didn't even know *how* to be careful in a swim like this. But I knew what he needed to hear. "Okay." It was a promise I wasn't sure I'd be able to keep. But I'd try.

He took in my greasy body, hugging it anyway. "I love you."

"I love you, too. Stop worrying, I'll be fine. I promise."

Then I was alone.

God, I thought. *Please let me be fine.*

21

THE PAILOLO

I got several curious stares as I strutted toward the bay clad only in flip-flops, an old Speedo LZR, and layers of lube. I could see the questions in people's eyes, wondering what on earth had happened to me. No one knew that it was *yet* to happen.

I beamed at anyone brave enough to meet my gaze, offering no explanation.

The boat was 500 meters out when I arrived. Shelley kayaked to shore, about to join me for the start.

I discarded my flip-flops, knowing I would never see them again, and sat on the beach as Shelley disembarked.

12:56 p.m.

"You're amazing!" Shelley proclaimed as she hurried toward me. I didn't think it was deserved—I hadn't done anything yet.

Shelley loudly informed our beach audience, "This girl is about to make history and swim from here to Molokai, then to Lanai, and then back to Maui!" She theatrically pointed out the course, all of which was visible, as she spoke.

A few people began taking pictures. I remained seated, paying no attention. My mind was calm. It felt like any other competition day. Even though I hadn't trained for *this* swim, my pre-race routine tricked my body into thinking I had. Into thinking this was any other open water race.

The eighty-degree water lapped at my feet as I took in the full course. I couldn't decide whether it looked long or short today. It didn't matter.

I was expecting it to take fifteen hours, finishing around 6 a.m. tomorrow. Just one afternoon—and one night—of my life.

It was only four days' worth of practices. When I broke it down that way, it didn't seem that bad.

Shelley counted down. At "one," I walked into the water, leaving Maui, wading toward the mass of land sixteen kilometers away. Molokai.

When I was waist-deep, I began swimming across the Pailolo Channel. I couldn't keep the smile off my face for the first ten minutes as I moved away from shore. The bay's protected waters were calm. I kept my stroke long and easy, using little-to-no effort.

This was my legacy. This swim, even though I hadn't known it, was what I had been training for my whole life. I wondered what my Olympic-obsessed thirteen-year-old self would've thought. I decided she would have been proud.

The moment I swam past the bay's protected point, a wave crashed into my side.

I sighted, lifting my head. I was surrounded by four-foot swells.

Shoot.

The waves pushed my body against its will. This was the untamed ocean, and I was a small, nonaquatic animal within it.

This was *real* open water.

And suddenly, I wasn't sure whether I was a real open water swimmer.

What if I start panicking right now and have to get out, and I've only been swimming for twenty minutes?

Familiar fear began clawing at my innards. It coursed through my nervous system, threatening to overload.

No. It was *too early* to have a panic attack. It would waste too much energy—maybe even so much that I wouldn't be able to finish.

But it was too late because the adrenaline was already coursing through my veins. Fight-or-flight response had already been activated.

What had I gotten myself into? I was barely twenty minutes in, and already I was being tossed around by the ocean. This wasn't even the hard leg of the journey! How was I going to make it? Why had I thought this was a good idea?

If you don't get out, you're going to go crazy. Or die. Get out, said my OCD. *Get out, get out, get out, get out.*

Shut up, I told it. *You're a liar.*

Get out, get out, get out.

I had to let the thoughts be. I had to not react. I began counting my strokes. *One. Two. Three. Four—get out—Five . . .*

The adrenaline eventually subsided because it was too hard to maintain. My brain and my body couldn't sustain it.

But I felt the aftermath, like a city ravaged by an earthquake. And I had only been swimming for thirty minutes.

You're fine, Becca. It doesn't matter if you're already tired. You're going to keep swimming.

I would have ups and downs; everything would pass. This was just one day of my life. I could swim for one day, even through panic attacks. One day of the highs and lows of a long channel swim. This time tomorrow, I'd be done.

Maybe it'll be even easier than the 25k. I grinned into the water.

It wouldn't be right—or rewarding—if it wasn't challenging.

Even if you have a panic attack the entire swim, you're going to keep swimming.

I started singing music from *Hamilton* to myself, starting at the beginning of the soundtrack, and just kept swimming.

But summoning the words to my favorite songs was torturous. My mind wanted to go elsewhere.

I forced the lyrics into my brain—Hamilton picturing his death. The beat in the open ocean had no melody.

A seed of unease planted in my stomach. *What if this is a sign that I'm going to die?*

Nope, I told it, squashing the seed. *That is my OCD. Go back to singing about death.*

Maybe I should have chosen a musical that *wasn't* about death, but it was too late for that now.

By the sixth song on the soundtrack, Miley Cyrus' *Wrecking Ball* came in like—well, a wrecking ball—transposing itself over *Hamilton*.

I only knew the chorus, so it became a chant reverberating through my mind that not even *Defying Gravity* could drown out.

I was shocked to find out that I had gone almost five kilometers in the first hour. I was making good time.

My mood mellowed, but the next hour was still difficult.

The waves were huge, I felt somewhat sick, and I had to force myself to feed every twenty minutes. My stomach did *not* want liquid. It was having trouble digesting. My mind almost fell down dozens of rabbit holes, my rationality just barely managing to catch it every time.

Whenever I began to spiral, I grounded myself in my tempo, stroking to the half-beat of *Wrecking Ball*. It centered me like a form of mindfulness. Pull, rotate, pull, rotate, pull, rotate.

Unless I was actively feeding, the support boat remained a few hundred meters ahead of me. I swam toward it, and every twenty minutes, I found myself even. I'd look up, and my mom would be waiting with a feed.

Until one feed, about two hours in, she wasn't. Instead, Shelley threw me my fuel.

I didn't ask what had happened. I already knew. The boat was at a standstill in the midst of five-foot swells. She *must've* been seasick.

My suspicions were confirmed a few minutes later when I cut through chunks of *something* that certainly had not come from the unsullied water. I lifted my head as I crested a wave. Sure enough, my mom was hanging over the side of the boat.

I was too engaged to be disgusted, and I couldn't expend energy worrying about her. I trusted she could take care of herself.

An hour later, she was back to feeding me, though I could tell that her nausea had not yet passed. A part of me thought it poetic—we would both be working through challenges together.

Hour three came and went. 4 p.m.

This is already hard, my body said. *You know it. You're thinking it too.*

Power through, said my brain. *Stay on track. It doesn't matter if it's hard.*

It would get easier at some point. It had to.

Just make it to the next feed. Chunk this.

I distracted myself by making up a backstory for Kainoa, one of my three kayakers. He paddled beside me, a complete enigma, as I had never met him until he was suddenly taking on the swells beside me.

Molokai got bigger and Maui got smaller. My joy metastasized into adrenaline. I was going to do it. I had been the sixth fastest 800 freestyler in the world one year. I could do *anything* in the water.

My slight nausea subsided. My stroke was strong. I appreciated the beauty of Hawaii as the mighty mountains of Molokai loomed ever closer. The beauty of the crystal-clear ocean. Several jellyfish floated peacefully below me. These waters of paradise were going to be my home for the next several hours. How amazing was *that*?

One of those jellyfish stung me. I ignored it, knowing the pain would subside after about ten minutes.

Around three and a half hours in, I swam for a feed and was told I was on pace to get the Pailolo Channel record. The possibility reinvigorated me further—I felt as if I had just jumped in the water.

Molokai is gorgeously untouched by tourism. I watched colorful fish as I swam the final distance to shore. 5:01 p.m. Four hours, one minute. Not the record, but an hour *under* my estimated arrival time. I was a fourth of the way through the swim. I was going to finish—and in under fifteen hours.

I landed with a man named Steve, my third and final kayaker. I was allowed a maximum of ten minutes on shore, but I wanted to be off in eight for peace of mind. I spent five minutes reapplying lanolin. My left armpit was starting to chafe, so I inserted a generous glob there. I ate half a slice of bread and two pieces of a sliced apple. I changed my goggles to a giant clear pair—big enough that it wouldn't put my already-swollen face in any more pain—which had the blinking red LED light laced through the straps. It was two hours prior to sunset, so I'd need the light soon.

Then I journeyed on toward Lanai.

Everything was going according to plan, minus my mother's seasickness. This was exactly what I hoped the swim would be. It was challenging, yes, but nothing I couldn't handle.

The hardest part of any race was always the beginning. Since that had gone so well, the rest of the swim would be smooth sailing.

I was a back-halfer. Even for forty-mile channel crossings.

Right?

22

THE KALOHI

I embarked on channel two—the Kalohi Channel—enthusiastically. I felt the current before I even started swimming.

The water pushed against my ankles as I waded back in. It was strong. *Weird.* Surely the current hadn't been *that* strong before?

Oh no.

This channel was going to be much more challenging than the last. And the last one hadn't been easy.

I belly-flopped back into the ocean. The ocean floor barely moved below me.

I feel like I'm in an endless pool.

Strong currents were the reason I'd *chosen* the triangle. *You wanted this,* I reminded myself. *And it's probably not as bad as you think it is.* On the bright side, the waves were in a more comfortable position, no longer interrupting my breathing pattern.

The eight-minute break had not helped my arms. My triceps were an odd mixture of sore and burning.

Oh well. My arms just needed to last another ten hours. Whether they worked after that didn't matter. This was it. This was the end of my swimming career and, therefore, the end of the life I had led up until this point.

After ten minutes, I became as numb to the current as I'd grown numb to the cold. A sea turtle swam under me as the ocean floor disappeared once more, replaced by the depthless cobalt blue.

I convinced myself that the current was gone. There was no way to gauge it now that I was surrounded by nothing but water once more.

The sky distracted me before I could convince myself otherwise.

The sun dipped toward the horizon off to my right, dyeing the sky orange and pink. My heart soared. My first foray into *night swimming* was about to commence. I was about to become a *real* open water swimmer.

The water darkened to indigo, then black.

But I could still see my hands—dozens of dots of gold, bioluminescent light would spark to life with every stroke I took.

My mouth flew open.

How was this even possible? How could a world as incredible as this exist? How lucky was I that I got to be engulfed in it?

There was bioluminescence several feet below. Something was moving beneath me. A hint of trepidation crept into my chest.

You like sharks, I reminded myself. *So much that you're swimming through their house.*

I did some backstroke and could make out bright lights through my foggy goggles. I stopped swimming, clearing them. I had a feeling I was about to see something *unbelievable*.

Every star in the galaxy illuminated the sky, glinting down at me. I could see the *entire* Milky Way. There were more stars than darkness. As I floated on my back, I felt like I could reach up and touch them.

People sometimes asked me which place I'd visited was the most beautiful. In that moment, I realized that I didn't necessarily find *places* beautiful. I found *moments* to be beautiful.

If I told someone the most beautiful place in the world was the middle of the ocean in Hawaii, they would not see what I saw, even if they managed to get a moonless night like this. The seven hours of fierce swimming leading up to this moment, the knowledge that I was doing something that no other human had ever done before, and the power that I felt as I cut through the ocean, all enhanced the sky in a way I couldn't put into words.

"Whoa," I murmured at the sky. "Just whoa." I sounded like a frat bro. I may as well have been—the stars had rendered me speechless. I supposed I should just let them *res ipsa loquitur.*

"Pretty cool, right?" Kainoa's voice sounded somewhere above the water.

I was intertwining swimming and life. There was no balance between them. Instead, they looped around each other like strands of a tapestry, each one strengthening the other.

Kainoa had paddled ahead, sensing my moment. It felt right that I was alone. My swimming career had been mine and mine only, just like this night sky. I didn't want to share it with others.

Except for one person. "This is incredible!" I said to my mom as she threw me the next feed. I could only see her head. She was lying on the deck, which gave her an ideal viewing spot. Her face was gaunt and her eyes exhausted.

All she gave me was a nod before her head disappeared once more.

The sky was just for me, then.

It's a good thing I never made the Olympics.

The thought caught me so off guard that my stroke hitched. I was shocked. This wasn't an intrusive OCD thought worming its way into my peaceful brain to wreak havoc. This thought was *true*.

If I'd made the team, I wouldn't have done this swim and wouldn't have experienced this beauty.

I felt grateful that this was my life. That my swimming career had led me here. If I had been an Olympian, I wouldn't have been crossing this channel.

I enjoyed the high of swimming beneath the canopy of stars, acknowledging that this peace wouldn't last long, yet relishing it all the same. While I could. The moonrise over Maui was spectacular— though I was sad to see the stars go—as I continued on my quest.

Steve told me I just had to push through the current for another two hours, which was when I would reach the protected waters between Lanai and Maui. I could do that. I just had two more hours of fighting the invisible current and the waves crashing on my back. Two hours of hard work, then just a 25k through the glassy, stagnant ocean.

And the 25k was easy.

I was at peace despite throwing up the bread and apple slices. I knew that I wasn't going to be able to stomach solid food during the rest of the journey.

Was my nose shrinking?

I flared my nostrils. Yes, definitely shrinking.

I stopped swimming and touched my nose. The sides of my nostrils had swollen together, blocking the canals.

Not vital to your success, my inner doctor decided.

I swam onward.

A few feeds later, I asked, "Am I over halfway to Lanai?" I'd kept myself from voicing the question until I was sure I was well past. I expected that I'd swum about twenty-one kilometers since leaving Molokai and only had five to go.

Shelley's voice shouted back at me, "You've gone ten kilometers since Molokai."

That couldn't be right. It *wasn't*.

I must have ten kilometers *left*. But even that felt wrong. I must've heard incorrectly.

It was either that or I had completely misjudged how much time had passed since Molokai. Was my brain playing tricks on me? Could the fabric of reality already be tearing my mind out of touch with time and space?

I put my head down. I tried to pick up my tempo. I'd wait until I knew I had covered a significant distance before asking again.

I zoned out, getting from one feed to the next. The twenty-minute increments between feeds bled into each other. I imagined I was on a long road trip, my mind wandering as the car rolled on. When I next looked at the clock, I would be surprised to see that hours had passed and I was almost at my destination.

Even as time melted, my biological clock always knew when it was almost time to feed.

And my biological clock was telling me that it was time, messing with my groove. It was the opposite of what I'd felt crossing the Au'au when I was ten. I'd learned from many 10ks that fuel was vital to my success.

I turned toward the light that was Kainoa in the kayak, trying to do some mental math. Both Shelley and Steve had kayaked with me since sunset, meaning the sun had set over four hours ago.

Right?

I didn't trust my math, but I did trust my stomach. And it shouted, *FEED ME!*

"How long till I feed?"

"I think it's coming up soon."

I put my head back down, peeved with the answer.

I kept swimming for several long minutes before I picked my head up again, looking at Kainoa.

"When is the feed?"

"Soon."

"*Now*. I want to feed *now*. They're *late*."

Or time is moving at half speed.

Was it moving at half speed? How would I *ever* finish if time moved at half speed?

Nothing changed. The boat stayed ahead. Whenever I got close, it moved forward.

When I finally swam up to the boat, I was livid.

"This is *late*." Had forty minutes passed? Had they forgotten my last feed altogether? Or had it been closer to twenty-five minutes?

I didn't know. There was no way to tell when I had been frozen in time and space with nothing but my parched tongue and empty stomach to center me.

"Here," my mom rasped, chucking the feed at me. She didn't look good, but I was sure I looked worse.

"I need to be fed *on time*," I ordered the entire boat. "*Not* late. Every twenty minutes. You keep going *way* ahead of me, so I can't just call to you that I need a feed."

My mom threw one of the ziplocks of oatmeal into a floating container as I guzzled the Gatorade.

"There's no way I can digest that."

A packet of baby food. I eyed it, internally shrugged, and squeezed it into my mouth. I was surprised that my body didn't immediately reject it.

"Give me the baby food every time."

My unsettled stomach had become like my swollen nostrils and my weary arms: *constant* in a way that I could ignore and absorb into my mood.

Which was *souring*.

Just make it to the baby food. Make it to your peach puree. That became my small goal. Get out of the time warp and to the baby food.

I swam through another six or seven feeds before I decided it was time to ask how much longer I had. I *must* be approaching Club Lanai. My guesstimation was that I was five kilometers away, though it looked no closer. But it *had* to be.

"How much longer do I have?" My throat was raw. I had zoned out for who knew how long.

"11.2 kilometers away!"

My heart stopped. I had been swimming the Kalohi Channel for almost six hours and was *barely* over halfway.

I'd been working hard—in pain, but *manageable* pain. *Manageable* because I'd been making progress. Progress made *everything* manageable. My physical pain, my emotions, my thoughts.

But you're not making progress, sang the devil in the back of my mind. *You're swimming in place.*

Anger and dread threatened to leak into the cracks.

"How long until I pass the current?"

"Another five kilometers."

I exhaled the negative emotions into the water and imagined the current taking them away, back toward Molokai.

I picked up the pace. *Just go faster. Only 5k. That's nothing.*

Sometimes there was a stall. I'd had one for two years, stuck at 8:27 in the 800 free before dropping five seconds. I'd stalled for two hours, and now I'd be able to go faster.

I was a badass. A badass with heavy, sluggish arms. But that was fine. Ten hours of swimming would do that.

I forced my thoughts toward the positive.

At my next feed, I asked how far Lanai was. I'd done *well* in that segment. I'd bet my life that I'd gone a kilometer. "10.7 kilometers!" someone called from the boat.

The calm exploded, transforming into a fury that impaled each member of my crew with a deathly shard.

"You mean," I yelled, "I've gone five hundred meters in twenty minutes?!"

"You're doing great!"

But the floodgates had burst open, and the rage had already poisoned me. "It certainly doesn't seem that way! You told me I'd be at the easy part hours ago!" I looked up at my mom, who looked miserable in her parka.

"Give me a pep talk," I ordered.

She didn't. She just threw me some baby food. I fixed her with a glare, and she met it for a moment before her head disappeared.

"*Give me,*" I repeated, knowing she could hear every venomous word. "A. Pep. Talk."

"What do you want me to say?" my mom asked, her eyes reappearing.

"I don't know! How about you tell me that I'm doing great? That I'm going to make it?"

"I'm hanging on for dear life here."

"Yeah, well, so am I!"

"You're doing great." I scoffed. I was *not* doing great. I had gone *four kilometers* in two hours. I should've been doing four kilometers in forty-five minutes!

I used up precious mental capacity to do *math*. I *hated* math. Why the hell was I the one doing math? I hadn't taken a math class in almost a decade.

"At this rate, it's going to take me SEVEN HOURS to swim this 10k! I'm not going that slow. I'm doing my job, so do yours and get me on a better course!"

I wasn't confident in my addition, but I *was* confident that my crew had failed at their jobs. I should have listened to Mike Spalding. I should have been aiming for Shipwreck Beach.

I swam away so I could get the last word. *Ha, that showed them!*

Was it too late to go to Shipwreck? Yes. I was parallel to Lanai. I'd already passed it.

I could have already been on the final stretch!

Lanai was *right* beside me. Why couldn't I just swim in? Why did we have to go all the way to Club Lanai?

Stop thinking like this, I told myself. *Keep moving forward. Just keep swimming.*

I watched the bioluminescence dance around my fingers.

I hate Finding Nemo. *I hate Dory, and the dad clownfish, and Nemo, and all the other annoying talking fish. They would've given up swimming a long time ago if they were here.*

I thought about sunset, which may as well have been a lifetime ago. How the water had gone from light to indigo to pure darkness. My spirits were doing the same.

I lifted my head out of the water and looked at the kayak. I found Shelley staring back at me. "Why can't I just go into Lanai right now? Can we at least go closer to get out of this current? Maybe the land will block it."

"There's a reef blocking it until Club Lanai."

I put my head back down. I was drenched in gasoline, just one tiny fiery comment away from igniting again.

You're not allowed to have a mental breakdown until hour twelve.

If I'd learned anything over my eight years on the National Team, it was how to delay my emotions. I bottled up my anger to be unleashed later.

For maybe the first time ever, it was the healthy thing to do. The longer I could go without being upset, the more energy I'd conserve. Two more hours. I had to keep it together for another two hours. If it took me three days to get back to Maui, it would take me three days. The only thing that mattered was getting to hour twelve so I could have the mental breakdown I so desperately wanted to have.

That would be my reward. I was looking forward to it. I was going to be the biggest baby on the face of the earth. I was going to scream and cry and probably throw up.

When I got to twelve hours, I would certainly be over halfway. And once I reached the hump that was the halfway point—once I got my emotions out—everything would be easy. There would be absolutely *no* pressure after hour twelve. It was long enough that, no matter if something went wrong, I would be able to say that I'd swum for twelve hours.

At one point, I noticed that Shelley was no longer kayaking beside me. I continued onward, trusting that she could take care of herself. She was an Olympic kayaker, after all.

Shelley made her way back to my side two or three minutes later. A wave had tipped her kayak, something that had never happened to her before. The waves were that big. I hadn't even noticed since they were at my back, despite the current being against me.

My internal radio clicked off, muting Miley Cyrus' *Wrecking Ball*, and silence enveloped my brain.

I was in a sensory deprivation tank. Time wasn't real. All I could see was darkness and random blinking lights. Smell and sound didn't work. I felt things in my body, but I'd been feeling them for so long that I didn't even *know* if I was feeling them.

As for taste, I was never putting salt on my food again. I hated salt.

Thoughts were difficult to hold on to. So I held none. I let them flow.

Left breath, Maui. Right breath, Lanai. Left breath, Maui. Right breath, Lanai.

Maui—wait, why did it seem like I was in the middle of the channel instead of hugging the shoreline of Lanai? The reef couldn't have been *that* big, could it?

I wanted to trust my crew, but the words of the other Hawaiian Channel swimmers echoed through my skull. Were they taking me the wrong way? Why was it still so rough?

Why are you trusting them? They've done nothing to earn it. And Mom's not in her right mind. She can't keep them on track.

What was I doing, not relying on my personally informed knowledge and instincts? Why was I blindly trusting these people that I only had limited knowledge of? What made *them* experts?

I swam up to the side of the boat for a feed.

"How much?"

"7.8 kilometers to Lanai."

I was still only going 500 meters per twenty minutes.

I tried to keep my voice even. "Why are we swimming toward Maui? You know we're going to Lanai, right?"

"We're on a direct course to Club Lanai," someone called, "And going closer to the middle of the channel to avoid currents."

"When are we going to be at the easy part?"

"There's no way to tell."

"You don't know?! What happened to swimming in the middle to avoid the currents? We're obviously not doing that! I want to go to Lanai!"

I put my head back down. The boat responded by pulling ahead about a hundred meters, as it had been doing the entire swim, still veering left. I stopped again and said to Kainoa, who was kayaking next to me, "I'm not going that way."

"There's a reef that the boat is avoiding."

"Shelley informed me. But we're literally in the middle of the ocean."

"You're doing awesome, Becca! Just keep—"

I put my head back down and mentally deleted the backstory I'd written for him, envisioning all the ways I could tip the kayak over.

I slapped my hands into the water with a vengeance every stroke. Tears of anger pooled into my goggles.

Stop crying. Crying isn't going to help.

I intellectually knew that I couldn't waste my energy on fury.

Midnight came and went. I still had an hour left before I was allowed to have my breakdown. My mind raced—I needed to change something, or I didn't know if I would be able to hold my meltdown at bay.

When have you ever blindly followed? I wondered. *Why are you going along with this?*

I stopped veering left and started aiming for Lanai. Kainoa kept paddling beside me. The boat lights grew smaller as I blazed my own path, a blinking red light in an ocean of darkness.

A surge of adrenaline powered me. I was alone in the ocean in the middle of the night. I wasn't afraid—the ocean was my sanctuary. It was my place of peace and comfort. It was why I loved open water swimming so much.

The boat seemingly corrected, joining me on my course.

The burning in my left armpit got worse. When I treaded water for a feed, I wheezed, "Can I get some lanolin?"

"We don't have any," my mom mumbled.

"Yes, we *do*."

"You used the last of it."

"I'm *100 percent positive* that I put *four* in the bag. So they're in there."

My mom's eyes were hollow and haunted as they reflected the moonlight.

My heart was even *more* hollow as it tried to conjure sympathy.

"I need it," I declared. "On the next feed. *Find it*."

I didn't care that I was being callous. My job was to swim across the ocean; hers was to make sure I had everything I needed to make that happen. I would have appreciated the lanolin to make it just a *little* less painful.

My hip flexors burned as I maintained my four-beat kick. My triceps were half their usual length, unable to extend.

But my ridiculous armpit hurt the *worst*.

The next feed was thrown out of the boat, though my mom didn't even lift her head over the side.

"How far have I gone?"

The boat was silent.

"I am *talking to you!* How far?!"

"400 meters."

I choked back a scream.

"What time is it?"

"1:02 a.m."

Relief spread through my body. It was time for my mental breakdown. I could have the most dramatic tantrum. It would be so satisfying.

But now that I had permission—

Not yet. Wait till the last channel. Hold it together just a little longer.

"Where's the lanolin?"

"I don't have it," came my mom's voice.

"Yes, you do! It is *on the boat,* and it *better* be out on my next feed because I am losing ground every second I'm not swimming!"

When it didn't come out at the next feed, I dropped it. Being mad about it wasn't going to make it appear. Though I vowed that I would make sure Beth Mann did not hear the end of it when this was over.

Just a short day of my life. That's all this was.

I calmed my anger, ignored the burning chafing, and swam on.

At the next feed—over an hour after I initially asked for the lanolin— my mom threw it into the dark ocean beside me. I scooped it up before it could sink.

The plastic safety wrap was still on.

"You didn't take the wrap off!" I exclaimed, the morsel of sympathy I had left for her evaporating.

But my mom was already lying down again.

My body and brain settled back into the repetitive motions. I struggled forward on the surface of the silver water, staring into the darkness beneath it. Even the glinting gold bubbles that my arms created every time they crashed into the water seemed to be getting tired of the recurring motion.

I still found it beautiful. Isolation and repetition held a tranquility. Earth was a foreign concept. I was in a different dimension, one where gravity didn't work. I was one with the water.

Water was in every direction. Yes, there were black blobs in the distance that I intellectually knew were land, but they were so far away that they didn't feel real. My wonder was tainted.

I was pulled into a world in which I could never stop swimming. All I could do was keep stroking, keep kicking, with no rest, and land just out of reach, never getting closer.

Maybe you're in hell, said my OCD. *Maybe a shark ate you and you've died.* What if that was now my reality? What if I had died and gone to hell and this was it? An endless sea, swimming in place for the rest of eternity?

I couldn't think of anything that would've put me into hell. *It's just by deciding that your moral code was too strict.*

Calm down, I told myself, panic beginning to spike in my bloodstream. *You're fine. You love swimming. You love the ocean. This is just one night of your life. You're enjoying this.*

I hadn't had existential OCD for years. *Your OCD is back, and it's never going to leave. Because you're in hell. Forever.*

I kept swimming. *Stop,* I told myself. I didn't even believe in hell.

You don't have to believe in it, my OCD replied. *Doesn't change the fact that you're in it.*

Dread weaved into my lungs, suffocating me. There was no distraction. Nothing to hold my distress at bay.

It'll pass, I thought. *Just ride through it. Just let it be.*

Or, my OCD chimed in, *it'll keep going like this forever because you're in hell.*

I tried to focus on the burning in my armpit. That pain was contained. I just had to get to the next feed. That would give me something else to think about.

Even before I caught up to the boat, my body couldn't hold on to the panic very long. The adrenaline faded into weariness.

"How far have I gone?" I demanded to the boat, more desperate than ever to get out of this ocean.

"1.2 kilometers."

I cried tears of happiness, all thoughts of eternal suffering forgotten. I was finally out of the hard part! The last 5k to Lanai passed in seconds. I had *done* it. Now I just needed to have enough endurance.

Only 20k left. Less than the easiest event at World Championships. In five hours, I could climb into my bed and lie motionless for as long as I wanted. Five hours was nothing. My body would only ache with pain for five more hours. I could do anything for five hours.

I imagined Ashley and Eva swimming beside me, matching me stroke for stroke, the three of us swimming the 25k together.

One kilometer out from Lanai, I shouted to my sick mom, "Put a new suit, lanolin, Vaseline, and energy chews in the land bag."

"I can't get the Vaseline."

"Why?" I choked back a string of profanities, determined not to say something I'd regret if I did, in fact, get eaten by a shark. I wouldn't need *that* to be my last words to my mother.

And that probably won't help me with not freaking out about hell.

"I can't stand."

"Have someone *else* get it, then!"

She threw up over the side of the boat in response.

"Hello, people!" I shouted. "Can someone *please* help my mother and get her the Vaseline? I'm not moving until someone does!"

Mike jumped away from the wheel to search the cabin, giving me a floating break.

I stared up at the sky. I was in good spirits, back to being in awe of my abilities and Hawaii.

I lifted my head. "Steve," I said, glancing at the kayak. "How long do you think the Au'au Channel's gonna take?"

My first and now my final crossing.

"Maybe four and a half?"

I could do that. If I did it in 6.5 when I was ten, I could do it in 4.5 at twenty-one.

When the land bag was ready, I continued stroking toward shore. But the short break had made my body feel much, much worse. My arms weighed a hundred pounds.

Before I could loosen, brightness appeared beneath me.

The ocean floor glinted in the moonlight.

It was low tide, so I had only about a foot of water separating me from the reef. It was all I needed.

I stood up—grateful that the hard part was over, and proud that I had persevered—and stumbled onto the beach of Club Lanai for the first time in eleven years.

23

RETURN TO THE AU'AU

It was somewhere around 2:20 a.m.

Steve ran to retrieve the strobe light while I stripped out of my old racing suit, praying the practice suit would chafe less.

I lifted my arms to take off the straps, then found my elbows wouldn't bend.

Shoot.

I looked at my left elbow, then manually bent it with my right arm, hissing in pain. I grasped the strap.

My elbow wasn't bent enough to pull the strap over my broad shoulders.

Come on, I chastised. I could swim for fourteen hours, but I couldn't get my swimsuit off?

I kept applying pressure. *Bend, elbows! Bend, bend, bend!*

My whole arm shook as I pulled. I shimmied, lowering my shoulder. My elbows were going to snap. Or break. I pushed them, bracing my whole body—

The strap rounded my shoulder, resting on my deltoid. I exhaled. The hard part was over.

I peeled it off, enjoying not having fabric chafing on my raw skin for about one second before I stepped into my other suit, pulling it on just before Steve returned with the strobe light.

I spent the next three minutes applying Lanolin and Vaseline and another three eating two energy chews.

"Where's my drink?"

"What?" Steve asked.

"My drink."

"There's nothing else in the bag."

"My mom forgot a drink?"

"I guess so."

My fists clenched. "I need another feed right when we're back by the boat, then." The boat was just a light in the distance. It had been well over twenty minutes since I'd hydrated.

It'll be fine. You deal with what you've been given.

Eight minutes. I had two more, but I wanted to be off the shore with plenty of time to spare, so I'd leave at nine.

I spent my final minute ashore staring at the dark water.

The ocean had never looked so unwelcoming. There was nothing I wanted to do less than submerge myself in it once more. I would rather be locked in a porta-potty. I would rather deep-clean a frat house. I'd rather talk about my feelings with Agnes. I would rather go back to Omaha to swim the 800 final in 2016—well, maybe not that.

No, I realized. *There is one thing you want to do less.*

Quit.

I was curious. Curious about what I could do. Curious how much faster my half-dead twenty-one-year-old body would cross this channel than my ten-year-old self.

I remembered standing in this very spot when I was ten, staring at Maui. The ocean had been a body of possibilities. Of my untouched potential.

I didn't want to wade back into the water, but I did it anyway. For her. For ten-year-old me. To see what I was capable of in the very same waters one more time.

I would start and finish my career with the same swim and the same desire to push myself. It didn't matter that *no one* had ever done it before. It mattered that *I* hadn't done it before.

There was no pressure. I had already proven my ability. This last channel was my victory lap. The *fun* lap.

Res ipsa loquitur. I waded back into the water.

I wanted to get back out.

My arms shook. They could barely complete a full stroke cycle. Waves smacked my face as I struggled over the reef. The ocean floor disappeared much more slowly than it'd appeared going in.

My crew had been wrong—this channel was *not* going to be easy. The lights of the boat were camouflaged by the lights of Maui, so I just kept swimming in the direction I assumed was straight.

The boat found me. Shelley switched out with Steve, and my destroyed arms started moving again. The boat passed me, moving ahead toward . . . Molokai?

Hell. No.

I was *not* doing that again. I was going to Maui. And I was going *straight* there.

I was infuriated and exhausted, and I was *not* about to take the long way to "avoid currents" when we hadn't managed to avoid a single current in the entire freaking ocean.

No, I was taking the most efficient route.

I ignored the boat and continued onward toward Maui. The boat did not budge.

Neither did I.

The game gave me a burst of adrenaline. I was here to *play*. This was the drama I needed to get my mind off the pain in my hip flexors, the chafing in my groin, and the inflammation in my throat.

Within minutes, the boat was parallel to me, 500 meters to my left.

Screw the boat.

Shelley continued paddling beside me. "Becca!" she called. I didn't pick up my head. I knew what she was going to say, so I didn't give her the chance to say it.

The moment she stopped shouting, Shelley began veering back toward the boat. I watched her apathetically, the light on the kayak getting smaller and smaller with each breath.

When I could no longer see the light, I grinned. I could do this without the crew. I didn't need them. I didn't need Shelley or her shark shockers to finish. I didn't need the boat either. It wouldn't be pleasant, but if they didn't come back to me, I could make it four more hours without feeds. I didn't need anyone except myself.

I should have listened to the other channel swimmers, but I was here now. And I would rather take the right course late than never.

All I could see was a dark blob in the distance. I couldn't see upcoming currents *or* a map, but I was still 87 percent sure I could make it to Maui without feeding. It would be brutal and *very* unsafe, and I would be severely dehydrated by the end, but I would get there.

The 13 percent chance of getting lost at sea, eaten by a shark, or drowning were odds that, in my emotionally unstable state, I was fine going against.

But my intellect hadn't been completely shut down, and it said to me, *Those aren't odds you want to go against. Not when it comes to your life.*

My emotions said, *But I'm mad! I can do this faster!*

You can do it slower and actually be safe, said my intellect.

I wonder if Mom even knows that I'm out here. I assumed she didn't. I couldn't imagine that the captains had told her, and I doubted that Shelley was back at the boat yet.

My emotions and intellect came to an agreement—we would play this game of chicken until the boat made a decision. Would they listen to me, or would they make me swim back toward them?

They wouldn't leave me out here. I was the talent. The star.

I kept swimming, a speck in the massive ocean. I was determined to make as much progress as possible. The longer I continued on this course—*my* course—the shorter the journey to Maui would be.

After what I thought must have been five minutes, Shelley cut me off with the kayak. She was done with this little game.

"Becca," she snapped. "You're going to miss Maui if you don't follow the boat."

"That's not even possible!"

"You need to follow the boat!" She then said something about two knots pushing me to the right, which went two knots to the right over my head. "You need to go left."

"No."

"Then I'm staying here."

Shelley was cutting me off. I didn't have a choice. I would run into the kayak, which would disqualify me. And I certainly wasn't going to be disqualified because of my pride or my temper.

Screw you, I thought. *Screw all of you.*

I started crying, the hot tears falling into my goggles like tiny, warm hugs. I had no idea that crying could feel so good.

Ironically, it made me stop crying. I settled into a trance, my body and mind on autopilot, going through the motions in a semiconscious state.

At the next feed, I barked, "When is the ocean going to be as calm as you claimed this channel would be? Or is it going to be like this the whole time?"

"6k till it calms down and 13k to the finish."

In normal circumstances, this wouldn't be a problem. But these weren't normal circumstances. My throat felt as if my tonsils and uvula had been dislodged into my trachea. And my nostrils were closed, so breathing out of them wouldn't be possible. My body was the Tinman waiting for Dorothy to come around with a can of oil.

I was back to only going 400 meters per twenty minutes. It wasn't fair. Forty-five of the sixty kilometers were going to be against the current.

If channel swimming were fair or easy, everyone would do it. The beauty was in the unfairness and in being able to get through it despite that.

I swam on. I sighted for the boat and moved my body despite its protests.

Was I aiming for the boat? Or just the lights of Maui? Did it matter?

I went in for the next feed—

When did it turn into dawn?

The sky was light, the sun beginning to peek above the horizon.

I gazed at it in confusion. It had been 4 a.m. when I'd last asked for the time. Was it really already after 6 a.m.?

Had I blacked out?

Time no longer had meaning. Only the water had meaning. I was part of it. I'd become part of the habitat at some point. I lived in the ocean now.

I ate my feed, not unhappy with the passage of time. I couldn't see the islands to tell how much channel I'd covered.

"How much farther?" I asked, still blinking at the sun.

"10.5k."

That was something.

I enjoyed the sunrise, my brain waking with the sun. *Had* I been asleep? A hint of joy seeped through the pain. The light would rejuvenate me. I knew it would.

"How much left?" I asked at my next feed.

"10.1k."

Why couldn't I swim more than 400 meters every twenty minutes?

"Give me the darker goggles."

I could see the islands again. Maui looked *very* far.

I continued my short, inefficient freestyle. Time once again blurred together—twenty years or twenty seconds may have passed before the next feed.

"How much?

"8.6k left."

My heart leaped in my chest. I may as well have been told that I'd won the lottery. I'd passed the current! I had gone 1.5k in those twenty minutes! I was going to be finished in two hours! Maui suddenly looked much closer. Just the length of one long swim practice, then I'd be there. Easy.

The world brightened, and not just from the sun.

This must be what drugs feel like. I was euphoric. The pain in my arms vanished. I was doing it. The hard part was over. I would get to enjoy the rest of the swim, just as I had enjoyed the end of my swimming career.

Only two more hours! I sang to myself.

At the next feed twenty minutes later, I asked again, expecting to hear 7.2k.

"9k."

My heart stopped. I repeated the question, shocked. It *couldn't* be . . .

"9k. Keep it up!"

I gaped at the boat, doing my best not to sob. After a long, tense moment, I said, "9k? Nine!? So I went *backward*?!"

No one answered me for several long seconds, and then my mom's head popped up.

She'd heard the hysteria in my voice. "You misheard last time. It was 9.6 at the last feed, not 8.6."

My soul shattered into a million pieces. I was livid. The angriest I'd ever been in my lifetime.

I put my head down, the adrenaline that had powered me through the previous ten minutes evaporating, leaving me more drained than before.

We're not on the best course. I'm swimming backward. I hate everyone. I'm never getting out of here. I don't know what time it is.

In my delirium, I thought this must be the worst version of myself. But the swim wouldn't have been complete without her coming out to play. I needed to persevere—to overcome my worst self to get back to my best.

I had been angry during my first swim of this channel too. I had thrown multiple tantrums.

Not a lot had changed since then. I was swimming in the same waters with the same vicious anger and the same burning desire to challenge myself in ways that I hadn't before.

The monster within me came out when I was tested, and I would fight it away, becoming stronger in the battle. The person I was now had learned true strength—with that first crossing, moving away, the peaks and valleys of my swimming career, and the people I'd met along the way—and had overcome every trial that had come my way.

That was why I loved doing swims like this. They stripped my character down to the core, then built it back up better than it was before.

This wasn't the worst version of myself—it was the best. I was finishing my swimming career better than I'd ever been in my life. I hadn't thought I'd ever be able to reach my best athletic self after getting overtrained. I thought that time had passed.

But this swim—the fact that I was swimming onward despite my fury and exhaustion and stings and muscular pain—proved otherwise. It proved that I had grown stronger through every challenge I'd endured.

Challenges make me feel alive, I realized, despite crying into my goggles. Despite feeling more anger toward my crew than I ever had at anyone in my life. But when I calmed down, I would apologize. I would learn. I would grow.

After I was done being mad.

At the next feed, I asked, "When will the current die?"

Young Captain Mike kindly replied, "Time doesn't matter, just finishing!"

I was beginning to hate coming in for feeds. Every word from the crew pissed me off. "I've been swimming for eighteen hours and my throat is closing! Time *does* matter!"

No one responded. My mom was the only one brave enough to meet my piercing gaze, but her eyes were vacant. She was so sick that she probably thought that if I got out now, she could go to sleep sooner.

I was still convinced I wasn't on the fastest route.

So, to get my crew in order, I said with all the fury I could muster, "I'm getting out if I'm not there in three hours."

I didn't mean it. Quitting was not on my radar, though I was a bit worried about my throat.

Just so no one could accuse me of wanting to quit, I whispered to my mom, though I'm sure everyone heard, "Not really. I just want them to get me there faster."

I settled back into the hypnotic rhythm of swimming. Time blurred, just as dizzying as my head when I lifted it to sight. I was just a few degrees away from normal reality—close enough to *normal* that I wasn't alarmed but far enough away that I felt myself flowing through it differently.

Time was a current, and it was finally pushing me in the right direction. Toward Maui.

Alone in the water, moving through a different dimension, galaxies away from the crew, I was calm. Nothing was coherent except the water. Tears pooled into my goggles, though not because I was upset—they soothed my swollen eyes, so my body kept producing them.

The current weakened.

I stayed in a trance of water and pain until I noticed the boat veering right—to the south.

I frowned, doing my best to pull myself back to reality. Land was straight ahead. I'd spent the past four hours veering left.

The visceral anger began to brew in my gut once more.

At my next feed, I asked, "Why are we going right?"

"We're going to Lahaina."

"Why?"

"What do you mean?"

"The land in front of us looks *way* closer."

"Just keep swimming!"

I looked at my mom, who was resting her head on the side of the boat. I pleaded with my eyes. An unspoken understanding passed between us.

Get us on the right course, I wordlessly begged. *I need to be done with this.*

My mom nodded. Instead of her head disappearing beneath the side, she turned to the others on the ship.

The next feed, Mike said, "We're going to Ka'anapali. It's 5.8 kilometers away."

I cried tears of happiness. It cut a kilometer off the course.

I grinned at my mom as I chugged my feed, and she nodded at me. *Thank you.*

She heaved over the side of the boat.

Now in glassy water, and *finally* on the right course, my attitude improved tremendously. It was much easier. Despite the near-constant pain, there was also peace. I appreciated the beauty of Hawaii. And how amazing was it that I had been swimming for so long?

The sun was fully up, the water a deep cobalt blue. I could make out houses. I was covering 800 meters per twenty minutes—2.4 kilometers per hour, which was still *extremely* slow—but it didn't matter to me anymore. The ocean was no longer abusing me.

So I did what I did best. I swam. And swam. And swam. I didn't think. I just kept moving forward.

Then, one feed, I looked ahead and saw the beach a few hundred meters ahead. I could make out individual people on the shore.

This was it.

I swam over another reef, finally bodysurfing some waves into shore.

I took two shaky steps onto the beach.

I'd done it.

I was too exhausted to feel emotional, but my soul was satiated, my heart happy, and my brain proud.

That was amazing. I would do it again. I will do something like it *again.*

I sat down in the sand, took off my cap and goggles, and touched my swollen face. My eyes were so puffy I could barely see.

Remember this moment, I told myself. *And let this swim speak for itself.*

That was fun.

Yes. More than anything, it had been *fun.*

This was what my eight-year-old self—who had watched the trees pass by and who had wanted to experience the world—had dreamed of.

I stared at the water as Shelley paddled in. There were hardly any people on the beach I'd landed on in Ka'anapali. Just like at the start, I preferred it that way.

The world had gone on while I'd swum. The ocean looked calm and beautiful—and probably welcoming to people who hadn't been submerged for almost a full day.

I looked over at Lanai. It looked so close, almost as if it were mocking me. I would have smiled if I could have felt my face.

I looked at the full course. It looked both short and long.

I swam that, I thought. *I just crossed the ocean.*

Shelley shoved a camera in my blobfish-like face as soon as she came ashore. I asked for the time.

It was 9:53 a.m. I'd swum for twenty hours, fifty-three minutes, and thirty-seven seconds. The Au'au Channel leg was significantly slower than the one I had done when I was ten, which was appropriate *and* hilarious.

"How do you feel?" Shelley asked.

I licked my lips, my voice coming out as a croak. "I feel wonderful . . . to be on land. And very swollen." I chuckled.

"And very amazing," Shelley added.

"Thanks." It was true. I knew it, and Shelley knew it, even if the few morning beachgoers didn't. "It was a journey. A good journey."

Swimming was a good journey. A journey that made me confident that I would thrive in whatever I decided to do with life.

I sat for a few minutes, peace enveloping me. Nothing hurt. Nothing mattered. The waves caressed my feet. Birds flew through the cloudless sky.

Life was good. I felt alive.

ACKNOWLEDGMENTS

Writing books and crossing oceans are team sports, and I have no clue what my life would look like without my team.

First, I want to thank my parents. My mom, Beth Mann, who has believed in me more than I've believed in myself. For teaching me that the world is my oyster, and I have the power to be whoever I want to be. My dad, Bob Mann, thank you for supporting me unconditionally, even when you don't agree. You have both made my life so much fun.

My sisters, Rachel and Julia, thank you for always being there at the drop of a dime whenever I need support, or to be moved, and for picking out family birthday gifts on my behalf. Rachel, thank you for all the Costco pizzas in between practices, for letting me draft off of you during that first 10k so I had the energy to beat you at the end, for all the early notes on this book, and for being the best role model I could have asked for. Julia, thank you for keeping me grounded, humble, and with my ego in check (for the most part). One day I will be as funny and generous as you.

Ashley Twichell, thank you for teaching me to lead with empathy and inspiring me to be a better person and a harder worker every day.

Eva Fabian—who has read every word of every draft of this book— thank you for entertaining every absurd idea I've ever had, especially that we're the same person from different multiverses.

Allison Schmitt, for teaching me how to be a friend and to love unabashedly.

Derek Wall, thanks for paying for my ice cream in Tiburon ten years ago, despite my embarrassing protests, and for letting me join your family, fixing everything I break, and letting me drink all your coffee.

To everyone at Blue Star Press, thank you for all the notes and the tireless work! To my editors, Lindsay Wilkes-Edrington, Avalon Radys, Rachel Kuck, Olivia Voutour, and Alison Dalafave; my design team, Brielle Stein and Bryce de Flamand; and my marketing team,

Brenna Licalzi and Bailey Dueitt. Thank you for making this process fun and easy.

Thank you to Bill Rose, John Payne, Mohammad Khadembashi, and Ivan Puskovitch for nourishing my love of swimming.

To Nate Gualtieri and Jo Macariola, for giving me notes on early drafts. To Peri Segel, Mary Bronaugh, Carolyn Bradley, and Wilke Macariola for the quick-turnaround notes when I knew something was wrong but couldn't diagnose what.

And big thanks to everyone who has shown me generosity in my swimming journey, especially Alex Meyer, Frank Dyer, Randy Reese, Bob Bowman, Erik Posegay, Urbie, Jack Roach, Tim Hochradel, Michael Phelps, the Katz family, Jake Sannem, Catherine Sanchez, Amy Dantzler, Ous Mellouli, Jack Fabian, Craig Sinel, Tiger, Jenny Zhu, Jordan Wilimovsky, Keith Dickson, Emma Nordin, Cat Salladin, and all my masters swim friends.

I also want to acknowledge everyone who has made me a better writer, especially Bob Tzudiker, Noni White, Irving Belateche, Vinnie Wilhelm, Nina Kim, Michael Ouzas, Michelle Askew, Yasmin Alammar, Nate Gualtieri, Shane Munson, Mckenna Martin, and Grainger David. Whether I learned from watching you craft stories, listening to you explain structure, or receiving notes—you made me the storyteller I am today.

And thank you to everyone who has shared in the joy of the ocean with me when I've looked at the water and said, "Want to go in?" regardless of the waves, weather, and time of day/night.

REFERENCES

Anderson, Jared. 2016. "2016 U.S. Olympic Trials: Official SwimSwam Preview Schedule." SwimSwam, June 26. https://swimswam.com/2016-u-s-olympic-trials-official-swimswam-preview-schedule/.

Keith, Braden. 2012a. "Lochte Wins 400 IM Final to Stamp First Ticket to London; American Record for Dana Vollmer." SwimSwam, June 25. https://swimswam.com/lochte-wins-400-im-to-stamp-first-ticket-to-london/.

Keith, Braden. 2012b. "Olympic Trials Day 1 – Live Updates and Recaps from Deck in Omaha." SwimSwam, June 25. https://swimswam.com/olympic-trials-day-1-live-updates-and-recaps-from-deck-in-omaha/.

Keith, Braden. 2012c. "15-Year Old Ledecky, Cullen Jones, Stun on 7th Night of Trials." SwimSwam, July 1. https://swimswam.com/day-7-sunday-night-finals-session-recap-live/.

Keith, Braden. 2013. "Christine Jennings, Becca Mann First Two for US World Championships Roster in Barcelona." SwimSwam, May 17. https://swimswam.com/christine-jennings-becca-mann-first-two-for-world-championships-roster-in-barcelona/.

McLean, Don. 1971. "American Pie," *American Pie*. United Artists Records. Originally released October 24.